CONTENTS

KU-611-397

Introduction iv

Contributors to this book v

1 Health, Safety and Welfare in Construction and Associated Industries 1

2 Knowledge of Technical Information, Quantities and Communication with Others 39

3 Knowledge of Construction Technology 65

4 Erect and Dismantle Access Equipment and Working Platforms 93

5 Prepare Common Surface Types for Decoration 121

6 Apply Basic Paint Systems by Brush and Roller 163

7 Apply Foundation and Plain Papers 199

8 Produce Standard Decorative Finishes 235

Index 261

INTRODUCTION

About this book

This book has been written for the Cskills Awards Level 1 Diploma in Painting and Decorating. It covers all the units of the qualification, so you can feel confident that your book fully covers the requirements of your course.

This book contains a number of features to help you acquire the knowledge you need. It also demonstrates the practical skills you will need to master to successfully complete your qualification. We've included additional features to show how the skills and knowledge can be applied to the workplace, as well as tips and advice on how you can improve your chances of gaining employment.

The features include:

* chapter openers which list the learning outcomes you must achieve in each unit

* key terms that provide explanations of important terminology that you will need to know and understand

* Did you know? margin notes to provide key facts that are helpful to your learning

* practical tips to explain facts or skills to remember when undertaking practical tasks

* Reed tips to offer advice about work, building your CV and how to apply the skills and knowledge you have learnt in the workplace

* case studies that are based on real tradespeople who have undertaken apprenticeships and explain why the skills and knowledge you learn with your training provider are useful in the workplace

* practical tasks that provide step-by-step directions and illustrations for a range of projects you may do during your course

* Test yourself multiple choice questions that appear at the end of each unit to give you the chance to revise what you have learnt and to practise your assessment (your tutor will give you the answers to these questions).

Further support for this book can be found at our website, www.planetvocational.com/subjects/build

REED
PROPERTY &
CONSTRUCTION

EXCLUS
EMPLOYMENT ADVICE

PAINTING & DECORATING

LEVEL 1

B|A
C|H
BRITISH ASSOCIATION
OF
CONSTRUCTION HEADS

OXFORD
UNIVERSITY PRESS

OXFORD
UNIVERSITY PRESS

Great Clarendon Street, Oxford, OX2 6DP, United Kingdom

Oxford University Press is a department of the University of Oxford.
It furthers the University's objective of excellence in research, scholarship, and education by publishing worldwide. Oxford is a registered trade mark of Oxford University Press in the UK and in certain other countries

© Oxford University Press 2014

The moral rights of the authors have been asserted

First published in 2014

British Library Cataloguing in Publication Data
Data available

978-1-40-852695-8

10 9 8 7 6 5 4 3 2 1

MIX
Paper from
responsible sources
FSC   FSC® C007785
www.fsc.org

Paper used in the production of this book is a natural, recyclable product made from wood grown in sustainable forests. The manufacturing process conforms to the environmental regulations of the country of origin.

Printed in Great Britain by Bell and Bain Ltd., Glasgow.

Acknowledgements
The publishers would like to thank the following for permissions to use their photographs:

© **Arcaid Images/Alamy**: 3.12; © **blickwinkel/Alamy**: 3.13; © **Peter Davey/Alamy**: 1.0; **ALAN OLIVER/Alamy**: 7.54; **andrewmedina/iStock**: 5.9; **Chotewang/Shutterstock**: 3.20; **Cynthia Farmer/Shutterstock**: 4.15; **David J. Green/ Alamy**: 5.64; **DGLowrie/iStock**: 3.19; **Energy Saving Trust © 2011 - marketing@est.org.uk**: 3.28; **EricVega/iStock**: 6.1; **ferrantraite/iStock**: 3.26; **ffotocymru/Alamy**: 4.22; **Fotolia**: 1.1, 1.2, 1.3, 1.5, 1.6, 1.7, 1.8, 1.14, 1.15, 1.16; **Hipped end roof. Chicago_bungalow[1] (Wikipedia)**: 3.15; **ictor/iStockphoto**: 3.22; **imageBROKER/Alamy**: 5.36; **Ivan Neru/Fotolia**: 6.3; **JasonDoiy/iStock**: 2.26; **katylh /iStock**: 3.27; **KjellBrynildsen/ iStock**: 3.16; **mark phillips/Alamy**: 6.2; **Monkey Business Images/Shutterstock**: 3.0; **ndoeljindoel/Shutterstock**: 2.0; **Nelson Thornes**: 1.9, 1.10, 1.12, 1.13; **Nomad_Soul/Fotolia**: 5.8; **ofbeautifulthings/iStock**: 3.18; **ognianmed/Fotolia**: 6.19; **ogressie/Fotolia**: 5.35; **Pavel L Photo and Video/ Shutterstock**: 3.23; **pejft/iStock**: 3.25; **Permission granted by David Crowley, Scafit Ltd (www.scafit.co.nz)**: 4.27; **PETER GARDINER/SCIENCE PHOTO LIBRARY**: 1.4; **photolia/iStock**: 1.11; **piyathep/iStock**: 6.9; **prill/iStock**: 4.8; **Richard Wilson/ Oxford University Press**: 4.0, 4.4, 4.5, 4.6, 4.7, 4.9, 4.10, 4.11, 4.12, 4.13, 4.26, 4.30, 4.31, 4.32, 4.33, 4.34, 4.35, 4.36, 4.37, 4.38, 5.0, 5.1, 5.2, 5.3, 5.4, 5.5, 5.6, 5.11, 5.12, 5.13, 5.14, 5.15, 5.16, 5.17, 5.18, 5.19, 5.20, 5.21, 5.22, 5.23, 5.24, 5.26, 5.27, 5.25, 5.28, 5.30, 5.31, 5.33, 5.34, 5.37, 5.38, 5.39, 5.40, 5.41, 5.42, 5.44, 5.45, 5.46, 5.47, 5.48, 5.49, 5.50, 5.51, 5.52, 5.53, 5.54, 5.55, 5.56, 5.57, 5.58, 5.59, 5.60, 5.61, 5.62, 5.63, 5.65, 5.66, 5.68, 5.69, 5.70, 5.71, 5.72, 5.73, 5.74, 5.75, 5.76, 5.77, 5.78, 5.79, 5.80, 5.81, 5.82, 6.0, 6.4, 6.6, 6.7, 6.8, 6.10, 6.11, 6.12, 6.14, 6.16, 6.20, 6.31, 6.32, 6.33, 6.34, 6.35, 6.36, 6.37, 6.38, 6.39, 6.40, 6.41, 6.42, 6.43, 6.44, 6.45, 6.46, 6.47, 6.48, 6.49, 6.50, 6.51, 6.52, 6.53, 6.54, 6.55, 6.56, 6.57, 6.58, 6.59, 6.60, 6.61, 6.62, 6.63, 6.64, 6.65, 6.67, 6.68, 7.0, 7.1, 7.2, 7.3, 7.4, 7.5, 7.6, 7.7, 7.8, 7.9, 7.10, 7.11, 7.12, 7.13, 7.15a, 7.35, 7.46, 7.15b, 7.36, 7.18, 7.20, 7.21, 7.22, 7.23, 7.24, 7.25, 7.26, 7.27, 7.28, 7.30, 7.31, 7.32, 7.33, 7.34, 7.35, 7.36, 7.37, 7.38, 7.39, 7.41, 7.42, 7.43, 7.44, 7.45, 7.46, 7.47, 7.48, 7.49, 7.50, 7.51, 7.52, 7.53, 7.55, 7.56, 7.57, 7.58, 7.59, 7.60, 7.81, 8.0, 8.1, 8.2, 8.3, 8.4, 8.5, 8.6, 8.7, 8.8, 8.9, 8.10, 8.11, 8.12, 8.13, 8.21, 8.22, 8.23, 8.24, 8.25, 8.26, 8.27, 8.28, 8.29, 8.30, 8.31, 8.32, 8.33, 8.34, 8.35, 8.36, 8.37, 8.38, 8.39, 8.40, 8.41, 8.42, 8.43, 8.44, 8.45, 8.46; **richsouthwales/Shutterstock**: 3.14; **Ron Ellis/Shutterstock**: 5.10; **Sandie Webster**: 8.20; **small_frog/iStock**: 3.4; **SSPL via Getty Images**: 6.30; **starekase/Fotolia**: 5.32; **Susan Law Cain/ Shutterstock**: 3.11; **titine974/iStock**: 3.21; **toschro/iStock**: 4.14; **VIEW Pictures Ltd/Alamy**: 8.17; **yenwen/iStock**: 5.7; **YK/ Shutterstock**: 3.24

Note to learners and tutors

This book clearly states that a risk assessment should be undertaken and the correct PPE worn for the particular activities before any practical activity is carried out. Risk assessments were carried out before photographs for this book were taken and the models are wearing the PPE deemed appropriate for the activity and situation. This was correct at the time of going to print. Colleges may prefer that their learners wear additional items of PPE not featured in the photographs in this book and should instruct learners to do so in the standard risk assessments they hold for activities undertaken by their learners. Learners should follow the standard risk assessments provided by their college for each activity they undertake which will determine the PPE they wear.

CONTRIBUTORS TO THIS BOOK

British Association of Construction Heads

The British Association of Construction Heads is an association formed largely from those managing and delivering the construction curriculum from pre-apprenticeship to post graduate level. The Association is a voluntary organisation and was formed in 1983 and has grown to a position where it can demonstrate that BACH members now manage over 90% of the Learners studying the construction curriculum and includes membership of 80% of the Colleges offering the Construction curriculum in England, Northern Ireland, Scotland and Wales. It accepts membership applications from Colleges and other organisations who are passionate about quality and standards in construction education and training. Visit www.bach.uk.com for more information.

A huge thank you to Paul Vowles at Weston College, Stuart Proctor at Coleg Sir Gar and Mike Wynn and his team at Vision West Nottinghamshire College for their technical expertise in reviewing, advising and facilitating the photo shoot.

Reed Property & Construction

Reed Property & Construction specialises in placing staff at all levels, in both temporary and permanent positions, across the complete lifecycle of the construction process. Our consultants work with most major construction companies in the UK and our clients are involved with the design, build and maintenance of infrastructure projects throughout the UK.

Expert help

As a leading recruitment consultancy for mid–senior level construction staff in the UK, Reed Property & Construction is ideally placed to advise new workers entering the sector, from building a CV to providing expertise and sharing our extensive sector knowledge with you. That's why you will find helpful hints from our highly experienced consultants, designed to help you find that first step on the construction career ladder. These tips range from advice on CV writing to interview tips and techniques, and are linked with the learning material in this book.

Work-related advice

Reed Property & Construction has gained insights from some of our biggest clients to help you understand the mind-set of potential employers. This includes the traits and skills that they would like to see in their new employees, why you need the skills taught in this book and how they are used on a day to day basis within their organisations.

Getting your first job

This invaluable information is not available anywhere else and is geared to helping you gain a position with an employer once you've completed your studies. Entry level positions are not usually offered by recruitment companies, but our advice will help you to apply for jobs in construction and hopefully gain your first position as a skilled worker.

CONTRIBUTORS TO THIS BOOK

The case studies in this book feature staff from Laing O'Rourke and South Tyneside Homes.

Laing O'Rourke is an international engineering company that constructs large-scale building projects all over the world. Originally formed from two companies, John Laing (founded in 1848) and R O'Rourke and Son (founded in 1978) joined forces in 2001.

At Laing O'Rourke, there is a strong and unique apprenticeship programme. It runs a four-year 'Apprenticeship Plus' scheme in the UK, combining formal college education with on-the-job training. Apprentices receive support and advice from mentors and experienced tradespeople, and are given the option of three different career pathways upon completion: remaining on site, continuing into a further education programme, or progressing into supervision and management.

The company prides itself on its people development, supporting educational initiatives and investing in its employees. Laing O'Rourke believes in collaboration and teamwork as a path to achieving greater success, and strives to maintain exceptionally high standards in workplace health and safety.

South Tyneside Council's
Housing Company

South Tyneside Homes was launched in 2006, and was previously part of South Tyneside Council. It now works in partnership with the council to repair and maintain 18,000 properties within the borough, including delivering parts of the Decent Homes Programme.

South Tyneside Homes believes in putting back into the community, with 90 per cent of its employees living in the borough itself. Equality and diversity, as well as health and wellbeing of staff, is a top priority, and it has achieved the Gold Status Investors in People Award.

South Tyneside Homes is committed to the development of its employees, providing opportunities for further education and training and great career paths within the company – 80 per cent of its management team started as apprentices with the company. As well as looking after its staff and their community, the company looks after the environment too, running a renewable energy scheme for council tenants in order to reduce carbon emissions and save tenants money.

The apprenticeship programme at South Tyneside Homes has been recognised nationally, having trained over 80 young people in five main trade areas over the past six years. One of the UK's Top 100 Apprenticeship Employers, it is an Ambassador on the panel of the National Apprentice Service. It has won the Large Employer of the Year Award at the National Apprenticeship Awards and several of its apprentices have been nominated for awards, including winning the Female Apprentice of the Year for the local authority.

Chapter 1

Unit CSA–L1Core01

HEALTH, SAFETY AND WELFARE IN CONSTRUCTION AND ASSOCIATED INDUSTRIES

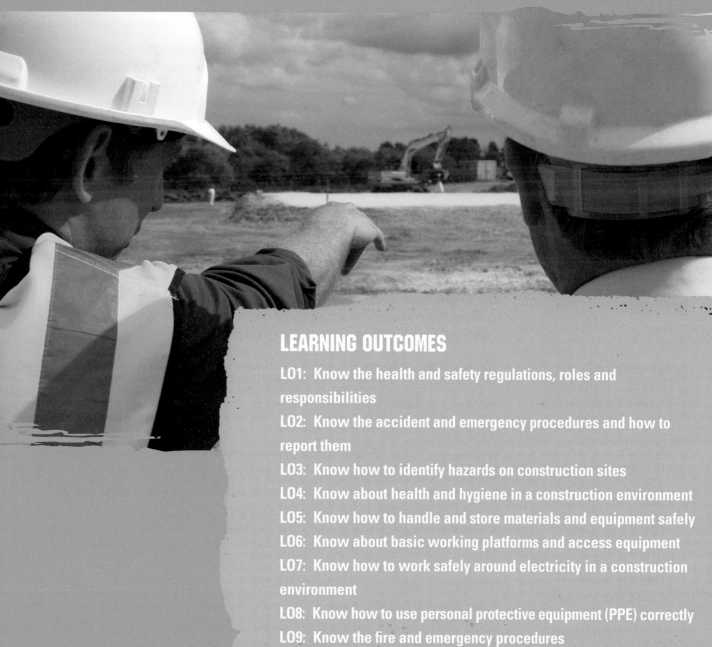

LEARNING OUTCOMES

LO1: Know the health and safety regulations, roles and responsibilities

LO2: Know the accident and emergency procedures and how to report them

LO3: Know how to identify hazards on construction sites

LO4: Know about health and hygiene in a construction environment

LO5: Know how to handle and store materials and equipment safely

LO6: Know about basic working platforms and access equipment

LO7: Know how to work safely around electricity in a construction environment

LO8: Know how to use personal protective equipment (PPE) correctly

LO9: Know the fire and emergency procedures

LO10: Know about signs and safety notices

INTRODUCTION

The aim of this chapter is to:

* help you to source relevant safety information
* help you to use the relevant safety procedures at work.

HEALTH AND SAFETY REGULATIONS, ROLES AND RESPONSIBILITIES

The construction industry can be dangerous, so keeping safe and healthy at work is very important. If you are not careful, you could injure yourself in an accident or perhaps use equipment or materials that could damage your health. Keeping safe and healthy will help ensure that you have a long and injury-free career.

Although the construction industry is much safer today than in the past, more than 2,000 people are injured and around 50 are killed on site every year. Many others suffer from long-term ill-health such as deafness, spinal damage, skin conditions or breathing problems.

Key health and safety legislation

Laws have been created in the UK to try to ensure safety at work. Ignoring the rules can mean injury or damage to health. It can also mean losing your job or being taken to court.

The two main laws are the Health and Safety at Work etc. Act (HASAWA) and the Control of Substances Hazardous to Health Regulations (COSHH).

The Health and Safety at Work etc. Act (HASAWA) (1974)

This law applies to all working environments and to all types of worker, sub-contractor, employer and all visitors to the workplace. It places a duty on everyone to follow rules in order to ensure health, safety and welfare. Businesses must manage health and safety risks, for example by providing appropriate training and facilities. The Act also covers first aid, accidents and ill health.

Reporting of Injuries, Diseases and Dangerous Occurrences Regulations (RIDDOR) (1995)

Under RIDDOR, employers are required to report any injuries, diseases or dangerous occurrences to the Health and Safety Executive (HSE). The regulations also state the need to maintain an accident book.

KEY TERMS

HASAWA

– the Health and Safety at Work etc. Act outlines your and your employer's health and safety responsibilities.

COSHH

– the Control of Substances Hazardous to Health Regulations are concerned with controlling exposure to hazardous materials.

DID YOU KNOW?

In 2011 to 2012, there were 49 fatal accidents in the construction industry in the UK. (*Source* HSE, www.hse.gov.uk)

KEY TERMS

HSE

– the Health and Safety Executive, which ensures that health and safety laws are followed.

Accident book

– this is required by law under the Social Security (Claims and Payments) Regulations 1979. Even minor accidents need to be recorded by the employer. For the purposes of RIDDOR, hard copy accident books or online records of incidents are equally acceptable.

Control of Substances Hazardous to Health (COSHH) (2002)

In construction, it is common to be exposed to substances that could cause ill health. For example, you may use oil-based paints or preservatives, or work in conditions where there is dust or bacteria.

Employers need to protect their employees from the risks associated with using hazardous substances. This means assessing the risks and deciding on the necessary precautions to take.

Any control measures (things that are being done to reduce the risk of people being hurt or becoming ill) have to be introduced into the workplace and maintained; this includes monitoring an employee's exposure to harmful substances. The employer will need to carry out health checks and ensure that employees are made aware of the dangers and are supervised.

Control of Asbestos at Work Regulations (2012)

Asbestos was a popular building material in the past because it was a good insulator, had good fire protection properties and also protected metals against corrosion. Any building that was constructed before 2000 is likely to have some asbestos. It can be found in pipe insulation, boilers and ceiling tiles. There is also asbestos cement roof sheeting and there is a small amount of asbestos in decorative coatings such as Artex.

Asbestos has been linked with lung cancer, other damage to the lungs and breathing problems. The regulations require you and your employer to take care when dealing with asbestos:

* You should always assume that materials contain asbestos unless it is obvious that they do not.

* A record of the location and condition of asbestos should be kept.

* A risk assessment should be carried out if there is a chance that anyone will be exposed to asbestos.

The general advice is as follows:

* Do not remove the asbestos. It is not a hazard unless it is removed or damaged.

* Remember that not all asbestos presents the same risk. Asbestos cement is less dangerous than pipe insulation.

* Call in a specialist if you are uncertain.

Provision and Use of Work Equipment Regulations (PUWER) (1998)

PUWER concerns health and safety risks related to equipment used at work. It states that any risks arising from the use of equipment must either be prevented or controlled, and all suitable safety measures must have been taken. In addition, tools need to be:

* suitable for their intended use

* safe

REED TIP

Employers will want to know that you understand the importance of health and safety. Make sure you know the reasons for each safe working practice.

* well maintained

* used only by those who have been trained to do so.

Manual Handling Operations Regulations (1992)

These regulations try to control the risk of injury when lifting or handling bulky or heavy equipment and materials. The regulations state as follows:

* Hazardous manual handling should be avoided if possible.

* An assessment of hazardous manual handling should be made to try to find alternatives.

* You should use mechanical assistance where possible.

* The main idea is to look at how manual handling is carried out and finding safer ways of doing it.

Personal Protection at Work Regulations (PPE) (1992)

This law states that employers must provide employees with personal protective equipment (PPE) at work whenever there is a risk to health and safety. PPE needs to be:

* suitable for the work being done

* well maintained and replaced if damaged

* properly stored

* correctly used (which means employees need to be trained in how to use the PPE properly).

Work at Height Regulations (2005)

Whenever a person works at any height there is a risk that they could fall and injure themselves. The regulations place a duty on employers or anyone who controls the work of others. This means that they need to:

* plan and organise the work

* make sure those working at height are competent

* assess the risks and provide appropriate equipment

* manage work near or on fragile surfaces

* ensure equipment is inspected and maintained.

In all cases the regulations suggest that, if it is possible, work at height should be avoided. Perhaps the job could be done from ground level? If it is not possible, then equipment and other measures are needed to prevent the risk of falling. When working at height measures also need to be put in place to minimise the distance someone might fall.

KEY TERMS

PPE

– personal protective equipment can include gloves, goggles and hard hats.

Competent

– to be competent an organisation or individual must have:

  • sufficient knowledge of the tasks to be undertaken and the risks involved

  • the experience and ability to carry out their duties in relation to the project, to recognise their limitations and take appropriate action to prevent harm to those carrying out construction work, or those affected by the work.

(*Source* HSE)

Figure 1.1 Examples of personal protective equipment

Employer responsibilities under HASAWA

HASAWA states that employers with five or more staff need their own health and safety policy. Employers must assess any risks that may be involved in their workplace and then introduce controls to reduce these risks. These risk assessments need to be reviewed regularly.

Employers also need to supply personal protective equipment (PPE) to all employees when it is needed and to ensure that it is worn when required.

Specific employer responsibilities are outlined in Table 1.1.

Employee responsibilities under HASAWA

HASAWA states that all those operating in the workplace must aim to work in a safe way. For example, they must wear any PPE provided and look after their equipment. Employees should not be charged for PPE or any actions that the employer needs to take to ensure safety.

Specific employer responsibilities are outlined in Table 1.1. Table 1.2 identifies the key employee responsibilities.

KEY TERMS

Risk

– the likelihood that a person may be harmed if they are exposed to a hazard.

Hazard

– a potential source of harm, injury or ill-health.

Near miss

– any incident, accident or emergency that did not result in an injury but could have done so.

Employer responsibility	Explanation
Safe working environment	Where possible all potential risks and hazards should be eliminated.
Adequate staff training	When new employees begin a job their induction should cover health and safety. There should be ongoing training for existing employees on risks and control measures.
Health and safety information	Relevant information related to health and safety should be available for employees to read and have their own copies.
Risk assessment	Each task or job should be investigated and potential risks identified so that measures can be put in place. A risk assessment and method statement should be produced. The method statement will tell you how to carry out the task, what PPE to wear, equipment to use and the sequence of its use.
Supervision	A competent and experienced individual should always be available to help ensure that health and safety problems are avoided.

Table 1.1 Employer responsibilities under HASAWA

Employee responsibility	Explanation
Working safely	Employees should take care of themselves, only do work that they are competent to carry out and remove obvious hazards if they are seen.
Working in partnership with the employer	Co-operation is important and you should never interfere with or misuse any health and safety signs or equipment. You should always follow the site rules.
Reporting hazards, near misses and accidents correctly	Any health and safety problems should be reported and discussed, particularly a near miss or an actual accident.

Table 1.2 Employee responsibilities under HASAWA

Health and Safety Executive

The Health and Safety Executive (HSE) is responsible for health, safety and welfare. It carries out spot checks on different workplaces to make sure that the law is being followed.

HSE inspectors have access to all areas of a construction site and can also bring in the police. If they find a problem then they can issue an **improvement notice**. This gives the employer a limited amount of time to put things right.

In serious cases, the HSE can issue a **prohibition notice**. This means all work has to stop until the problem is dealt with. An employer, the employees or **sub-contractors** could be taken to court.

The roles and responsibilities of the HSE are outlined in Table 1.3.

Responsibility	Explanation
Enforcement	It is the HSE's responsibility to reduce work-related death, injury and ill health. It will use the law against those who put others at risk.
Legislation and advice	The HSE will use health and safety legislation to serve improvement or prohibition notices or even to prosecute those who break health and safety rules. Inspectors will provide advice either face-to-face or in writing on health and safety matters.
Inspection	The HSE will look at site conditions, standards and practices and inspect documents to make sure that businesses and individuals are complying with health and safety law.

Table 1.3 HSE roles and responsibilities

Sources of health and safety information

There is a wide variety of health and safety information. Most of it is available free of charge, while other organisations may make a charge to provide information and advice. Table 1.4 outlines the key sources of health and safety information.

Source	Types of information	Website
Health and Safety Executive (HSE)	The HSE is the primary source of work-related health and safety information. It covers all possible topics and industries.	www.hse.gov.uk
Construction Industry Training Board (CITB)	The national training organisation provides key information on legislation and site safety.	www.citb.co.uk
British Standards Institute (BSI)	Provides guidelines for risk management, PPE, fire hazards and many other health and safety-related areas.	www.bsigroup.com
Royal Society for the Prevention of Accidents (RoSPA)	Provides training, consultancy and advice on a wide range of health and safety issues that are aimed to reduce work related accidents and ill health.	www.rospa.com
Royal Society for Public Health (RSPH)	Has a range of qualifications and training programmes focusing on health and safety.	www.rsph.org.uk

Table 1.4 Health and safety information

Informing the HSE

The HSE requires the reporting of:

* deaths and injuries – any major injury, over 7-day injury or death
* occupational disease
* dangerous occurrence – a collapse, explosion, fire or collision
* gas accidents – any accidental leaks or other incident related to gas.

Enforcing guidance

Work-related injuries and illnesses affect huge numbers of people. According to the HSE, 1.1 million working people in the UK suffered from a work-related illness in 2011 to 2012. Across all industries, 173 workers were killed, 111,000 other injuries were reported and 27 million working days were lost.

The construction industry is a high risk one and, although only around 5 per cent of the working population is in construction, it accounts for 10 per cent of all major injuries and 22 per cent of fatal injuries.

The good news is that enforcing guidance on health and safety has driven down the numbers of injuries and deaths in the industry. Only 20 years ago over 120 construction workers died in workplace accidents each year. This is now reduced to fewer than 60 a year.

However, there is still more work to be done and it is vital that organisations such as the HSE continue to enforce health and safety and continue to reduce risks in the industry.

On-site safety inductions and toolbox talks

The HSE suggests that all new workers arriving on site should attend a short induction session on health and safety. It should:

* show the commitment of the company to health and safety
* explain the health and safety policy
* explain the roles individuals play in the policy
* state that each individual has a legal duty to contribute to safe working
* cover issues like excavations, work at height, electricity and fire risk
* provide a layout of the site and show evacuation routes
* identify where fire fighting equipment is located
* ensure that all employees have evidence of their skills
* stress the importance of signing in and out of the site.

KEY TERMS

Major injury

– any fractures, amputations, dislocations, loss of sight or other severe injury.

Over 7-day injury

– an injury that has kept someone off work for more than seven days.

DID YOU KNOW?

Workplace injuries cost the UK £13.4bn in 2010 to 2011.

DID YOU KNOW?

Toolbox talks are normally given by a supervisor and often take place on site, either during the course of a normal working day or when someone has been seen working in an unsafe way. CITB produces a book called *GT700 Toolbox Talks* which covers a range of health and safety topics, from trying a new process and using new equipment to particular hazards or work practices.

Behaviour and actions that could affect others

It is the responsibility of everyone on site not only to look after their own health and safety, but also to ensure that their actions do not put anyone else at risk.

Trying to carry out work that you are not competent to do is not only dangerous to yourself but could compromise the safety of others.

Simple actions, such as ensuring that all of your rubbish and waste is properly disposed of, will go a long way to removing hazards on site that could affect others.

Just as you should not create a hazard, ignoring an obvious one is just as dangerous. You should always obey site rules and particularly the health and safety rules. You should follow any instructions you are given.

ACCIDENT AND EMERGENCY PROCEDURES

PRACTICAL TIP

If you come across any health and safety problems you should report them so that they can be controlled.

All sites will have specific procedures for dealing with accidents and emergencies. An emergency will often mean that the site needs to be evacuated, so you should know in advance where to assemble and who to report to. The site should never be re-entered without authorisation from an individual in charge or the emergency services.

Types of emergencies

Emergencies are incidents that require immediate action. They can include:

* fires
* spillages or leaks of chemicals or other hazardous substances, such as gas
* failure of a scaffold
* collapse of a wall or trench
* a health problem
* an injury
* bombs and security alerts.

Figure 1.2 It's important that you know where your company's fire-fighting equipment is located

Legislation and reporting accidents

RIDDOR (1995) puts a duty on employers, anyone who is self-employed, or an individual in control of the work, to report any serious workplace accidents, occupational diseases or dangerous occurrences (also known as near misses).

The report has to be made by these individuals and, if it is serious enough, the responsible person may have to fill out a RIDDOR report.

Injuries, diseases and dangerous occurrences

Construction sites can be dangerous places, as we have seen. The HSE maintains a list of all possible injuries, diseases and dangerous occurrences, particularly those that need to be reported.

Injuries

There are two main classifications of injuries: minor and major. A minor injury can usually be handled by a competent first aider, although it is often a good idea to refer the individual to their doctor or to the hospital. Typical minor injuries can include:

* minor cuts
* minor burns
* exposure to fumes.

Major injuries are more dangerous and will usually require the presence of an ambulance with paramedics. Major injuries can include:

* bone fracture
* concussion
* unconsciousness
* electric shock.

Diseases

There are several different diseases and health issues that have to be reported, particularly if a doctor notifies that a disease has been diagnosed. These include:

* poisoning
* infections
* skin diseases
* occupational cancer
* lung diseases
* hand/arm vibration syndrome.

Dangerous occurrences

Even if something happens that does not result in an injury, but could easily have done so, it is classed as a dangerous occurrence. It needs to be reported immediately and then followed up by an accident report form. Dangerous occurrences can include:

* accidental release of a substance that could damage health
* anything coming into contact with overhead power lines
* an electrical problem that caused a fire or explosion
* collapse or partial collapse of scaffolding over 5m high.

PRACTICAL TIP

An up-to-date list of dangerous occurrences is maintained by the Health and Safety Executive.

Recording accidents and emergencies

The Reporting of Injuries, Diseases and Dangerous Occurrences Regulations (RIDDOR) (1995) requires employers to:

* report any relevant injuries, diseases or dangerous occurrences to the Health and Safety Executive (HSE)
* keep records of incidents in a formal and organised manner (for example, in an accident book or online database).

After an accident, you may need to complete an accident report form – either in writing or online. This form may be completed by the person who was injured or the first aider.

On the accident report form you need to note down:

* the casualty's personal details, e.g. name, address, occupation

* the name of the person filling in the report form

* the details of the accident.

In addition, the person reporting the accident will need to sign the form.

On site a trained first aider will be the first individual to try and deal with the situation. In addition to trying to save life, stop the condition from getting worse and getting help, they will also record the occurrence.

On larger sites there will be a safety officer, but all businesses should keep records and documentation that details any accident or emergency that has taken place under RIDDOR and to provide that information if the HSE requests it.

Importance of reporting accidents and near misses

Reporting incidents is not just about complying with the law or providing information for statistics. Each time an accident or near miss takes place it means lessons can be learned and future problems avoided.

The accident or near miss can alert the business or organisation to a potential problem. They can then take steps to ensure that it does not occur in the future.

Major and minor injuries and near misses

RIDDOR defines a major injury as:

* a fracture (but not to a finger, thumb or toes)

* a dislocation

* an amputation

* a loss of sight in an eye

* a chemical or hot metal burn to the eye

* a penetrating injury to the eye

* an electric shock or electric burn leading to unconsciousness and/or requiring resuscitation

* hyperthermia, heat-induced illness or unconsciousness

* asphyxia

* exposure to a harmful substance

* inhalation of a substance

* acute illness after exposure to toxins or infected materials.

A minor injury could be considered as any occurrence that does not fall into any of the above categories.

A near miss is any incident that did not actually result in an injury but which could have caused a major injury if it had done so. Non-reportable near misses are useful to record as they can help to identify potential problems. Looking at a list of near misses might show patterns for potential risk.

Accident trends

We have already seen that the HSE maintains statistics on the number and types of construction accidents. The following are among the 2011/2012 construction statistics:

* There were 49 fatalities.

* There were 5,000 occupational cancer patients.

* There were 74,000 cases of work-related ill health.

* The most common types of injury were caused by falls, although many injuries were caused by falling objects, collapses and electricity. A number of construction workers were also hurt when they slipped or tripped, or were injured while lifting heavy objects.

Accidents, emergencies and the employer

Even less serious accidents and injuries can cost a business a great deal of money. But there are other costs too:

* Poor company image – if a business does not have health and safety controls in place then it may get a reputation for not caring about its employees. The number of accidents and injuries may be far higher than average.

* Loss of production – the injured individual might have to be treated and then may need a period of time off work to recover. The loss of production can include those who have to take time out from working to help the injured person and the time of a manager or supervisor who has to deal with all the paperwork and problems.

* Insurance – each time there is an accident or injury claim against the company's insurance the premiums will go up. If there are many accidents and injuries the business may find it impossible to get insurance. It is a legal requirement for a business to have insurance so in the end that company might have to close down.

* Closure of site – if there is a serious accident or injury then the site may have to be closed while investigations take place to discover the reason, or who was responsible. This could cause serious delays and loss of income for workers and the business.

DID YOU KNOW?

RoSPA (the Royal Society for the Prevention of Accidents) uses many of the statistics from the HSE. The latest figures that RoSPA has analysed date back to 2008/2009. In that year, 1.2 million people in the UK were suffering from work-related illnesses. With fewer than 132,000 reportable injuries at work, this is believed to be around half of the real figure.

DID YOU KNOW?

An employee working in a small business broke two bones in his arm. He could not return to proper duties for eight months. He lost out on wages while he was off sick and, in total, it cost the business over £45,000.

REED TIP

On some construction sites, you may get a Health and Safety Inspector come to look round without any notice – one more reason to always be thinking about working safely.

Accident and emergency authorised personnel

Several different groups of people could be involved in dealing with accident and emergency situations. These are listed in Table 1.5.

Authorised personnel	Role
First aiders and emergency responders	These are employees on site and in the workforce who have been trained to be the first to respond to accidents and injuries. The minimum provision of an appointed person would be someone who has had basic first aid training. The appointment of a first aider is someone who has attained a higher or specific level of training. A construction site with fewer than 5 employees needs an appointed first aider. A construction site with up to 50 employees requires a trained first aider, and for bigger sites at least one trained first aider is required for every 50 people.
Supervisors and managers	These have the responsibility of managing the site and would have to organise the response and contact emergency services if necessary. They would also ensure that records of any accidents are completed and up to date and notify the HSE if required.
Health and Safety Executive	The HSE requires businesses to investigate all accidents and emergencies. The HSE may send an inspector, or even a team, to investigate and take action if the law has been broken.
Emergency services	Calling the emergency services depends on the seriousness of the accident. Paramedics will take charge of the situation if there is a serious injury and if they feel it necessary will take the individual to hospital.

Table 1.5 People who deal with accident and emergency situations

DID YOU KNOW?

The three main emergency services in the UK are: the Fire Service (for fire and rescue); the Ambulance Service (for medical emergencies); the Police (for an immediate police response). Call them on 999 only if it is an emergency.

The basic first aid kit

BS 8599 relates to first aid kits, but it is not legally binding. The contents of a first aid box will depend on an employer's assessment of their likely needs. The HSE does not have to approve the contents of a first aid box but it states that where the work involves low level hazards the minimum contents of a first aid box should be:

* a copy of its leaflet on first aid – *HSE Basic advice on first aid at work*
* 20 sterile plasters of assorted size
* 2 sterile eye pads
* 4 sterile triangular bandages
* 6 safety pins
* 2 large sterile, unmedicated wound dressings
* 6 medium-sized sterile unmedicated wound dressings
* 1 pair of disposable gloves.

The HSE also recommends that no tablets or medicines are kept in the first aid box.

Figure 1.3 A typical first aid box

What to do if you discover an accident

When an accident happens it may not only injure the person involved directly, but it may also create a hazard that could then injure others. You need to make sure that the area is safe enough for you or someone else to help the injured person. It may be necessary to turn off the electrical supply or remove obstructions to the site of the accident.

The first thing that needs to be done if there is an accident is to raise the alarm. This could mean:

* calling for the first aider

* phoning for the emergency services

* dealing with the problem yourself.

How you respond will depend on the severity of the injury.

You should follow this procedure if you need to contact the emergency services:

* Find a telephone away from the emergency.

* Dial 999.

* You may have to go through a switchboard. Carefully listen to what the operator is saying to you and try to stay calm.

* When asked, give the operator your name and location, and the name of the emergency service or services you require.

* You will then be transferred to the appropriate emergency service, who will ask you questions about the accident and its location. Answer the questions in a clear and calm way.

* Once the call is over, make sure someone is available to help direct the emergency services to the location of the accident.

IDENTIFYING HAZARDS

As we have already seen, construction sites are potentially dangerous places. The most effective way of handling health and safety on a construction site is to spot the hazards and deal with them before they can cause an accident or an injury. This begins with basic housekeeping and carrying out risk assessments. It also means having a procedure in place to report hazards so that they can be dealt with.

Good housekeeping

Work areas should always be clean and tidy. Sites that are messy, strewn with materials, equipment, wires and other hazards can prove to be very dangerous. You should:

* always work in a tidy way

* never block fire exits or emergency escape routes

* never leave nails and screws scattered around

* ensure you clean and sweep up at the end of each working day

* not block walkways

* never overfill skips or bins

* never leave food waste on site.

Risk assessments and method statements

It is a legal requirement for employers to carry out risk assessments. This covers not only those who are actually working on a particular job, but other workers in the immediate area, and others who might be affected by the work.

It is important to remember that when you are carrying out work your actions may affect the safety of other people. It is important, therefore, to know whether there are any potential hazards. Once you know what these hazards are you can do something to either prevent or reduce them as a risk. Every job has potential hazards.

There are five simple steps to carrying out a risk assessment, which are shown in Table 1.6, using the example of repointing brickwork on the front face of a dwelling.

Step	Action	Example
1	Identify hazards	The property is on a street with a narrow pavement. The damaged brickwork and loose mortar need to be removed and placed in a skip below. Scaffolding has been erected. The road is not closed to traffic.
2	Identify who is at risk	The workers repointing are at risk as they are working at height. Pedestrians and vehicles passing are at risk from the positioning of the skip and the chance that debris could fall from height.
3	What is the risk from the hazard that may cause an accident?	The risk to the workers is relatively low as they have PPE and the scaffolding has been correctly erected. The risk to those passing by is higher, as they are unaware of the work being carried out above them.
4	Measures to be taken to reduce the risk	Station someone near the skip to direct pedestrians and vehicles away from the skip while the work is being carried out. Fix a secure barrier to the edge of the scaffolding to reduce the chance of debris falling down. Lower the bricks and mortar debris using a bucket or bag into the skip and not throwing them from the scaffolding. Consider carrying out the work when there are fewer pedestrians and less traffic on the road.
5	Monitor the risk	If there are problems with the first stages of the job, you need to take steps to solve them. If necessary consider taking the debris by hand through the building after removal.

Table 1.6 A five-step risk assessment for repointing brickwork

These working practices can help to prevent accidents or dangerous situations occurring in the workplace:

* *Risk assessments* look carefully at what could cause an individual harm and how to prevent this. This is to ensure that no one should be injured or become ill as a result of their work. Risk assessments identify how likely it is that an accident might happen and the consequences of it happening. A risk factor is worked out and control measures created to try to offset them.

* *Method statements,* however brief, should be available for every risk assessment. They summarise risk assessments and other findings to provide guidance on how the work should be carried out.

* *Permit to work systems* are used for very high risk or even potentially fatal activities. They are checklists that need to be completed before the work begins. They must be signed by a supervisor.

* *A hazard book* lists standard tasks and identifies common hazards. These are useful tools to help quickly identify hazards related to particular tasks.

Types of hazards

Typical construction accidents can include:

* fires and explosions
* slips, trips and falls.
* burns, including those from chemicals
* falls from scaffolding, ladders and roofs
* electrocution
* injury from faulty machinery
* power tool accidents
* being hit by construction debris
* falling through holes in flooring

We will look at some of the more common hazards in a little more detail.

Fires
Fires need oxygen, heat and fuel to burn. Even a spark can provide enough heat needed to start a fire, and anything flammable, such as petrol, paper or wood, provides the fuel. It may help to remember the 'triangle of fire' – heat, oxygen and fuel are all needed to make fire so remove one or more to help prevent or stop the fire.

Tripping

Leaving equipment and materials lying around can cause accidents, as can trailing cables and spilt water or oil. Some of these materials are also potential fire hazards.

Chemical spills

If the chemicals are not hazardous then they just need to be mopped up. But sometimes they do involve hazardous materials and there will be an existing plan on how to deal with them. A risk assessment will have been carried out.

Falls from height

A fall even from a low height can cause serious injuries. Precautions need to be taken when working at height to avoid permanent injury. You should also consider falls into open excavations as falls from height. All the same precautions need to be in place to prevent a fall.

Burns

Burns can be caused not only by fires and heat, but also from chemicals and solvents. Electricity and wet concrete and cement can also burn skin. PPE is often the best way to avoid these dangers. Sunburn is a common and uncomfortable form of burning and sunscreen should be made available. Keeping covered up, for example keeping skin covered up will help to prevent sunburn. You might think a tan looks good, but it could lead to skin cancer.

Electrical

Electricity is hazardous and electric shocks can cause burns and muscle damage, and can kill.

Exposure to hazardous substances

We look at hazardous substances in more detail on pages 20–1. COSHH regulations identify hazardous substances and require them to be labelled. You should always follow the instructions when using them.

Plant and vehicles

On busy sites there is always a danger from moving vehicles and heavy plant. Although many are fitted with reversing alarms, it may not be easy to hear them over other machinery and equipment. You should always ensure you are not blocking routes or exits. Designated walkways separate site traffic and pedestrians – this includes workers who are walking around the site. Crossing points should be in place for ease of movement on site.

Reporting hazards

We have already seen that hazards have the potential to cause serious accidents and injuries. It is therefore important to report hazards and there are different methods of doing this.

The first major reason to report hazards is to prevent danger to others, whether they are other employees or visitors to the site. It is vital to prevent accidents from taking place and to quickly correct any dangerous situations.

Injuries, diseases and actual accidents all need to be reported and so do dangerous occurrences. These are incidents that do not result in an actual injury, but could easily have hurt someone.

Accidents need to be recorded in an accident book, computer database or other secure recording system, as do near misses. Again it is a legal requirement to keep appropriate records of accidents and every company will have a procedure for this which they should tell you about. Everyone should know where the book is kept or how the records are made. Anyone that has been hurt or has taken part in dealing with an occurrence should complete the details of what has happened. Typically this will require you to fill in:

* the date, time and place of the incident

* how it happened

* what was the cause

* how it was dealt with

* who was involved

* signature and date.

The details in the book have to be transferred onto an official HSE report form.

As far as is possible, the site, company or workplace will have set procedures in place for reporting hazards and accidents. These procedures will usually be found in the place where the accident book or records are stored. The location tends to be posted on the site notice board.

How hazards are created

Construction sites are busy places. There are constantly new stages in development. As each stage is begun a whole new set of potential hazards need to be considered.

At the same time, new workers will always be joining the site. It is mandatory for them to be given health and safety instruction during induction. But sometimes this is impossible due to pressure of work or availability of trainers.

Construction sites can become even more hazardous in times of extreme weather:

* Flooding – long periods of rain can cause trenches to fill with water, cellars to be flooded and smooth surfaces to become extremely wet and slippery.

* Wind – strong winds may prevent all work at height. Scaffolding may have become unstable, unsecured roofing materials may come loose, dry-stored materials such as sand and cement may have been blown across the site.

* Heat – this can change the behaviour of materials: setting quicker, failing to cure and melting. It can also seriously affect the health of the workforce through dehydration and heat exhaustion.

* Snow – this can add enormous weight to roofs and other structures and could cause collapse. Snow can also prevent access or block exits and can mean that simple and routine work becomes impossible due to frozen conditions.

Storing combustibles and chemicals

A combustible substance can be both flammable and explosive. There are some basic suggestions from the HSE about storing these:

* Ventilation – the area should be well ventilated to disperse any vapours that could trigger off an explosion.

* Ignition – an ignition is any spark or flame that could trigger off the vapours, so materials should be stored away from any area that uses electrical equipment or any tool that heats up.

* Containment – the materials should always be kept in proper containers with lids and there should be spillage trays to prevent any leak seeping into other parts of the site.

* Exchange – in many cases it can be possible to find an alternative material that is less dangerous. This option should be taken if possible.

* Separation – always keep flammable substances away from general work areas. If possible they should be partitioned off.

Combustible materials can include a large number of commonly used substances, such as cleaning agents, paints and adhesives.

HEALTH AND HYGIENE

Just as hazards can be a major problem on site, other less obvious problems relating to health and hygiene can also be an issue. It is both your responsibility and that of your employer to make sure that you stay healthy.

The employer will need to provide basic welfare facilities, no matter where you are working and these must have minimum standards.

Welfare facilities

Welfare facilities can include a wide range of different considerations, as can be seen in Table 1.7.

DID YOU KNOW?

You do not have to be involved in specialist work to come into contact with combustibles.

KEY TERMS

Contamination

– this is when a substance has been polluted by some harmful substance or chemical.

Facilities	Purpose and minimum standards
Toilets	If there is a lock on the door there is no need to have separate male and female toilets. There should be enough for the site workforce. If there is no flushing water on site they must be chemical toilets.
Washing facilities	There should be a wash basin large enough to be able to wash up to the elbow. There should be soap, hot and cold water and, if you are working with dangerous substances, then showers are needed.
Drinking water	Clean drinking water should be available; either directly connected to the mains or bottled water. Employers must ensure that there is no contamination.
Dry room	This can operate also as a store room, which needs to be secure so that workers can leave their belongings there and also use it as a place to dry out if they have been working in wet weather, in which case a heater needs to be provided.
Work break area	This is a shelter out of the wind and rain, with a kettle, a microwave, tables and chairs. It should also have heating.

Table 1.7 Welfare facilities in the workplace

CASE STUDY

South Tyneside Homes

South Tyneside Council's Housing Company

Staying safe on site

Johnny McErlane finished his apprenticeship at South Tyneside Homes a year ago.

'I've been working on sheltered accommodation for the last year, so there are a lot of vulnerable and elderly people around. All the things I learnt at college from doing the health and safety exams comes into practice really, like taking care when using extension leads, wearing high-vis and correct footwear. It's not just about your health and safety, but looking out for others as well.

On the shelters, you can get a health and safety inspector who just comes around randomly, so you have to always be ready. It just becomes a habit once it's been drilled into you. You're health and safety conscious all the time.

The shelters also have a fire alarm drill every second Monday, so you've got to know the procedure involved there. When it comes to the more specialised skills, such as mouth-to-mouth and CPR, you might have a designated first aider on site who will have their skills refreshed regularly. Having a full first aid certificate would be valuable if you're working in construction.

You cover quite a bit of the first aid skills in college and you really have to know them because you're not always working on large sites. For example, you might be on the repairs team, working in people's houses where you wouldn't have a first aider, so you've got to have the basic knowledge yourself, just in case. All our vans have a basic first aid kit that's kept fully stocked.

The company keeps our knowledge current with these "toolbox talks", which are like refresher courses. They give you any new information that needs to be passed on to all the trades. It's a good way of keeping everyone up to date.'

Noise

Ear defenders are the best precaution to protect the ears from loud noises on site. Ear defenders are either basic ear plugs or ear muffs, which can be seen in Fig 1.13 on page 32.

The long-term impact of noise depends on the intensity and duration of the noise. Basically, the louder and longer the noise exposure, the more damage is caused. There are ways of dealing with this:

* Remove the source of the noise.

* Move the equipment away from those not directly working with it.

* Put the source of the noise into a soundproof area or cover it with soundproof material.

* Ask a supervisor if they can move all other employees away from that part of the site until the noise stops.

Substances hazardous to health

COSHH Regulations (see page 3) identify a wide variety of substances and materials that must be labelled in different ways.

Controlling the use of these substances is always difficult. Ideally, their use should be eliminated (stopped) or they should be replaced with something less harmful. Failing this, they should only be used in controlled or restricted areas. If none of this is possible then they should only be used in controlled situations.

If a hazardous situation occurs at work, then you should:

* ensure the area is made safe

* inform the supervisor, site manager, safety officer or other nominated person.

You will also need to report any potential hazards or near misses.

Personal hygiene

Construction sites can be dirty places to work. Some jobs will expose you to dust, chemicals or substances that can make contact with your skin or may stain your work clothing. It is good practice to wear suitable PPE as a first line of defence as chemicals can penetrate your skin. Whenever you have finished a job you should always wash your hands. This is certainly true before eating lunch or travelling home. It can be good practice to have dedicated work clothing, which should be washed regularly.

Always ensure you wash your hands and face and scrub your nails. This will prevent dirt, chemicals and other substances from contaminating your food and your home.

Make sure that you regularly wash your work clothing and either repair it or replace it if it becomes too worn or stained.

Health risks

The construction industry uses a wide variety of substances that could harm your health. You will also be carrying out work that could be a health risk to you, and you should always be aware that certain activities could cause long-term damage or even kill you if things go wrong. Unfortunately not all health risks are immediately obvious. It is important to make sure that from time to time you have health checks, particularly if you have been using hazardous substances. Table 1.8 outlines some potential health risks in a typical construction site.

KEY TERMS

Dermatitis

– this is an inflammation of the skin. The skin will become red and sore, particularly if you scratch the area. A GP should be consulted.

Leptospirosis

– this is also known as Weil's disease. It is spread by touching soil or water contaminated with the urine of wild animals infected with the leptospira bacteria. Symptoms are usually flu-like but in extreme cases it can cause organ failure.

Health risk	Potential future problems
Dust	The most dangerous potential dust is, of course, asbestos, which **should only be handled by specialists under controlled conditions**. But even brick dust and other fine particles can cause eye injuries, problems with breathing and even cancer.
Chemicals	Inhaling or swallowing dangerous chemicals could cause immediate, long-term damage to lungs and other internal organs. Skin problems include burns or skin can become very inflamed and sore. This is known as dermatitis.
Bacteria	Contact with waste water or soil could lead to a bacterial infection. The germs in the water or dirt could cause infection which will require treatment if they enter the body. The most extreme version is leptospirosis.
Heavy objects	Lifting heavy, bulky or awkward objects can lead to permanent back injuries that could require surgery. Heavy objects can also damage the muscles in all areas of the body.
Noise	Failure to wear ear defenders when you are exposed to loud noises can permanently affect your hearing. This could lead to deafness in the future.
Vibrating tools	Using machines that vibrate can cause a condition known as hand/arm vibration syndrome (HAVS) or vibration white finger, which is caused by injury to nerves and blood vessels. You will feel tingling that could lead to permanent numbness in the fingers and hands, as well as muscle weakness.
Cuts	Any open wound, no matter how small, leaves your body exposed to potential infections. Cuts should always be cleaned and covered, preferably with a waterproof dressing. The blood loss from deep cuts could make you feel faint and weak, which may be dangerous if you are working at height or operating machinery.
Sunlight	Most construction work involves working outside. There is a temptation to take advantage of hot weather and get a tan. But long-term exposure to sunshine means risking skin cancer so you should cover up and apply sun cream.
Head injuries	You should seek medical attention after any bump to the head. Severe head injuries could cause epilepsy, hearing problems, brain damage or death.

Table 1.8 Health risks in construction

HANDLING AND STORING MATERIALS AND EQUIPMENT

On a busy construction site it is often tempting not to even think about the potential dangers of handling equipment and materials. If something needs to be moved or collected you will just pick it up without any thought. It is also tempting just to drop your tools and other equipment when you have finished with them to deal with later. But abandoned equipment and tools can cause hazards both for you and for other people.

Safe lifting

Lifting or handling heavy or bulky items is a major cause of injuries on construction sites. So whenever you are dealing with a heavy load, it is important to carry out a basic risk assessment.

The first thing you need to do is to think about the job to be done and ask:

* Do I need to lift it manually or is there another way of getting the object to where I need it?

Consider any mechanical methods of transporting loads or picking up materials. If there really is no alternative, then ask yourself:

1. Do I need to bend or twist?
2. Does the object need to be lifted or put down from high up?
3. Does the object need to be carried a long way?
4. Does the object need to be pushed or pulled for a long distance?
5. Is the object likely to shift around while it is being moved?

If the answer to any of these questions is 'yes', you may need to adjust the way the task is done to make it safer.

Think about the object itself. Ask:

1. Is it just heavy or is it also bulky and an awkward shape?
2. How easy is it to get a good hand-hold on the object?
3. Is the object a single item or are there parts that might move around and shift the weight?
4. Is the object hot or does it have sharp edges?

Again, if you have answered 'yes' to any of these questions, then you need to take steps to address these issues.

It is also important to think about the working environment and where the lifting and carrying is taking place. Ask yourself:

1. Are the floors stable?
2. Are the surfaces slippery?
3. Will a lack of space restrict my movement?
4. Are there any steps or slopes?
5. What is the lighting like?

Before lifting and moving an object, think about the following:

* Check that your pathway is clear to where the load needs to be taken.

* Look at the product data sheet and assess the weight. If you think the object is too heavy or difficult to move then ask someone to help you. Alternatively, you may need to use a mechanical lifting device.

When you are ready to lift, gently raise the load. Take care to ensure the correct posture – you should have a straight back, with your elbows tucked in, your knees bent and your feet slightly apart.

Once you have picked up the load, move slowly towards your destination. When you get there, make sure that you do not drop the load but carefully place it down.

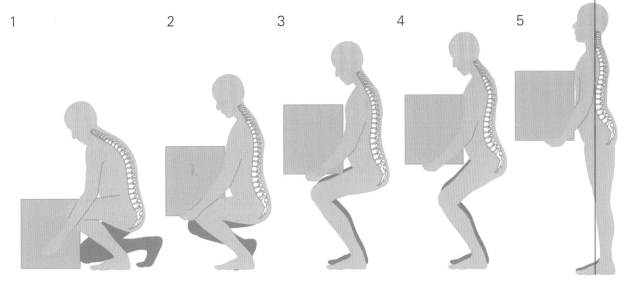

1   2   3   4   5

Figure 1.4 Take care to follow the correct procedure for lifting

Sack trolleys are useful for moving heavy and bulky items around. Gently slide the bottom of the sack trolley under the object and then raise the trolley to an angle of 45° before moving off. Make sure that the object is properly balanced and is not too big for the trolley.

Trailers and forklift trucks are often used on large construction sites, as are dump trucks. Never use these without proper training.

Figure 1.5 Pallet truck

Figure 1.6 Sack trolley

Site safety equipment

You should always read the construction site safety rules and when required wear your PPE. Simple things, such as wearing the right footwear for the right job, are important.

Safety equipment falls into two main categories:

* PPE – including hard hats, footwear, gloves, glasses and safety vests

* perimeter safety – this includes screens, netting and guards or clamps to prevent materials from falling or spreading.

Construction safety is also directed by signs, which will highlight potential hazards.

Safe handling of materials and equipment

All tools and equipment are potentially dangerous. It is up to you to make sure that they do not cause harm to yourself or others. You should always know how to use tools and equipment. This means either instruction from someone else who is experienced, or at least reading the manufacturer's instructions.

You should always make sure that you:

* use the right tool – don't be tempted to use a tool that is close to hand instead of the one that is right for the job

* wear your PPE – the one time you decide not to bother could be the time that you injure yourself

* never try to use a tool or a piece of equipment that you have not been trained to use.

You should always remember that if you are working on a building that was constructed before 2000 it may contain asbestos.

Correct storage

We have already seen that tools and equipment need to be treated with respect. Damaged tools and equipment are not only less effective at doing their job, they could also cause you to injure yourself.

Table 1.9 provides some pointers on how to store and handle different types of materials and equipment.

Materials and equipment	Safe storage and handling
Hand tools	Store hand tools with sharp edges either in a cover or a roll. They should be stored in bags or boxes. They should always be dried before putting them away as they will rust.
Power tools	Never carry them by the cable. Store them in their original carrying case. Always follow the manufacturer's instructions.
Wheelbarrows	Check the tyres and metal stays regularly. Always clean out after use and never overload.
Bricks and blocks	Never store more than two packs high. When cutting open a pack, be careful as the bricks could collapse.
Slabs and curbs	Store slabs flat on their edges on level ground, preferably with wood underneath to prevent damage. Store curbs the same way. To prevent weather damage, cover them with a sheet.
Tiles	Always cover them and protect them from damage as they are relatively fragile. Ideally store them in a hut or container.
Aggregates	Never store aggregates under trees as leaves will drop on them and contaminate them. Cover them with plastic sheets.
Plaster and plasterboard	Plaster needs to be kept dry, so even if stored inside you should take the precaution of putting the bags on pallets. To prevent moisture do not store against walls and do not pile higher than five bags. Plasterboard can be awkward to manage and move around. It also needs to be stored in a waterproof area. It should be stored flat and off the ground but should not be stored against walls as it may bend. Use a rotation system so that the materials are not stored in the same place for long periods.
Wood	Always keep wood in dry, well-ventilated conditions. If it needs to be stored outside it should be stored on bearers that may be on concrete. If wood gets wet and bends it is virtually useless. Always be careful when moving large cuts of wood or sheets of ply or MDF as they can easily become damaged.
Adhesives and paint	Always read the manufacturer's instructions. Ideally they should always be stored on clearly marked shelves. Make sure you rotate the stock using the older stock first. Always make sure that containers are tightly sealed. Storage areas must comply with fire regulations and display signs to advise of their contents.

Table 1.9 Safe storing and handling of materials and equipment

Waste control

The expectation within the building services industry is increasingly that working practices conserve energy and protect the environment. Everyone can play a part in this. For example, you can contribute by turning off hose pipes when you have finished using water, or not running electrical items when you don't need to.

Simple things, such as keeping construction sites neat and orderly, can go a long way to conserving energy and protecting the environment. A good way to remember this is Sort, Set, Shine, Standardise:

* Sort – sort and store items in your work area, eliminate clutter and manage deliveries.

* Set – everything should have its own place and be clearly marked and easy to access. In other words, be neat!

Figure 1.7 It's important to create as little waste as possible on the construction site

* Shine – clean your work area and you will be able to see potential problems far more easily.

* Standardise – by using standardised working practices you can keep organised, clean and safe.

Reducing waste is all about good working practice. By reducing wastage disposal, and recycling materials on site, you will benefit from savings on raw materials and lower transportation costs.

Planning ahead, and accurately measuring and cutting materials, means that you will be able to reduce wastage.

BASIC WORKING PLATFORMS AND ACCESS EQUIPMENT

Working at height should be eliminated or the work carried out using other methods where possible. However, there may be situations where you may need to work at height. These situations can include:

* roofing

* repair and maintenance above ground level

* working on high ceilings.

Any work at height must be carefully planned. Access equipment includes all types of ladder, scaffold and platform. You must always use a working platform that is safe. Sometimes a simple step ladder will be sufficient, but at other times you may have to use a tower scaffold.

Generally, ladders are fine for small, quick jobs of less than 30 minutes. However, for larger, longer jobs a more permanent piece of access equipment will be necessary.

Working platforms and access equipment: good practice and dangers of working at height

Table 1.10 outlines the common types of equipment used to allow you to work at heights, along with the basic safety checks necessary.

Equipment	Main features	Safety checks
Step ladder	Ideal for confined spaces. Four legs give stability	• Knee should remain below top of steps • Check hinges, cords or ropes • Position only to face work
Ladder	Ideal for basic access, short-term work. Made from aluminium, fibreglass or wood	• Check rungs, tie rods, repairs, and ropes and cords on stepladders • Ensure it is placed on firm, level ground • Angle should be no greater than 75° or 1 in 4
Mobile mini towers or scaffolds	These are usually aluminium and foldable, with lockable wheels	• Ensure the ground is even and the wheels are locked • Never move the platform while it has tools, equipment or people on it
Roof ladders and crawling boards	The roof ladder allows access while crawling boards provide a safe passage over tiles	• The ladder needs to be long enough and supported • Check boards are in good condition • Check the welds are intact • Ensure all clips function correctly
Mobile tower scaffolds	These larger versions of mini towers usually have edge protection	• Ensure the ground is even and the wheels are locked • Never move the platform while it has tools, equipment or people on it • Base width to height ratio should be no greater than 1:3
Fixed scaffolds and edge protection	Scaffolds fitted and sized to the specific job, with edge protection and guard rails	• There needs to be sufficient braces, guard rails and scaffold boards • The tubes should be level • There should be proper access using a ladder
Mobile elevated work platforms	Known as scissor lifts or cherry pickers	• Specialist training is required before use • Use guard rails and toe boards • Care needs to be taken to avoid overhead hazards such as cables

Table 1.10 Equipment for working at height and safety checks

You must be trained in the use of certain types of access equipment, like mobile scaffolds. Care needs to be taken when assembling and using access equipment. These are all examples of good practice:

• Step ladders should always rest firmly on the ground. Only use the top step if the ladder is part of a platform.

• Do not rest ladders against fragile surfaces, and always use both hands to climb. It is best if the ladder is steadied (footed) by someone at the foot of the ladder. Always maintain three points of contact – two feet and one hand.

• A roof ladder is positioned by turning it on its wheels and pushing it up the roof. It then hooks over the ridge tiles. Ensure that the access ladder to the roof is directly beside the roof ladder.

• A mobile scaffold is put together by slotting sections until the required height is reached. The working platform needs to have a suitable edge protection such as guard-rails and toe-boards. Always push from the bottom of the base and not from the top to move it, otherwise it may lean or topple over.

Figure 1.8 A tower scaffold

WORKING SAFELY WITH ELECTRICITY

It is essential whenever you work with electricity that you are competent and that you understand the common dangers. Electrical tools must be used in a safe manner on site. There are precautions that you can take to prevent possible injury, or even death.

Precautions

Whether you are using electrical tools or equipment on site, you should always remember the following:

* Use the right tool for the job.

* Use a transformer with equipment that runs on 110V.

* Keep the two voltages separate from each other. You should avoid using 230V where possible but use a residual current device (RCD) if you have to use 230V.

* When using 100V, ensure that leads are yellow in colour.

* Check the plug is in good order

* Confirm that the fuse is the correct rating for the equipment.

* Check the cable (including making sure that it does not present a tripping hazard).

* Find out where the mains switch is, in case you need to turn off the power in the event of an emergency.

* Never attempt to repair electrical equipment yourself.

* Disconnect from the mains power before making adjustments, such as changing a drill bit.

* Make sure that the electrical equipment has a sticker that displays a recent test date.

Visual inspection and testing is a three-stage process:

1. The user should check for potential danger signs, such as a frayed cable or cracked plug.

2. A formal visual inspection should then take place. If this is done correctly then most faults can be detected.

3. Combined inspections and **PAT** should take place at regular intervals by a competent person.

Watch out for the following causes of accidents – they would also fail a safety check:

KEY TERMS

PAT

– Portable Appliance Testing – regular testing is a health and safety requirement under the Electricity at Work Regulations (1989).

* damage to the power cable or plug

* taped joints on the cable

* wet or rusty tools and equipment

* weak external casing

* loose parts or screws

* signs of overheating

* the incorrect fuse

* lack of cord grip

* electrical wires attached to incorrect terminals

* bare wires.

DID YOU KNOW?

All power tools should be checked by the user before use. A PAT programme of maintenance, inspection and testing is necessary. The frequency of inspection and testing will depend on the appliance. Equipment is usually used for a maximum of three months between tests.

When preparing to work on an electrical circuit, do not start until a permit to work has been issued by a supervisor or manager to a competent person.

Make sure the circuit is broken before you begin. A 'dead' circuit will not cause you, or anybody else, harm. These steps must be followed:

* Switch off – ensure the supply to the circuit is switched off by disconnecting the supply cables or using an isolating switch.

* Isolate – disconnect the power cables or use an isolating switch.

* Warn others – to avoid someone reconnecting the circuit, place warning signs at the isolation point.

* Lock off – this step physically prevents others from reconnecting the circuit.

* Testing – is carried out by electricians but you should be aware that it involves three parts:

  1. testing a voltmeter on a known good source (a live circuit) so you know it is working properly

  2. checking that the circuit to be worked on is dead

  3. rechecking your voltmeter on the known live source, to prove that it is still working properly.

It is important to make sure that the correct point of isolation is identified. Isolation can be next to a local isolation device, such as a plug or socket, or a circuit breaker or fuse.

The isolation should be locked off using a unique key or combination. This will prevent access to a main isolator until the work has been completed. Alternatively, the handle can be made detachable in the OFF position so that it can be physically removed once the circuit is switched off.

Dangers

You are likely to encounter a number of potential dangers when working with electricity on construction sites or in private houses. Table 1.11 outlines the most common dangers.

Danger	Identifying the danger
Faulty electrical equipment	Visually inspect for signs of damage. Equipment should be double insulated or incorporate an earth cable.
Damaged or worn cables	Check for signs of wear or damage regularly. This includes checking power tools and any wiring in the property.
Trailing cables	Cables lying on the ground, or worse, stretched too far, can present a tripping hazard. They could also be cut or damaged easily.
Cables and pipe work	Always treat services you find as though they are live. This is very important as services can be mistaken for one another. You may have been trained to use a cable and pipe locator that finds cables and metal pipes.
Buried or hidden cables	Make sure you have plans. Alternatively, use a cable and pipe locator, mark the positions, look out for signs of service connection cables or pipes and hand-dig trial holes to confirm positions.
Inadequate over-current protection	Check circuit breakers and fuses are the correct size current rating for the circuit. A qualified electrician may have to identify and label these.

Table 1.11 Common dangers when working with electricity

Each year there are around 1,000 accidents at work involving electric shocks or burns from electricity. If you are working in a construction site you are part of a group that is most at risk. Electrical accidents happen when you are working close to equipment that you think is disconnected but which is, in fact, live.

Another major danger is when electrical equipment is either misused or is faulty. Electricity can cause fires and contact with the live parts can give you an electric shock or burn you.

Different voltages

The two most common voltages that are used in the UK are 230V and 110V:

* 230V: this is the standard domestic voltage. But on construction sites it is considered to be unsafe and therefore 110V is commonly used.

* 110V: these plugs are marked with a yellow casement and they have a different shaped plug. A transformer is required to convert 230V to 110V.

Some larger homes, as well as industrial and commercial buildings, may have 415V supplies. This is the same voltage that is found on overhead electricity cables. In most houses and other buildings the voltage from these cables is reduced to 230V. This is what most electrical equipment works from. Some larger machinery actually needs 415V.

In these buildings the 415V comes into the building and then can either be used directly or it is reduced so that normal 230V appliances can be used.

Colour coded cables

Normally you will come across three differently coloured wires: Live, Neutral and Earth. These have standard colours that comply with European safety standards and to ensure that they are easily identifiable. However, in some older buildings the colours are different.

Wire type	Modern colour	Older colour
Live	Brown	Red
Neutral	Blue	Black
Earth	Yellow and Green	Yellow and Green

Table 1.12 Colour coding of cables

Working with equipment with different electrical voltages

You should always check that the electrical equipment that you are going to use is suitable for the available electrical supply. The equipment's power requirements are shown on its rating plate. The voltage from the supply needs to match the voltage that is required by the equipment.

Storing electrical equipment

Electrical equipment should be stored in dry and secure conditions. Electrical equipment should never get wet but – if it does happen – it should be dried before storage. You should always clean and adjust the equipment before connecting it to the electricity supply.

PERSONAL PROTECTIVE EQUIPMENT (PPE)

Personal protective equipment, or PPE, is a general term that is used to describe a variety of different types of clothing and equipment that aim to help protect against injuries or accidents. Some PPE you will use on a daily basis and others you may use from time to time. The type of PPE you wear depends on what you are doing and where you are. For example, the practical exercises in this book were photographed at a college, which has rules and requirements for PPE that are different to those on large construction sites. Follow your tutor's or employer's instructions at all times.

Types of PPE

PPE literally covers from head to foot. Here are the main PPE types.

Figure 1.9 A hi-vis jacket

Figure 1.10 Safety glasses and goggles

Figure 1.11 Hand protection

Figure 1.12 Head protection

Figure 1.13 Hearing protection

Protective clothing

Clothing protection such as overalls:

* provides some protection from spills, dust and irritants
* can help protect you from minor cuts and abrasions
* reduces wear to work clothing underneath.

Sometimes you may need waterproof or chemical-resistant overalls.

High visibility (hi-vis) clothing stands out against any background or in any weather conditions. It is important to wear high visibility clothing on a construction site to ensure that people can see you easily. In addition, workers should always try to wear light-coloured clothing underneath, as it is easier to see.

You need to keep your high visibility and protective clothing clean and in good condition.

Employers need to make sure that employees understand the reasons for wearing high visibility clothing and the consequences of not doing so.

Eye protection

For many jobs, it is essential to wear goggles or safety glasses to prevent small objects, such as dust, wood or metal, from getting into the eyes. As goggles tend to steam up, particularly if they are being worn with a mask, safety glasses can often be a good alternative.

Hand protection

Wearing gloves will help to prevent damage or injury to the hands or fingers. For example, general purpose gloves can prevent cuts, and rubber gloves can prevent skin irritation and inflammation, such as contact dermatitis caused by handling hazardous substances. There are many different types of gloves available, including specialist gloves for working with chemicals.

Head protection

Hard hats or safety helmets are compulsory on building sites. They can protect you from falling objects or banging your head. They need to fit well and they should be regularly inspected and checked for cracks. Worn straps mean that the helmet should be replaced, as a blow to the head can be fatal. Hard hats bear a date of manufacture and should be replaced after about 3 years.

Hearing protection

Ear defenders, such as ear protectors or plugs, aim to prevent damage to your hearing or hearing loss when you are working with loud tools or are involved in a very noisy job.

Respiratory protection

Breathing in fibre, dust or some gases could damage the lungs. Dust is a very common danger, so a dust mask, face mask or respirator may be necessary.

Make sure you have the right mask for the job. It needs to fit properly otherwise it will not give you sufficient protection.

Foot protection

Foot protection is compulsory on site. Footwear should include steel toecaps (or equivalent) to protect feet from dropped objects, midsole protection (usually a steel plate) to protect against puncture or penetration from things like nails on the floor, and soles with good grip to help prevent slips on wet surfaces.

Legislation covering PPE

The most important piece of legislation is the Personal Protective Equipment at Work Regulations (1992). It covers all sorts of PPE and sets out your responsibilities and those of the employer. Linked to this are the Control of Substances Hazardous to Health (2002) and the Provision and Use of Work Equipment Regulations (1992 and 1998).

Figure 1.14 Respiratory protection

Storing and maintaining PPE

All forms of PPE will be less effective if they are not properly maintained. This may mean examining the PPE and either replacing or cleaning it, or if relevant testing or repairing it. PPE needs to be stored properly so that it is not damaged, contaminated or lost. Each type of PPE should have a CE mark. This shows that it has met the necessary safety requirements.

Importance of PPE

PPE needs to be suitable for its intended use and it needs to be used in the correct way. As a worker or an employee you need to:

* make sure you are trained to use PPE

* follow your employer's instructions when using the PPE and always wear it when you are told to do so

* look after the PPE and if there is a problem with it report it.

Your employer will:

* know the risks that the PPE will either reduce or avoid

* know how the PPE should be maintained

* know its limitations.

Consequences of not using PPE

The consequences of not using PPE can be immediate or long-term. Immediate problems are more obvious, as you may injure yourself. The longer-term consequences could be ill health in the future. If your employer has provided PPE, you have a legal responsibility to wear it.

FIRE AND EMERGENCY PROCEDURES

KEY TERMS

Assembly point

– an agreed place outside the building to go to if there is an emergency.

If there is a fire or an emergency, it is vital that you raise the alarm quickly. You should leave the building or site and then head for the **assembly point.**

When there is an emergency a general alarm should sound. If you are working on a larger and more complex construction site, evacuation may begin by evacuating the area closest to the emergency. Areas will then be evacuated one-by-one to avoid congestion of the escape routes.

Figure 1.15 Assembly point sign

Three elements essential to creating a fire

Three ingredients are needed to make something combust (burn):

* oxygen   * heat   * fuel.

The fuel can be anything which burns, such as wood, paper or flammable liquids or gases, and oxygen is in the air around us, so all that is needed is sufficient heat to start a fire.

The fire triangle represents these three elements visually. By removing one of the three elements the fire can be prevented or extinguished.

Figure 1.16 The fire triangle

How fire is spread

Fire can easily move from one area to another by finding more fuel. You need to consider this when you are storing or using materials on site, and be aware that untidiness can be a fire risk. For example, if there are wood shavings on the ground the fire can move across them, burning up the shavings.

Heat can also transfer from one source of fuel to another. If a piece of wood is on fire and is against or close to another piece of wood, that too will catch fire and the fire will have spread.

On site, fires are classified according to the type of material that is on fire. This will determine the type of fire-fighting equipment you will need to use. The five different types of fire are shown in Table 1.13.

Class of fire	Fuel or material on fire
A	Wood, paper and textiles
B	Petrol, oil and other flammable liquids
C	LPG, propane and other flammable gases
D	Metals and metal powder
E	Electrical equipment

Table 1.13 Different classes of fire

There is also F, cooking oil, but this is less likely to be found on site, except in a kitchen.

Taking action if you discover a fire and fire evacuation procedures

During induction, you will have been shown what to do in the event of a fire and told about assembly points. These are marked by signs and somewhere on the site there will be a map showing their location.

If you discover a fire you should:

* sound the alarm

* not attempt to fight the fire unless you have had fire marshal training

* otherwise stop work, do not collect your belongings, do not run, and do not re-enter the site until the all clear has been given.

Different types of fire extinguishers

Extinguishers can be effective when tackling small localised fires. However, you must use the correct type of extinguisher. For example, putting water on an oil fire could make it explode. For this reason, you should not attempt to use a fire extinguisher unless you have had proper training.

When using an extinguisher it is important to remember the following safety points:

* Only use an extinguisher at the early stages of a fire, when it is small.

* The instructions for use appear on the extinguisher.

* If you do choose to fight the fire because it is small enough, and you are sure you know what is burning, position yourself between the fire and the exit, so that if it doesn't work you can still get out.

Type of fire risk	Fire class Symbol	White label Water	Cream label Foam	Black label Carbon dioxide	Blue label Dry powder	Yellow label Wet chemical
A – Solid (e.g. wood or paper)	A	✓	✓	✗	✓	✓
B – Liquid (e.g. petrol)	B	✗	✓	✓	✓	✗
C – Gas (e.g. propane)	C	✗	✗	✓	✓	✗
D – Metal (e.g. aluminium)	D METAL	✗	✗	✗	✓	✗
E – Electrical (i.e. any electrical equipment)	E	✗	✗	✓	✓	✗
F – Cooking oil (e.g. a chip pan)	F	✗	✗	✗	✗	✓

Table 1.14 Types of fire extinguishers

There are some differences you should be aware of when using different types of extinguisher:

* CO_2 extinguishers – do not touch the nozzle; simply operate by holding the handle. This is because the nozzle gets extremely cold when ejecting the CO_2, as does the canister. Fires put out with a CO_2 extinguisher may reignite, and you will need to ventilate the room after use.

* Powder extinguishers – these can be used on lots of kinds of fire, but can seriously reduce visibility by throwing powder into the air as well as on the fire.

SIGNS AND SAFETY NOTICES

In a well-organised working environment safety signs will warn you of potential dangers and tell you what to do to stay safe. They are used to warn you of hazards. Their purpose is to prevent accidents. Some will tell you what to do (or not to do) in particular parts of the site and some will show you where things are, such as the location of a first aid box or a fire exit.

Types of signs and safety notices

There are five basic types of safety sign, as well as signs that are a combination of two or more of these types. These are shown in Table 1.15.

Type of safety sign	What it tells you	What it looks like	Example
Prohibition sign	Tells you what you must *not* do	Usually round, in red and white	Do not use ladder
Hazard sign	Warns you about hazards	Triangular, in yellow and black	Caution Slippery floor
Mandatory sign	Tells you what you *must* do	Round, usually blue and white	Masks must be worn in this area
Safe condition or information sign	Gives important information, e.g. about where to find fire exits, assembly points or first aid kit, or about safe working practices	Green and white	First aid
Firefighting sign	Gives information about extinguishers, hydrants, hoses and fire alarm call points, etc.	Red with white lettering	Fire alarm call point
Combination sign	These have two or more of the elements of the other types of sign, e.g. hazard, prohibition and mandatory		DANGER Isolate before removing cover

Table 1.15 Different types of safety signs

TEST YOURSELF

1. Which of the following requires you to tell the HSE about any injuries or diseases?

   a. HASAWA

   b. COSHH

   c. RIDDOR

   d. PUWER

2. What is a prohibition notice?

   a. An instruction from the HSE to stop all work until a problem is dealt with

   b. A manufacturer's announcement to stop all work using faulty equipment

   c. A site contractor's decision not to use particular materials

   d. A local authority banning the use of a particular type of brick

3. Which of the following is considered a major injury?

   a. Bruising on the knee

   b. Cut

   c. Concussion

   d. Exposure to fumes

4. If there is an accident on a site who is likely to be the first to respond?

   a. First aider

   b. Police

   c. Paramedics

   d. HSE

5. Which of the following is a summary of risk assessments and is used for high risk activities?

   a. Permit to work

   b. Hazard book

   c. Monitoring statement

   d. Method statement

6. Some substances are combustible. Which of the following are examples of combustible materials?

   a. Adhesives

   b. Paints

   c. Cleaning agents

   d. All of these

7. What is dermatitis?

   a. Inflammation of the skin

   b. Inflammation of the ear

   c. Inflammation of the eye

   d. Inflammation of the nose

8. Screens, netting and guards on a site are all examples of which of the following?

   a. PPE

   b. Signs

   c. Perimeter safety

   d. Electrical equipment

9. Which of the following are also known as scissor lifts or cherry pickers?

   a. Bench saws

   b. Hand-held power tools

   c. Cement additives

   d. Mobile elevated work platforms

10. In older properties the neutral electricity wire is which colour?

    a. Black

    b. Red

    c. Blue

    d. Brown

Chapter 2

Unit CSA–L1Core02

KNOWLEDGE OF TECHNICAL INFORMATION, QUANTITIES AND COMMUNICATION WITH OTHERS

LEARNING OUTCOMES

LO1: Know how to interpret construction related technical information

LO2: Know how to determine quantities of materials

LO3: Know how to relay information in the construction environment

LO4: Know how to communicate with others in the construction environment

INTRODUCTION

The aim of this chapter is to:

* show you the processes of passing on information

* show you the concepts of effective communication.

INTERPRETING CONSTRUCTION-RELATED TECHNICAL INFORMATION

Even quite simple construction projects will require documents. These provide you with the necessary information you will need to do the job. The documents are produced by a range of different people and each document has a different purpose. Together they give you the full picture of the job, from the basic outline through to the technical specifications.

Importance of documentation

In many industries a great deal of information is only ever stored electronically. This is not always an option in the construction industry. Many documents, such as working drawings, will need to be referred to on site. Detailed drawings of components that need to be made will have to be measured and checked before making joints, for example, in the workshop.

It is not always easy to store and look after working documents. The following advice is worth remembering:

* Always ensure you have the latest version of a document to work from before you begin to follow its instructions.

* If you are not going to need to use a document until later then get into the habit of storing it somewhere safe.

* Try to make sure that you do not leave documents lying around on site, where they could get lost or damaged.

* Try to make sure you always have a second copy of the document. You should keep this away from the site, in reserve, in case you lose your working copy.

* You should store any documents that you have used on a particular job at least until that job is completely finished.

* You might need to store the documents for some time after in case you need to refer back to them for repair and servicing.

Interpreting construction specifications

Obviously it would be impossible to put in all of the details in full, so symbols, hatchings and abbreviations are used to simplify the drawings. All of these symbols or hatchings are drawn to follow a British Standards-approved format, BS 1192. The symbols cover various types of brickwork and blockwork, as well as concrete, hard core and insulation, as can be seen in Fig 2.1.

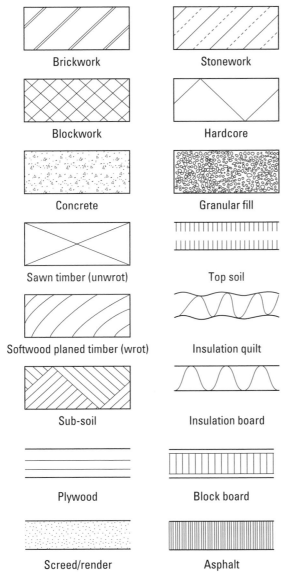

Figure 2.1 Symbols used on drawings

Common abbreviations

For the same reason, abbreviations are often used. Table 2.1 outlines some examples that you will need to become familiar with.

Abbreviation	Meaning
bwk	Brickwork
conc	Areas that will be concreted
dpc	Damp-proof course
fdn	Foundations
insul	Insulation
rwg	Rainwater gulleys
svp	Soil and vent pipe

Table 2.1

Types of documentation

Supporting information can be found in a variety of different types of documents. These include:

* drawings and plans
* programmes of work
* procedures
* specifications
* policies
* schedules
* manufacturers' technical information
* organisational documentation
* training and development records
* risk and method statements
* Construction (Design and Management) (CDM) Regulations
* Building Regulations.

Drawings and plans

Drawings are an important part of construction work. You will need to understand how drawings provide you with the information you need to carry out the work. The drawings show what the building will look like and how it will be constructed. This means that there are several different drawings of the building from different viewpoints.

Block plans

Block plans show the construction site and the surrounding area. Normally block plans are at a ratio of 1:2500 (usually in rural areas) and 1:1250 (usually in urban areas). This means that 1 mm on a block plan is equal to 2,500 mm or 1,250 mm on the ground.

Site plan

The site plan drawing shows what is basically planned for the site. It is an important drawing because it has been created in order to get approval for the project from planning committees or funding sources. In most cases the site plan is an architectural plan, showing the basic arrangement of buildings and any landscaping.

The site plan will usually show:

* directional orientation (i.e. the north point)

* location and size of the building or buildings

* existing structures

* clear measurements.

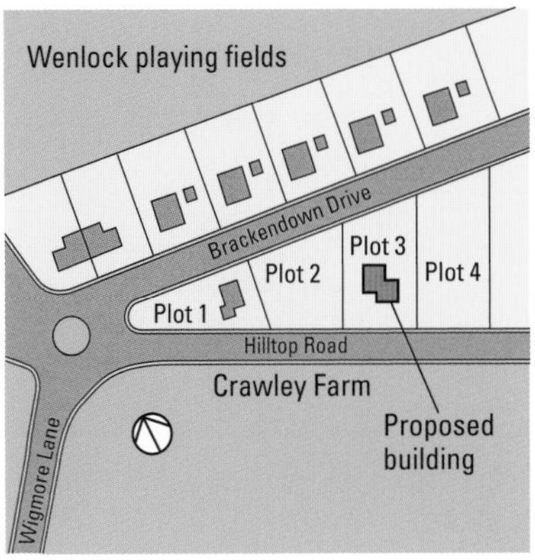

Figure 2.2 Block plan

General location

Location drawings show the site or building in relation to its surroundings. It will therefore show details such as boundaries, other buildings and roads. It will also contain other vital information, including:

* access
* sewers

* drainage
* the north point.

The scale will also be shown and the drawing will have a title. It will also be given a job or project number to help identify it easily, as well as an address, the date of the drawing and the name of the client. A version number will also be on the drawing with an amendment date if there have been any changes. You'll need to make sure you have the latest drawing.

Normally location drawings are either 1:500 or 1:200 (that is, 1 mm of the drawing represents 500 mm or 200 mm on the ground).

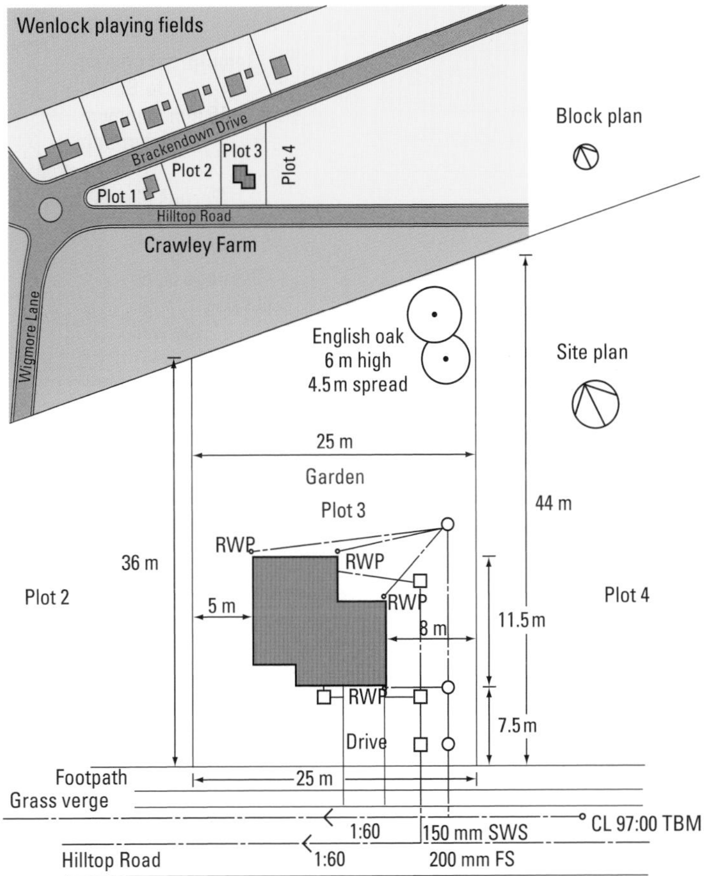

Assembly

These are detailed drawings that illustrate the different elements and components of the construction. They tend to be 1:20, 1:10 or 1:5 (1 cm of the drawing represents 20 mm, 10 mm or 5 mm on the ground). This larger scale allows more detail to be shown, to ensure accurate construction.

Figure 2.3 Location plan

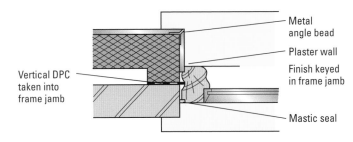

Figure 2.4 Assembly drawing

Sectional

These drawings aim to provide:

* vertical dimensions

* horizontal dimensions

* constructional details.

They can be used to show the height of ground levels, damp-proof courses, foundations and other aspects of the construction.

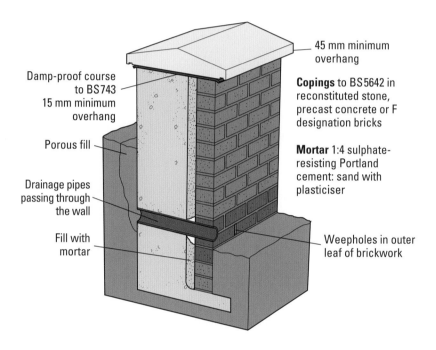

Damp-proof course
to BS743
15 mm minimum
overhang

Porous fill

Drainage pipes
passing through
the wall

Fill with
mortar

45 mm minimum
overhang

Copings to BS5642 in
reconstituted stone,
precast concrete or F
designation bricks

Mortar 1:4 sulphate-
resisting Portland
cement: sand with
plasticiser

Weepholes in outer
leaf of brickwork

Figure 2.5 Section drawing of an earth retaining wall

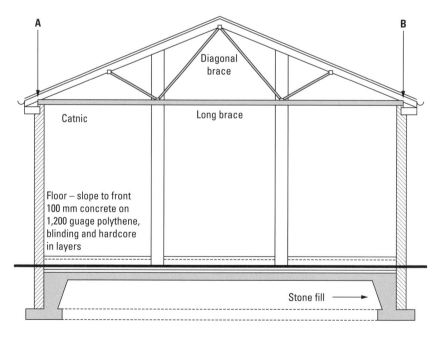

A

B

Diagonal
brace

Catnic

Long brace

Floor – slope to front
100 mm concrete on
1,200 guage polythene,
blinding and hardcore
in layers

Stone fill

Figure 2.6 Section drawing of a garage

Detail drawings

These drawings show how a component needs to be manufactured. They are used to show the relationship between different components within the fabric of the building. For instance, an eaves detail would show rafters, wall plate, roof coverings, inner and outer masonry, insulation and much more. Details can be shown in various scales, but mainly 1:10, 1:5 and 1:1 (the same size as the actual component if it is small).

Orthographic projection (first angle)

First angle projection is a view that represents the side view, the front view and the plan view from above, as can be seen in Fig 2.8.

Serving hatch   Vertical section

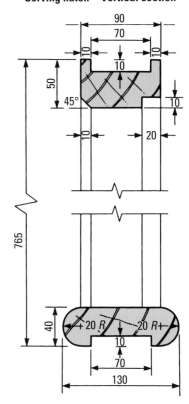

Figure 2.8 Detail drawing (measurements in mm)

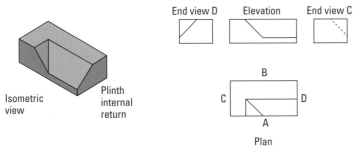

Figure 2.7 First angle projection

Isometric projection

Isometric projection is a way of representing three dimensional objects in two dimensions, as can also be seen in Fig 2.8. All horizontal lines are drawn at 30°.

Programmes of work

Programmes of work show the actual sequence of any work activities on a construction project. Part of the work programme plan is to show target times. They are usually shown in the form of a bar or Gantt chart (a special kind of bar chart), as can be seen in Fig 2.9.

DID YOU KNOW?

First angle is also known as European projection because Americans use third angle projection, which shows the views from a different position.

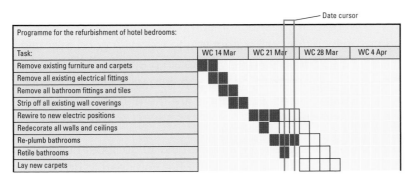

Figure 2.9 Single line contract plan Gantt chart

This figure shows the following:

* On the left hand side all of the tasks are listed – note this is ordered in the sequence of construction.

- On the right the blocks show the target start and end date for each of the individual tasks.

- The timescale can be either days, weeks or months.

Far more complex forms of work programmes can also be created. Fig 2.10 shows the construction of a house.

This more complex example of a Gantt chart shows the following:

- There are two lines – they show the target dates and actual dates. The actual dates are shaded, showing when the work actually began and how long it actually took.

- If this Gantt chart is kept up to date an accurate picture of progress and estimated completion time can be seen.

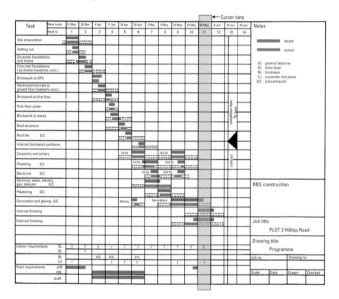

Figure 2.10 Gantt chart for the construction of a house

Procedures

When you work for a construction company there will be a series of procedures, which they will expect you to follow. A good example is the emergency procedure. This will explain precisely what is required in the case of an emergency on site and who will have responsibility to carry out particular duties. Procedures are there to show you the right way of doing something.

A construction procedure could outline how to go about building a wall or hanging a door, taking into account what you need to do beforehand, the materials and tools that are required, and the order in which you must carry out each step.

Another good example of a procedure is the procurement or buying procedure. This will outline:

- who is authorised to buy what, and how much individuals are allowed to spend

- any forms or documents that have to be completed when buying.

Specifications

In addition to drawings it is usually necessary to have documents known as specifications. These provide much more information, as can be seen in Fig 2.11.

The specifications give you a precise description. They will include:

* the address and description of the site

* on-site services (e.g. water and electricity)

* materials description, outlining the size, finish, quality and tolerances

* specific requirements, such as the individual who will authorise or approve work carried out

* any restrictions on site, such as working hours.

Policies

Policies are sets of principles or a programme of actions. The following are two good examples:

* The environmental policy outlines how the business goes about protecting the environment.

* The safety policy outlines how the business deals with health and safety matters and who is responsible for monitoring and maintaining it.

You will normally find both policies and procedures in site rules. These are usually explained to each new employee when they first join the company. Sometimes there may be additional site rules, depending on the job and the location of the work.

Schedules

Schedules are cross-referenced to drawings that have been prepared by an architect. They will show specific design information. Usually they are prepared for jobs that will be carried out regularly on site, such as:

* working on windows, doors, floors, walls or ceilings

* working on drainage, lintels or sanitary ware.

A schedule can be seen in Fig 2.12.

The schedule is very useful for:

* working out the quantities of materials needed

* ordering materials and components and then checking them against deliveries

* locating where specific materials will be used.

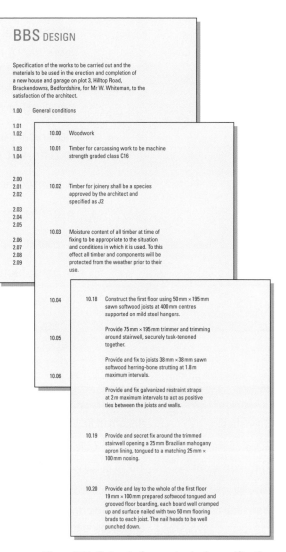

Figure 2.11 Extracts from a typical specification

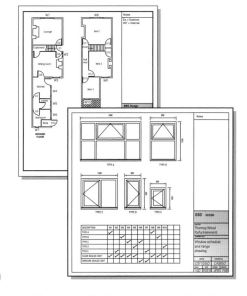

Figure 2.12 Typical windows schedule, range drawing and floor plans

Manufacturers' technical information

Almost everything that is bought to be used on site will come with a variety of information. The basic technical information provided will show what the equipment or material is intended to be used for, how it should be stored and any particular requirements it may have, such as handling or maintenance.

Technical information from the manufacturer can come from a variety of different sources:

* printed or downloadable data sheets

* printed or downloadable user instructions

* manufacturers' catalogues or brochures

* manufacturers' websites.

Organisational documentation

There is a huge potential list of organisational documentation and paperwork. Examples are outlined in Table 2.2. Visual examples can be seen in Fig 2.13 to 2.17.

Document	Purpose
Timesheet	Record of hours that you have worked and the jobs that you have carried out. This is used to help work out your wages and the total cost of the job.
Day worksheet	These detail work that has been carried out without providing an estimate beforehand. They usually include repairs or extra work and alterations.
Variation order	These are provided by the architect and given to the builder, showing any alterations, additions or omissions to the original job.
Confirmation notice	Provided by the architect to confirm any verbal instructions.
Daily report or site diary	These record things that might affect the project like detailed weather conditions, late deliveries or site visitors.
Orders and requisitions	These are order forms, requesting the delivery of materials.
Delivery notes	These are provided by the supplier of materials as a list of all materials being delivered. These need to be checked against materials actually delivered. The buyer will sign the delivery note when they are happy with the delivery.
Delivery record	These are lists of all materials that have been delivered on site.
Memorandum	These are used for internal communications and are usually brief.
Letters	These are used for external communications, usually to customers or suppliers.
Fax	Even though email is commonly used, the industry is still in favour of using faxes, as they provide an exact copy of an original document.

Table 2.2

Figure 2.13 Timesheet

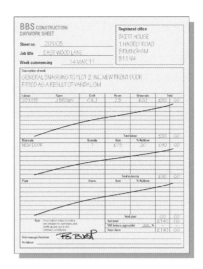

Figure 2.14 Day worksheet

Figure 2.15 Variation order

Figure 2.16 Confirmation notice

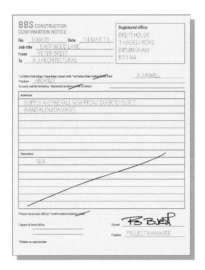

Figure 2.17 Daily report or site diary

Training and development records

Training and development is an important part of any job, as it ensures that employees have all the skills and knowledge that they need to do their work. Most medium to large employers will have training policies that set out how they intend to do this.

To make sure that they are on track and to keep records they will have a range of different documents. These will record all the training that an employee has undertaken.

Training can take place in a number of different ways:

* induction
* toolbox talks
* in-house training
* specialist training
* training or education leading to formal qualifications.

Scales used to produce construction drawings

When the plans for individual buildings or construction sites are drawn up they have to be scaled down so that they will fit on a manageable size of paper. It is important to remember that drawings are not sketches and that they are drawn to scale. This means that they are:

* exact and accurate

* in proportion to the real construction.

You can work out the dimensions by using the scale rule when measuring the drawings. There are several common scales used and the measurement is usually metric:

* 1:2500 – the drawing is 2,500 times smaller than the real object

* 1:100 – the drawing is 100 times smaller than the real object

* 1:50 – the drawing is 50 times smaller than the real object

* 1:20 – the drawing is 20 times smaller than the real object

* 1:10 – the drawing is 10 times smaller than the real object

* 1:5 – the drawing is 5 times smaller than the real object

* 1:2 – the drawing is 2 times smaller than the real object (also called 'half full size').

These drawings would clearly show the dimensions and these would be the actual measurements required (not the scaled-down measurements).

Selecting information

Various documents will provide you with the information you will need. The following examples show you how this works.

Location drawings and specifications

Location drawings are also known as block plans or site plans. The block plan shows the site presented as if you are looking down from above. It will show you where the site is in relation to other buildings and landmarks, such as roads.

The site plan will give you better detail of the site itself. It will contain measurements of the exact dimensions of the plot of land. It will also show you the routes of services and drainage.

The specifications are produced alongside the location drawings of the site. After giving you a brief description of the site, which includes the address, you will find:

* information about any services running into and through the site and whether or not they are connected or need to be connected

* whether there are restrictions about access or working hours on site

* materials that will be needed in order to carry out jobs on site (this will contain quite a lot of detail and will tell you what types of materials are needed, their size, quality and other technical details)

* information about the required workmanship, including what work needs to be done, what quality of work is expected and what the final finish should look like.

Schedules

Schedules can be quite big documents if you are working on a large site with lots of tasks to be done. There is usually a schedule for each different type of job. The schedules are there to record design information. They ensure that you do not accidentally use the wrong components or fittings.

Schedules cover all types of job, such as the types of doors, windows, joinery, heating components and other specific features.

Schedules usually have suitable drawings and usually a floor plan showing where the different features will appear.

PRACTICAL TIP

The same schedule can be used by several trades. For example, a window as far as a bricklayer is concerned means creating an opening that is large enough to take the window that has been selected. For the carpenter the window type and size is important, as they may have to construct a window of a specific size with particular openings and types of glass.

DETERMINE QUANTITIES OF MATERIALS

Working out the quantity and cost of resources that are needed to do a particular job is, perhaps, one of the most difficult tasks. In most cases you or the company you work for will be asked to provide a price for the work. It is generally accepted that there are three ways of doing this:

* **An estimate** is an approximate cost produced from the information available before construction begins.

* **A quotation** is a fixed price.

* **A tender** is a bid for the job at your price.

These three ways of costing are very different and each of them has its own problems.

Checking deliveries of building materials

It is important that all deliveries are thoroughly checked as they arrive. Your suppliers will need to have access to the site. It is important to inform suppliers whether the site has any access problems. Construction materials usually arrive on site on large and heavy lorries, so always check if the ground they will have to cross is soft or uneven and warn them if this is the case. Trees and overhead wires could also be a problem, as could finding space to reverse and turn the lorry.

If you are expecting a delivery to arrive, you should be prepared for it. This means ensuring there is:

* clear access to the site

* somewhere ready to store the materials and equipment being delivered

* enough help on hand to assist moving the materials from the delivery point to the storage area.

There are two documents that you will need in order to check the delivery:

* your order, which is a purchase order or confirmation of the materials and equipment that you have ordered from the supplier

* a delivery note, which should be handed to you by the delivery driver.

The first thing to do is check that the two documents match. If they do then what is on the delivery truck should be what you ordered. You now need to check and tick off each item on the delivery note. It needs to be:

* the right specification
* the right quantity
* the right size
* undamaged.

You should not accept items that do not match these four points. You should not sign the delivery ticket or delivery note unless you are satisfied with what has been delivered.

Methods used to estimate quantities

Numerous factors determine the cost of a construction project, whatever its size, but getting the best price on the ideal quantities should not be guesswork. Some possible considerations, according to the size and significance of the project, would be:

* the availability of labour and materials

* the lead time on materials

* the economy and borrowing rates

* the time of year

* cost of plant

* the duration of the project – really large projects can go on for years.

Obviously experience means that you can more quickly estimate the quantities of materials that will be needed on particular (small) construction projects. This is also true of working out the best place to buy materials and how much the labour costs will be to get the job finished.

Many businesses will use the *Hutchins UK Building Blackbook* (published by Franklin-Andrews), which provides a construction cost guide. It breaks down all types of work and shows an average cost for each of them.

Computerised estimating packages are available, which will give a comprehensive detailed estimate that looks very professional. This will also help to estimate quantities and timescales.

The alternative is of course to carry out a numerical calculation. So it is important to have the right resources upon which to base these calculations. These could be working drawings, schedules or other documents.

Usually this involves making additions, subtractions, multiplications and divisions. In order to work out the amount of materials you will need for a construction project you will need to know some basic information:

* What does the job entail? How complex is it, and how much labour is required?

* What materials will be used?

* What are the costs of the materials?

Measurement

The standard unit for measurement is the metre (m). There are 100 centimetres (cm) and 1,000 millimetres (mm) in a metre. It is important to remember that drawings and plans have different scales, so these need to be converted to work out quantities of materials.

The most basic thing to work out is length, from which you can calculate perimeter, area and then volume, capacity, mass and weight, as can be seen in Table 2.3.

Measurement	Explanation
Length	This is the distance from one end to the other. This could be measured in metres or milimetres, depending on the job.
Perimeter	This is the total distance around the outside of a shape. For example, you might need to know the length of the perimeter around a site to work out how much security fencing you need before work starts. You can work out the perimeter by adding the lengths of each side of the shape together. For most jobs, perimeter will be measured in metres (see Fig 2.20).
Area	This is the amount of surface a shape covers. For example you might need to work out the area of a room or a wall to calculate what quantity of materials you will need. You can work out the area of a room by measuring the length and the width of the room and multiplying the two figures together. You can work out the area of a wall by measuring the length and the height of the wall and multiplying the two figures together. For most jobs, area will be measured in square metres (m²) (see Fig 2.21).
Volume and capacity	This shows how much space is taken up by an object or room. You can work out the volume of a room by multiplying the width by the length and then by the height. For most jobs, volume will be measured in cubic metres (m³). Capacity works in exactly the same way as volume, but instead of showing the figure as cubic metres you may show it as litres (l). This is ideal if you are trying to work out the capacity of a water tank or a garden pond.
Mass or weight	Mass is measured usually in kilograms or in grams. Mass is the actual weight of a particular object, such as a brick.

Table 2.3

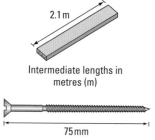

2.1 m

Intermediate lengths in metres (m)

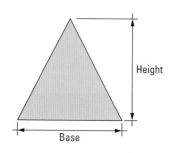

75 mm

Small lengths in millimetres (mm)

Figure 2.18 Length in metres and millimetres

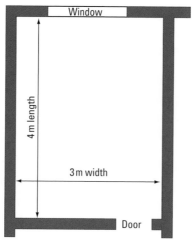

Figure 2.19 Measuring area and perimeter

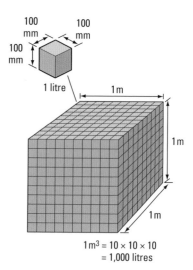

$1 m^3 = 10 \times 10 \times 10$
$= 1,000$ litres

Figure 2.20 Relationship between volume and capacity

Formulae

These can appear to be complicated, but using formulae is essential for working out quantities of materials. Each of the formulae is related to different shapes. In construction you will often have to work out quantities of materials needed for odd shaped areas.

Area

To work out the area of a triangular shape, you use the following formula:

$$\text{Area (A)} = \text{Base (B)} \times \frac{\text{Height (H)}}{2}$$

So if a triangle has a base of 4.5 and a height of 3.5 the calculation is:

$$4.5 \times \frac{3.5}{2}$$

$$\text{Or } 4.5 \times 3.5 = \frac{15.75}{2} = 7.875 \, m^2$$

Figure 2.21 Triangle

Height

If you want to work out the height of a triangle you switch the formulae around. To give:

$$\text{Height} = 2 \times \frac{\text{Area}}{\text{Base}}$$

Perimeter

To work out the perimeter of a rectangle we use the formula:

$$\text{Perimeter} = 2 \times (\text{Length} + \text{Width})$$

It is important to remember this because you need to count the length and the width twice to ensure you have calculated the total distance around the object.

Circles

To work out the circumference or perimeter of a circle you use the formula:

$$\text{Circumference} = \pi \text{ (pi)} \times \text{diameter}$$

π (pi) is always the same for all circles and is 3.142.

Diameter is the length of the widest part and is twice the radius.

If we know the circumference and need to work out the diameter of the circle the formula is:

$$\text{Diameter} = \frac{\text{circumference}}{\pi \ (\text{pi})}$$

For example if a circle has a circumference of 15.39 m then to work out the diameter:

$$\frac{15.39}{3.142} = 4.89 \, \text{m}$$

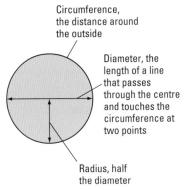

Figure 2.22 Parts of a circle

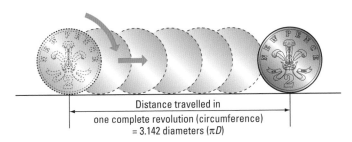

Figure 2.23 Relationship between circumference and diameter

Complex areas

Land, for example, is rarely square or rectangular. It is made up of odd shapes. Never be overwhelmed by complex areas, as all you need to do is break them down into regular shapes.

By accurately measuring the perimeter you can then break down the shape into a series of triangles or rectangles. All that is then necessary is to work out the area of each of the shapes within the overall shape and then add them together.

Shape	Area equals	Perimeter equals
Square	AA (or A multiplied by A)	4A (or A multiplied by 4)
Rectangle	LB (or L multiplied by B)	2(L+B) (or L plus B multiplied by 2)
Trapezium	$\dfrac{(A+B)H}{2}$ (or A plus B multiplied by H then divided by 2)	A+B+C+D

Shape	Area equals	Perimeter equals
Triangle	$\dfrac{BH}{2}$ (or B multiplied by H and then divided by 2)	A + B + C
Circle	πR^2 (or Pi (3.142) × R × R)	πD or $2\pi R$ (or Pi (3.142) × D or 2 × 3.142 × R)

Table 2.4

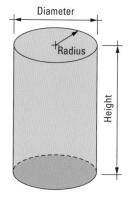

Figure 2.24 Cylinder

Volume

Sometimes it is necessary to work out the volume of an object, such as a cylinder or the amount of concrete needed. All that needs to be done is to work out the base area and then multiply that by the height.

For a concrete area, if a 1.2 m square needs 3 m of height then the calculation is:

$$1.2 \times 1.2 \times 3 = 4.32\,m^3$$

To work out the volume of a cylinder you need to know the base area × the height. The formula is:

$$\pi r^2 \times H$$

So if a cylinder has a radius (r) of 0.8 and a height of 3.5 m then the calculation is:

$$3.142 \times 0.8 \times 0.8 \times 3.5 = 7.038\,m^3$$

Pythagoras

Pythagoras' theorem is used to work out the length of the sides of right angled triangles. It states that:

In all right angled triangles the square of the longest side is equal to the sum of the squares of the other two sides (that is, the length of a side multiplied by itself).

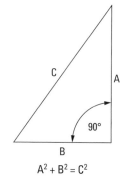

Figure 2.25 Pythagoras' theorem

Measuring materials

Using simple measurements and formulae can help you work out the amount of materials you will need. This is all summarised in the following table.

Material	Measurement
Timber	To work out the linear run of a cubic metre of timber of a given cross sectional area, divide a square metre by the cross sectional area of one piece.
Flooring	To work out the amount of flooring for a particular area metres^2 multiply the width of the floor by the length of the floor.
Stud walling, rafters and joists	Measure the distance that the stud partition will cover then divide that distance by a specified spacing and add 1. This will give you the number of spaces between each stud.
Fascias, barges and soffits	Measure the length and then add 10% for waste; however, this will depend on the nearest standard metric size of timber available.
Skirting, dado, picture rails and coving	You need to work out the perimeter of the room and then subtract any doorways or other openings. Again, add 10% for waste.
Bricks and mortar	Half brick walls use 60 bricks per metre squared and one brick walls use double that amount. You should add 5 per cent to take into account any cutting or damage. For mortar assume that you will need 1 kg for each brick.

Table 2.5

How to cost materials

Once you have found out the quantity of materials necessary you need to find out the price of those materials. It is then simply a case of multiplying those prices by the amount of materials actually needed.

Materials and purchasing systems

Many builders and companies will have preferred suppliers of materials. Many of them will already have negotiated discounts based on their likely spending with that supplier over the course of a year. The supplier will be geared up to supply them at an agreed price.

In other cases builders may shop around to find the best price for the materials that match the specification. It is not always the case that the lowest price is necessarily the best. All materials need to be of a sufficient quality. The other key consideration is whether the materials are immediately available for delivery.

DID YOU KNOW?

Many businesses that fail do so as a result of not working out their costs properly. They may have plenty of work but they are making very little money.

CASE STUDY

LAING O'ROURKE

What you learned at school comes in handy for work

Joshua Richardson is an apprentice in his third year at Laing O'Rourke in Leeds.

'I got an A in Resistant Materials (Design and Technology) at school and then decided it was a good idea to apply for a joinery apprenticeship. I applied for a few apprenticeships and eventually got one with Laing O'Rourke. They gave me a phone interview, and then I had to go to an assessment day where we did things like spatial tests, group activities and a 10-minute presentation. I'm glad I got to do similar tests with my other applications, because if this was the first place I'd done them, maybe I wouldn't have made it.

You had to have GCSEs in Maths, English and Science at A–C. There's some people at college who didn't have these so they have to do Functional Skills on top of everything.

It's important because you do use your Maths and English skills at work every day.

Not only do you need to use your English for college work-based evidence, but also just talking to people. I found that having done talks and presentations at school, it really helped communication skills, and I can talk quite easily with different people now.

With Maths, you definitely need that every day. When you're doing any job, you need to work out how to use a measuring tape, and what kind of Maths you're going to have to use. You have to measure up properly and know each calculation you'll need. It's all on your tape, but you've got to think about it and add it all together, and it's especially important to get it right when you're cutting.

If you're not too good with numbers, you just have to practise it – it's something that can come to you, and not everyone gets it straight away. Every so often, a guy will shout out a couple of measurements and say, "Add that!" So it's not as if you get to pull out your calculator every time.'

It is vital that suppliers are reliable and that they have sufficient materials in stock. Delays in deliveries can cause major setbacks on site. It is not always possible to warn suppliers that materials will be needed, but a well-run site should be able to anticipate needed materials and put the orders in within good time.

Large quantities may be delivered direct from the manufacturer straight to site. This is preferable when dealing with items where consistency is essential.

RELAYING INFORMATION IN THE CONSTRUCTION ENVIRONMENT

Communication is all about passing on accurate information. No matter who you are communicating with, you must understand what is being asked. You also need to be able to give them a clear answer. Sometimes you do not have the information or it is not your decision to make. In these cases you will need to take a message.

Whatever the situation, you always need to be positive and efficient. You also need to be clear. Poor communication and negative communication nearly always lead to confusion, delays and extra costs.

Basic content and requirements for recording a message

Message taking is an important skill. You are the way in which information is passed from one person to another. Providing you remember to pass the message on it may not need to be written down. In many cases, however, messages can be complicated and these do need to be written down. In fact it is a wise plan to record the fact that the message was received in the first place:

* Note the date and time that the message was received.

* Clearly write down the actual message. Someone will have to read this, so make sure it is legible.

* Write down the person's name and their contact details.

If you are taking a message and you are in the site office then there may be a telephone answering pad to hand, or perhaps sticky notes.

If the questions are complicated it will be best to get them to call back or to promise them that the person with the knowledge will call them back.

> **PRACTICAL TIP**
>
> Many people who leave a message will tell you that it is urgent. It is not for you to decide whether it is or not. It is just down to you to pass the message on and mark it urgent if they have said so.

Positive and negative communication

Construction is an industry that relies on communication.

Positive communication means:

* being courteous and respectful when you are talking to others

* being considerate, particularly if the other person is under pressure

* listening to what others are saying

* being clear on key points

* keeping a sense of humour.

Showing these positive communication skills should mean that others will show positive communication towards you.

On the other hand, if you are:

* rude and disrespectful

* unwilling to listen or pay attention

* incapable of making a decision

* bad tempered

then you are communicating in a negative way. This could lead to confusion, arguments and problems.

Clear and effective communication

Communication in all types of work is essential. It needs to be clear and to the point, as well as accurate. Above all it needs to be a two-way process. This means that any communication you have with anyone must be understood. Think before communicating and never assume that someone understands you unless they have confirmed that they do. Negative or poor communication can damage the confidence that others have in you to do your job.

In construction work everything is about time and following strict instructions and specifications. Failing to communicate will always cause confusion, extra cost and delays. In an industry such as this these are unacceptable and very easy to avoid.

Good communication means efficiency and achievement.

COMMUNICATING WITH OTHERS IN THE CONSTRUCTION ENVIRONMENT

Communication can be split into two different types:

* **Verbal communication** includes face-to-face conversations, discussions in meetings or performance reviews and talking on the telephone.

* **Written communication** includes all forms of documents, from letters and emails to drawings and work schedules.

Each of these forms of communication needs to be clear, accurate and designed in such a way as to make sure that whoever has to use it or refer to it understands it.

Communicating in the appropriate way with others

Each construction job will require the services of a team of professionals. They will need to be able to work and communicate with one another. Each has different roles and responsibilities. They can be broken down into three particular groups:

* on site
* off site
* visitors.

These are described in Tables 2.6, 2.7 and 2.8.

On site

Role	Responsibilities
Apprentices	They can work for any of the main building services trades under supervision. They only carry out work that has been specifically assigned to them by a trainer, a skilled operative or a supervisor.
Skilled or trade operative	A specialist in a particular trade, such as bricklaying or carpentry. They will be qualified in that trade, or working towards their qualification
Unskilled operatives	Also known as labourers, these are entry level operatives without any formal training. They may be experienced on sites and will take instructions from the supervisor or site manager.
Building services engineers	They are involved in the design, installation and maintenance of heating, water, electrics, lighting, gas and communications. They work either for the main contractor or the architect and give instruction to building services operatives.
Building services operatives	They include all the main trades involved in installation, maintenance and servicing. They take instruction from the building services engineers and work with other individuals, such as the supervisor and charge-hand.
Sub-contractor	They carry out work on behalf of the main contractor and are usually specialist tradespeople or professionals, such as electricians. Essentially, they provide a service and are contracted to complete their part of the project.
Charge-hand	This person supervises a specific trade, such as carpenters and bricklayers.
Site manager	This person runs the construction site, makes plans to avoid problems and meet deadlines, and ensures all processes are carried out safely. They communicate directly with the client.
Supervisor	The supervisor works directly for the site manager on larger projects and carries out some of the site manager's duties on their behalf.
Health and safety officer	This person is responsible for managing the safety and welfare of the construction site. They will carry out inspections, provide training and correct hazards.

Table 2.6

Off site

Role	Responsibilities
Client	The client, such as a local authority, commissions the job. They define the scope of the work and agree on the timescale and schedule of payments.
Customer	For domestic dwellings, the customer may be the same as the client, but for larger projects a customer may be the end user of the building, such as a tenant renting local authority housing or a business renting an office. These individuals are most affected by any work on site. They should be considered and informed, with a view to them suffering as little disruption as possible.
Architect	They are involved in designing new buildings, extensions and alterations. They work closely with clients and customers to ensure the designs match their needs. They also work closely with other construction professionals, such as surveyors and engineers.

Consultant	Consultants such as civil engineers work with clients to plan, manage, design or supervise construction projects. There are many different types of consultant, all with particular specialisms.
Main contractor	This is the main business or organisation employed to head up the construction work. They organise the on-site building team and pull together all necessary expertise. They manage the whole project, taking full responsibility for its progress and costs.
Clerk of works	This person is employed by the architect on behalf of a client. They oversee the construction work and ensure that it represents the interests of the client and follows agreed specifications and designs.
Quantity surveyor	Quantity surveyors are concerned with building costs. They balance maintaining standards and quality against minimising the costs of any project. They need to make choices in line with Building Regulations. They may work either for the client or for the contractor, and clients and contractors may both have quantity surveyors on site.
Estimator	Estimators calculate detailed cost breakdowns of work based on specifications provided by the architect and main contractor. They work out the quantity and costs of all building materials, plant required and labour costs.
Supplier/wholesaler contracts manager	They work for materials suppliers or stockists, providing materials that match required specifications. They agree prices and delivery dates.

Table 2.7

Visitors

Site visitor	Role and responsibility
Training officers and assessors	These people work for approved training providers. They visit the site to observe and talk to apprentices and their mentors or supervisors. They assess apprentices' competence and help them to put together the paperwork needed to show evidence of their skills.
Building control inspector	This person works for the local authority to ensure that the construction work conforms to regulations, particularly the Building Regulations. They check plans, carry out inspections, issue completion certificates, work with architects and engineers and provide technical knowledge on site.
Water inspector	This person carries out checks of plumbing and drainage systems on construction sites.
Health and Safety Executive (HSE) inspector	An HSE inspector from the local authority can enter any workplace without giving notice. They will look at the workplace, the activities and the management of health and safety to ensure that the site complies with health and safety laws. They can take action if they find there is a risk to health and safety on site.
Electrical services inspector	Inspectors are approved by the National Inspection Council for Electrical Installation Contracting. They check all electrical installation has been carried out in accordance with legislation, particularly Part P of the Building Regulations.

Table 2.8

Maintaining good working relationships

It is important to have a good working relationship with colleagues at work. An important part of this is to communicate in a clear way with them. This helps everyone understand what is going on and what decisions have been made. It also means being clear. Most communication with colleagues will be verbal (spoken). Good communication means:

* cutting out mistakes and stoppages (saving money)

* avoiding delays

* making sure that the job is done right the first time and every time.

Equality and diversity in communication

Equality and diversity is not simply about treating everyone in the same way. It is actually recognising that people are different. Each of us is unique. This could mean that we might have a different culture, be of different ages or follow different religions. It might refer to our marital status or gender, our sexual orientation or our first language.

In all your actions and your communications you should:

* recognise and respect other people's backgrounds

* recognise that everyone has rights and responsibilities

* not harass or be offensive and use language or behaviour that discriminates.

Figure 2.26 A water inspection

You should also remember that not everyone's first language will be English so they may not understand everything or be able to communicate clearly with you. You might also find that some colleagues may have hearing impairments (or may not hear what you're saying because they are in a noisy environment). It's best to use simple language and check that both you and the person you're communicating with have understood what you need to know.

CASE STUDY

Using writing and maths in the real world

Gary Kirsop, Head of Property Services says:

'People seem to think that trades are all about your hands, but it's more than that. You're measuring complicated things – all the trades need to have about the same technical level for planning, calculation and writing reports. You need that level to get through your exams for the future too. When you have one day a week in college, but four days a week working with customers in the real world, without communications skills, it would all fall apart. You have to understand that people come from different backgrounds and that they have their own communication modes. Having good GCSEs will really help you get by in the trade.'

TEST YOURSELF

1. If a drawing is at a scale of 1:500, each millimetre in the drawing represents how much on the ground?

   a. 1m

   b. 1mm

   c. 500mm

   d. 500m

2. What is the other term used to describe an orthographic projection?

   a. First angle

   b. Second angle

   c. Third angle

   d. Isometric

3. What is a variation order?

   a. A list of all materials that have been delivered to site

   b. A document showing work that has been carried out without a prior estimate

   c. A document that confirms any verbal instructions

   d. A document provided by the architect to the builder to show any changes to the original job

4. On a drawing, if you were to see the letters FDN, what would that mean?

   a. The signature of the architect

   b. Foundation Design Network

   c. Foundations

   d. Full distance

5. If a drawing is at a scale of 1:5, how many times smaller is the drawing than the real object?

   a. 5 times

   b. 50 times

   c. Half the size

   d. 500 times

6. Which of the following values is pi?

   a. 3.121

   b. 3.424

   c. 3.142

   d. 3.421

7. Which document is used to give detailed sets of requirements that cover the construction, features, materials and finishes?

   a. Work programme

   b. Purchase order

   c. Policy document

   d. Job specification

8. How do you work out the amount of flooring necessary for a room?

   a. Divide width by length

   b. Add width to length

   c. Multiply length by height

   d. Multiply width by length

9. Which individual on a typical site would sign off timesheets?

   a. Architect

   b. Site manager/supervisor

   c. Delivery person

   d. Customer

10. Which are the two main types of communication?

    a. Verbal and written

    b. Telephones and emails

    c. Meetings and memorandum

    d. Plans and faxes

Chapter 3

Unit CSA–L1Core03
KNOWLEDGE OF CONSTRUCTION TECHNOLOGY

LEARNING OUTCOMES

LO1: Know about foundation construction

LO2: Know about floor construction

LO3: Know about wall construction

LO4: Know about roof construction

LO5: Know about utilities and services within construction

LO6: Know about sustainability within construction

INTRODUCTION

The aim of this chapter is to:

* help you understand the range of building materials used within the construction industry

* help you understand their suitability to the construction of modern buildings.

* help you understand the role of sustainability in the construction industry

* help you to be aware of different construction methods.

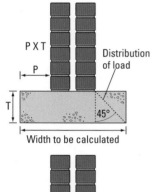

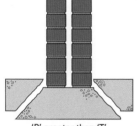

'P' greater than 'T'
leads to shear failure

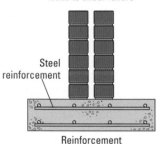

Reinforcement
used to reduce 'T'

Figure 3.1 Foundation properties

FOUNDATION CONSTRUCTION

Foundations are a primary element of a building, and form part of the substructure (the element of the building which is below ground and cannot be seen once the structure has been completed). Foundations spread the load of the superstructure (the visible part of the completed building), transferring it to the subsoil ground below. They provide structural stability and help to prevent damage to the building in the event of ground movement. They can range from a concrete strip to pre-cast reinforced concrete-driven piles.

Purpose of foundations

Foundations are designed to counteract factors such as ground movement, which could damage the building. It is important to work out the necessary width of foundation. This depends on the total load of the structure and the load-bearing capacity of the ground or subsoil on which the building is being constructed:

* Wide foundations are used when the construction is on weak ground, or the superstructure will be heavy.

* Narrow foundations are used when the subsoil is capable of carrying a heavy weight, or the building is a relatively light load.

The load that is placed on strip and pad foundations spreads into the ground at 45°. Shear failure will take place if the thickness of the foundations is less than the projection of the wall or column face on the edge of the foundations. This is what leads to subsidence (the ground under the structure sinking or collapsing).

As we will see in this section, the depth of the foundation is dependent on the load-bearing capacity of the subsoil. As a general rule of thumb, foundations should be 200 mm to 300 mm thick.

KEY TERMS

Shear failure

– when the load from the superstructure of the building bears down on the foundation. Underneath the foundation the soil will settle and there could be a failure of the soil to support the foundation. This will cause it to crack and part of the building will sink with it.

Different types of foundation

Generally there are several different types of foundation, which can be seen in Fig 3.2.

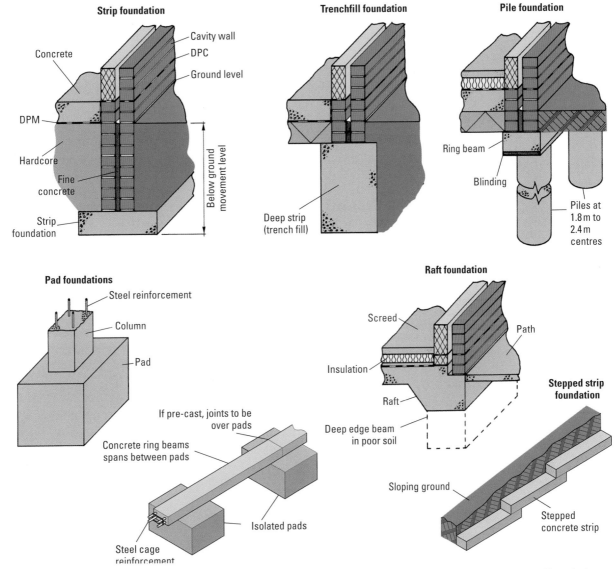

Figure 3.2 Foundation types

* The traditional **strip foundation** is quite narrow and tends to be used for low-rise buildings and dwellings. A thin strip of concrete is laid and then brick or block is built up to the DPC level. These can be reinforced where the ground is weak. They can also be stepped on sloping ground, in order to cut down on the amount of excavation needed. It can also be deep, which uses more concrete but reduces the number of bricks used below ground level. An alternative to deep strip foundations is a trench fill foundation.

* Trench fill foundations are constructed by digging a narrow trench to the foundation depth and then filled with concrete. This reduces the labour and materials required to lay the foundation, as no bricks or blocks have to be laid into the trench. Trench fill:

* reduces the need to have a wide foundation

* reduces construction time

* speeds up the construction of the foundation.

* **Pad foundations** tend to be used for structures that have either a concrete or a steel frame. The pads are placed to support the columns, which transfer the load of the building into the subsoil.

* **Pile foundations** tend to be used for high-rise buildings or where the subsoil is unstable. Holes are bored into the ground and filled with concrete or pre-cast concrete, steel or timber posts are driven into the ground. These piles are then spanned with concrete ring beams with steel reinforcement so that the load of the building is transferred deeper into the ground below. Pile foundations can be short or long depending on how high the building is or how bad the soil conditions are.

* **Raft foundations** are used when there is a danger that the subsoil is unstable. A large concrete slab reinforced with steel bars is used to outline the whole footprint of the building. It has an edge beam to take the load from the walls which is transferred over the whole raft. This means that the building effectively 'floats' on the ground surface on top of the concrete raft.

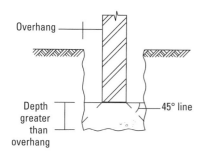

Figure 3.3 Unreinforced strip foundation

Selecting a foundation

One of the first things that a structural engineer will look at when they investigate a site is the nature of the soil, the ground conditions, the likelihood of ground movement and issues such as the water table (where groundwater begins).

Table 3.1 shows different types of subsoil and how they can affect the choice of foundation.

Subsoil type	Characteristics
Rock	High load bearing but there may be cracks or faults in the rock, which could collapse.
Granular	Medium to high load bearing and can be compacted sand or gravel. If there is a danger of flooding the sand can be washed away.
Cohesive	Low to medium load bearing, such as clay and silt. These are relatively stable, but there may be problems with water.
Organic	Low load bearing, such as peat and topsoil. There is also a great deal of air and water present in the soil so organic material must be removed before starting the foundations.

Table 3.1

The ground may move, particularly if the conditions are wet, extremely dry or there are extremes of temperature. Clay, for example, will shrink in the hot summer months and swell up again in the wet winter months. Frost can affect the water in the ground, causing it to expand (frost heave).

Ground movement is also affected by the proximity of trees and large shrubs. They will absorb water from the soil, which can dry out the subsoil. This causes the soil underneath the foundations to collapse. This may not be a problem until the tree or shrub is removed or new ones planted.

As we have seen above, the other key factor when selecting a foundation is the end use of the building:

* Strip foundations – this is the most common and cheapest type of foundation. It is a strip of concrete that runs under the load-bearing walls. The actual depth and width of the strip depends on the ground and the load from the building. They are used for low to medium rise domestic and industrial buildings, as the load bearing requirement will not be high.

* Piled foundations – tend to be used for high rise buildings or where subsoil is unstable if the ground directly under the building is weak or unstable then concrete or steel piles can be driven through this weak ground and into more solid ground beneath it. Reinforced concrete ring beams are placed over the piles as a direct support for the building.

* Raft foundations – these are very expensive and are only ever really used when the ground on which the building is being constructed is very soft. It is also sometimes used when the ground across the area is likely to react in different ways because of the weight of the building. In areas of the UK where there has been mining, for example, raft foundations are quite common, as the building could subside.

Concrete

Concrete is the most common material used for foundations as it is strong and durable. It is usually cast directly on site.

The concrete needs to be poured into the foundation with some care. The size of the foundation will usually determine whether the concrete is actually mixed on site or brought in, in a ready-mixed state, from a supplier. For smaller foundations a concrete mixer and wheelbarrows are usually sufficient. The concrete is then poured into the foundation using a chute (a long trough with a rounded bottom and open ends that directs the concrete to where it is needed).

Concrete consists of both fine and coarse aggregate, along with water.

Aggregates

Aggregates are basically fillers. Coarse aggregate is usually either crushed rock or gravel. The grains are 5mm or larger.

The fine aggregate fills up any gaps between the particles in the coarse aggregate.

Fine aggregate is usually sand that has grains smaller than 5mm.

Cement

Cement is an adhesive or binder. It is Portland stone, crushed, burnt and crushed again and mixed with limestone. The materials are powdered and then mixed together to create a fine powder, which is then fired in a kiln. It may be mixed with other materials for different purposes, such as creating masonry mortar.

Water

Potable water, which is water that is suitable for drinking, should be used when making concrete. The reason for this is that drinkable water has not been contaminated and it does not have organic material in it that could rot and cause the concrete to crack. The water mixes with the cement and then coats the aggregate. This effectively bonds everything together.

Additives

Additives, or admixtures, make it possible to control the setting time and other aspects of fresh concrete allowing you to have greater control over the concrete. They can:

* give you higher strength concrete

* provide protection against degradation of concrete or corrosion of reinforced concrete, which will weaken the structure

* speed up the time the concrete needs to set

* reduce the time the concrete takes to set

* provide protection against cracking as the concrete sets (by preventing shrinkage)

* improve the flow (workability) of the concrete

* improve the finish of the concrete

* provide hot or cold weather protection (a drop or rise in temperature can change the amount of time that concrete needs to set, so these admixtures compensate for that).

You might need this flexibility if, for example, the schedule or weather changes or the job has an unusual specification.

DID YOU KNOW?

Ordinary Portland cement is Portland stone crushed and burnt until all the water disappears. This is taken to site where the water is added again to reconstitute the stone to the form required.

Figure 3.4 Reinforcement using steel bars (or mesh)

Reinforcement

Steel bars or mesh can be used to give the foundation additional strength and support. It can also help to stop the foundation from cracking. Concrete is a good material under direct weight loads, but where concrete foundations are wide and parts of them are under additional tension there is a danger they may crack.

Natural and artificial stone

Both of these products can be placed over the top of plain foundations hardcore fill that is put into the substructure to fill the gap up to the ground floor level hardcore fill that is put into the substructure to fill the gap up to the ground floor level. The synthetic stone weighs far less than natural stone. The other advantage with the synthetic products is that the foundations do not need to be as substantial.

FLOOR CONSTRUCTION

A floor is a level surface that provides some insulation and carries any loads on it (for example, from furniture) and then to transfer those loads.

Ground floors also have additional purposes. They need to stop moisture from entering the building from the ground. They also need to prevent plant or tree roots from entering the building.

Ground floors

For ground floors there are two options:

* Solid – in contact with the ground

* Suspended – does not touch the ground and spans between walls in the building (effectively there is a void beneath the floor)

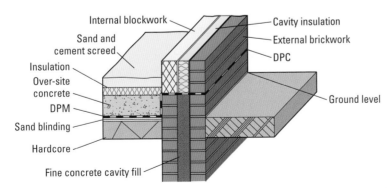

Figure 3.5 Solid ground floors

Floating floor

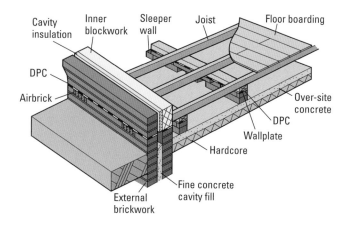

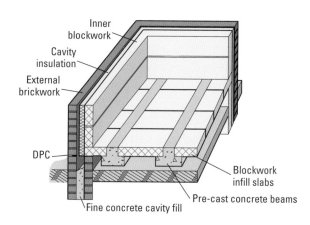

Figure 3.6 Suspended ground floors

The options for ground floors can be complicated because they need to perform several functions. While new builds don't tend to have timber joists and floorboards, extensions to existing buildings usually need to match existing construction styles. Suspended ground floors and traditional timber floors tend to be seen in older buildings. It is far more common to have solid ground floors, or to have timber floors over concrete floors, which are known as floating ground floors.

The key options are outlined in Table 3.2.

Type of floor	Construction and characteristics
Solid	The ground is compacted, and compacted hard core is used as the base, with a binding layer of sand, which is covered with a damp-proof membrane (dpm). A layer of insulation board, usually 100 mm thick, is then placed onto the dpm and concrete is poured on top. To provide a smooth finish for floor finishes a cement and sand screed is applied, usually after the building has been made watertight.
Suspended	Timber – a similar process to a solid ground floor is carried out but then, on top of this, dwarf walls or sleepers are built. These are used to support the timber floor. Air bricks are also added to provide necessary ventilation. Joists are then spaced out along the dwarf walls. A damp-proof course is inserted under the floor joists and then floorboards or sheets placed on top of the joists. Beam and block – concrete beams and lightweight concrete slabs or blocks are used to create the basic flooring. The beams are evenly spaced across the foundation and gaps between the beams are filled with blocks to form the floor. The blocks and beams are then insulated and it is finished off with a cement screed.
Floating	This is a timber construction which goes over the top of a solid concrete floor. Bearers are put down and then the boarding or sheets are fixed to the bearers. The weight of the boards themselves hold them in place.

Table 3.2

Upper floors

Usually for dwellings timber is used for these suspended floors. In industrial buildings beam and block or concrete floor slabs tend to be used.

Timber suspended upper floor

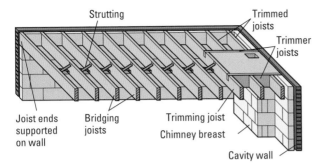

Concrete suspended upper floor

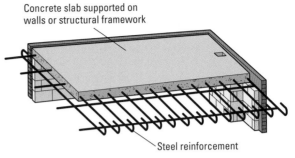

Figure 3.7 Upper floors

For dwellings, bridging joists (horizontal timbers that support the ceiling) are the most common joists used in suspended timber floors. These joists are supported at their ends by load-bearing walls. On the top of the joists, boarding or sheets provide the flooring for the room. Underneath the joists, plasterboard creates the basis of the ceiling for the room below.

When joists have to go into cavity walls (two walls with a hollow space between them) joist hangers are used (U-shaped metal brackets that are used to support the ends of floor joists). There are also complications when joists are in and around stairs and chimney breasts. Bridging joists are used so that these openings are not blocked. Openings in floors require the use of different types of joist called trimmers, trimming and trimmed joists. A trimmed joist is a shortened bridging joist. Any opening in a floor is treated in this way. When the span of a bridging joist exceeds 2 m then struts will be required in line with Building Regulations.

The voids between the floorboards and the plasterboard must be filled with insulation. This not only reduces heat loss, but can also reduce noise.

Concrete suspended floors are usually either cast on site or available as ready-cast units. They are effectively locked into the structure of the building by steel reinforcement. If the concrete floors are being cast on site then **formwork** is needed. Concrete floors are common because they offer greater load bearing capacity, have greater fire resistance and are more sound resistant.

KEY TERMS

Formwork

– this can also be known as shuttering. It is a temporary structure that supports and shapes wet concrete until it cures and is able to be self-supporting.

REED TIP

Try to remember that an effective team can produce more combined that a person can do on their own. Working with other people is also good for your personal well-being.

WALL CONSTRUCTION

Walls have a number of different purposes as they:

* hold up the roof

* provide protection against the elements

* keep the occupants of the building warm

* divide the building into rooms, providing privacy and different spaces.

External walls

Many buildings now have cavity walls which means:

* The outside wall is a wet one because it is exposed to the elements outside the building.

* The internal wall is dry but it needs to be kept separate from the outside wall by a cavity.

* The cavity or gap acts as a barrier against damp and also provides some heat insulation.

* The cavity can be completely filled or part-filled depending on the insulation value required by Building Regulations.

Internal walls

Internal walls divide up the space within the building. These do not have all of the demands of the external walls. They are less likely to be load bearing and they do not have to be insulated so are, therefore, thinner. (However, they are commonly insulated in areas such as the toilet or party walls in semi-detached or terrace construction.) They can be brick or block (particularly if they are load bearing), which is then covered with plaster. Alternatively they can be a timber or metal framework, known as stud work, which is covered plasterboard, to form a wall.

Different types of wall construction and structural considerations

In addition to walls being external or internal, they can also be classed as being load bearing or non-load bearing.

Internal walls can be either load bearing or non-load bearing. In both external and internal load bearing walls, any gaps or openings for windows or doors have to be bridged. This is achieved by using either arches or lintels. These support the weight of the wall above the opening.

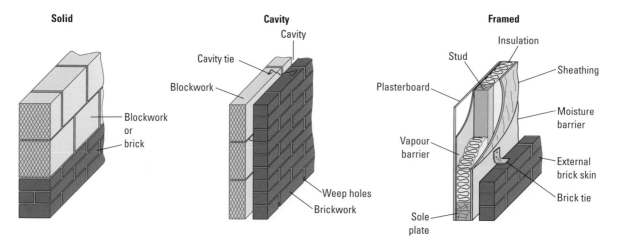

Figure 3.8 Some examples of external wall construction

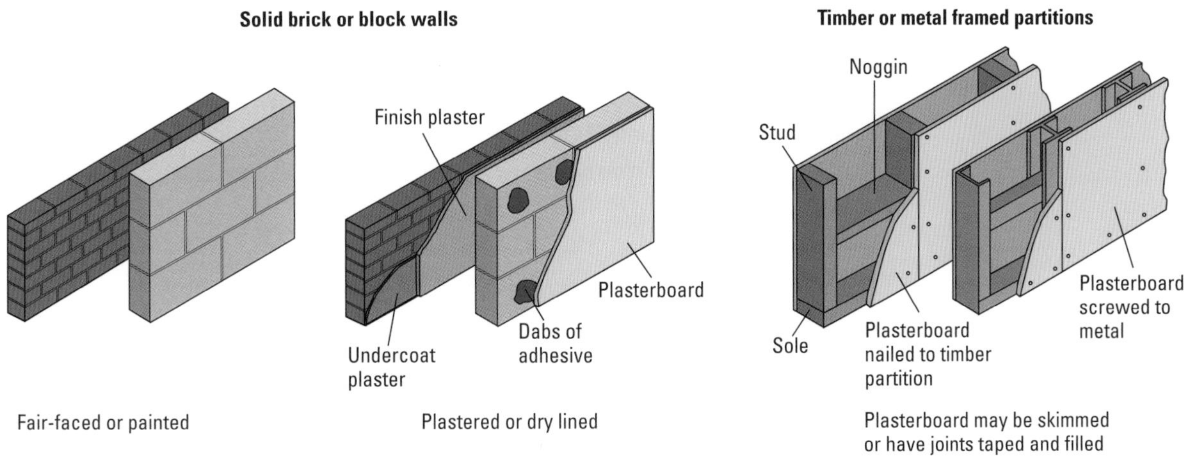

Solid brick or block walls

Timber or metal framed partitions

Finish plaster

Plasterboard

Dabs of adhesive

Undercoat plaster

Noggin

Stud

Sole

Plasterboard nailed to timber partition

Plasterboard screwed to metal

Fair-faced or painted

Plastered or dry lined

Plasterboard may be skimmed or have joints taped and filled

Figure 3.9 Some examples of internal wall construction

Solid walls

In modern builds construction of solid external walls is quite rare. External solid walls tend to be much thinner and made from lightweight blocks in modern builds. They will have some kind of waterproof surface over the top of them, which could be made of render, or plastic, metal or timber cladding.

Cavity walls

As we have seen, cavity walls have an outer and an inner wall and a cavity between them. Usually solid walling, or blockwork, is built up to ground level and then the cavity walling continues to the full height of the building. Alternatively a filled cavity wall is constructed up to ground level. Cavity walls are ideal for most buildings up to medium height.

Many industrial buildings have cavity walls for the lower part of the building and then have insulated steel panels for the top part of the building.

The usual technique is to have brick for the outer wall and an insulating block for the inner wall. The gap or cavity can then be partially filled with an insulation material.

Timber framed walls

Panels made of timber, or in some cases steel, are used to construct walls. They can either be load bearing or non-load bearing and can also be used for the outside of the building or for internal walling. Timber frames are also often clad in brickwork. The panels are solid structures and the spaces between the vertical struts (studs) and the horizontal struts (head or sole plates) are filled with insulation material.

Internal walls

Internal walls are either solid or framed. Solid walls can be made up from blocks or bricks. In many industrial buildings the blocks are actually exposed and can be left in their natural state or painted. In domestic buildings plasterboard is usually bonded to the surface and then plastered over to provide a smoother finish.

It is more common for domestic buildings to have timber or metal-framed internal walls, made from either timber or metal, which are known as stud partitions. These are exactly the same as other framed walling, but will usually have plasterboard fixed to them. They would then receive a skimmed coat of plaster to provide the smooth finish.

Damp-proof membrane (DPM) and damp-proof course (DPC)

Damp-proof membranes are installed under the concrete in ground floors in order to ensure that ground moisture does not enter the building. Effectively it waterproofs the building.

Damp-proof courses are a continuation of the damp-proof membrane. They are built into a horizontal course of either block or brickwork, which is a minimum of 150mm above the exterior ground level. DPCs are also designed to stop moisture from coming up from the ground, entering the wall and then getting into the building. The most common DPC is a polythene sheet damp-proof membrane, which comes in rolls the width of the blockwork or brickwork. In older buildings lead, bitumen or slate would have been used as a DPC.

ROOF CONSTRUCTION

In a country such as the UK, with a great deal of rain and snow, it makes sense for roofs to be pitched. Pitched means built at an angle. The idea is that the rain and snow falls down the angle and off the edge of the roof or into gutters rather than lying on the roof.

This is not to say that all roofs are pitched. In fact many domestic dwelling extensions have flat roofs. A great number of industrial buildings have entirely flat roofs. The problem with a flat roof is that it needs to be able to support itself, but as importantly it needs to be able to carry the additional weight of snow or rain. This means that large flat roofs may have to have steel sections (known as trusses) or even reinforced concrete and beams to increase their load-bearing capacity.

Roofs also provide stability to the walls by tying them together. As we will see, there are several different types of roof. These are usually identified by their pitch or shape.

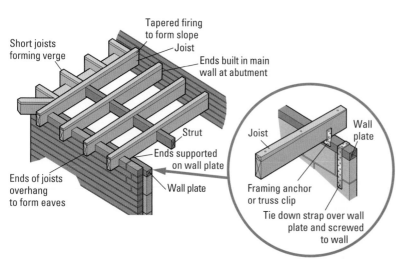

Short joists forming verge

Tapered firing to form slope

Joist

Ends built in main wall at abutment

Strut

Ends supported on wall plate

Ends of joists overhang to form eaves

Wall plate

Joist

Wall plate

Framing anchor or truss clip

Tie down strap over wall plate and screwed to wall

Figure 3.10 Flat roof structure

Types of roof construction

The roof is made up of the rafters and beams, Everything above the framework is regarded as a roof covering, such as slates, tiles and felt. Generally speaking, roofs are either pitched or flat. This will depend on the angle or slope of the roof.

Table 3.3 outlines some of the key characteristics of different types of roof.

Flat	This is a roof that has a slope of less than 10°. Generally flat roofs are used for smaller extensions to dwellings and on garages. Traditionally they would have had bitumen felt, although it is becoming more common for fibreglass to be used.	 Figure 3.11
Mono-pitch	This is a roof that has a single sloping surface but is not fixed to another building or wall. The front and back walls could be different heights, or the other exposed surface of the roof is perpendicular.	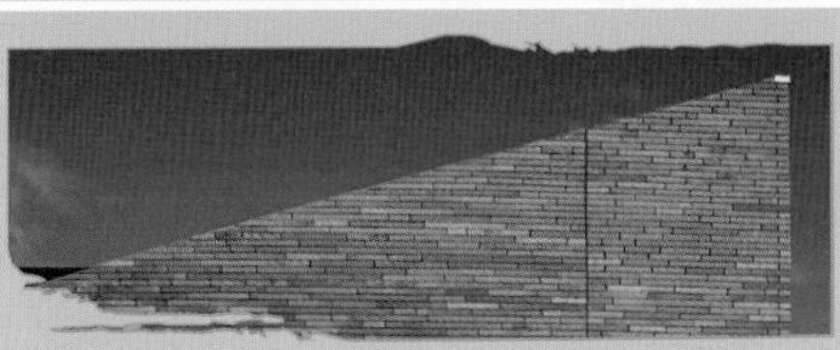 Figure 3.12
Double pitched	This is a roof that has two differently angled slopes. Usually the upper part of the roof has a fairly shallow pitch or slope and the lower part of the roof has a steeper slope.	 Figure 3.13
Couple roof	This is often called gable end and is one of the most common types of roof for dwellings. A gable is a wall with a triangular upper part. This supports the roof in construction using purlins. This means that the roof has two sloping surfaces, which come down from the ridge to the eaves.	 Figure 3.14
Hipped roof	Hipped roofs have slopes on three or four four sides. There are also hipped roofs with single, straight gables.	 Figure 3.15
Lean-to	A lean to is similar to a mono-pitched roof except it is abutted to a wall. The slope is greater than 10°. The higher part of the roof is fixed to a higher wall.	 Figure 3.16

Table 3.3 Different types of roof

Roofing components

Each part of a roof has a specific name and purpose. Table 3.4 explains each of these individual features.

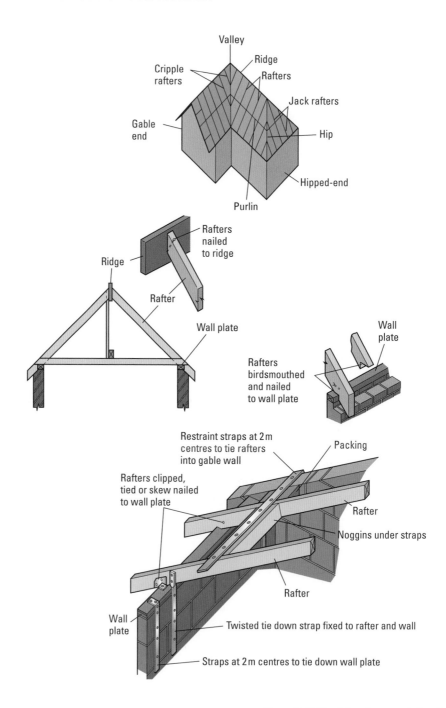

Figure 3.17 Traditional cut roof details

Roof feature	Description
Ridge	This is the top of the roof and the junction of the sloping sides. It is the apex, where the rafters meet.
Purlin	This is a beam that supports the mid-span section of rafters.
Firings	These are angled pieces of timber that are placed on the rafters to create a slope.
Batten	Roof battens are thin strips, usually of wood, which provide a fixing point for either roofing sheets or roof tiles.
Tile	These are artificial products that can be made from clay, concrete or plastic. They are placed in regular, overlapping rows and fixed to the battens.
Fascia	This is a horizontal board that closes and protects the rafter ends and provides a fixing for guttering. It is also decorative as it covers the rafter ends. It is fixed to the ends of the rafters at eaves level and is both a decorative feature and a fixing for rainwater goods.
Wall plate	This is a piece of horizontal timber that is placed at the top of a wall at eaves level. It provides a fixing for joists or rafters.
Bracings	Roof rafters may need to be braced to make them more rigid and stable. These bracings prevent the roof from buckling.
Felt	Roofing felt has two elements – it has a waterproofing agent (bitumen) and what is known as a carrier. The carrier can be either a polyester sheet or a glass fibre sheet. Roofing felt tends to be used for flat roofs and for roofs with a shallow pitch.
Slate	Slate roofing tiles are natural products and are usually fixed to timber battens with double nails. They have a lifespan of between 80 and 100 years.
Flashings	Wherever there is a joint or angle on a roof, a thin sheet of either lead or another waterproof material is added. In the past this tended always to be made from lead. Many different types of flashing can now be used but all have the role of preventing water penetrating into joints. Flashings are normally found where roofs abut a wall or where chimneys protrude through a roof.
Rafter	Roof rafters are the main structural components of the roof. They are the framework. They rest on supporting walls. The rafters are set at an angle on sloped roofs or horizontal on a flat roof.
Apex	The apex is the highest point of the roof, usually the ridge line.
Soffit	Soffits are the lower part, or overhanging part, of the eaves. In other words they are the underside of the eaves.
Bargeboard	This is a functional and ornamental feature, which is fixed to the gable end of a roof in order to hide the ends of roof timbers and to support the verge details.
Eaves	These are the area found at the foot of the rafter. They are not always visible as they can be flush. In modern construction, the eaves have two parts: the visible eaves projection and the hidden eaves projection.

Table 3.4

Roof coverings

There are many different types of materials that can be used to cover the roof. Even tiles and slates come in a wide variety of shapes and sizes, along with colours and different finishes.

In many cases the type of roof covering is determined by the traditional and local styles in the area. Local authorities usually want roof coverings that are not too far from the common style in the area. This does not stop manufacturers from coming up with new ideas, however, which can add benefits during construction and during the use of the building (such as better insulation properties).

Table 3.5 outlines some of the more common types of roof covering and describes their main characteristics and use.

Roof covering	Description
Felt  Figure 3.18	Felt is used as a waterproof barrier. Internal felt is rolled over the top of the rafters. The strips are overlapped to provide a permanent waterproof barrier. They are then battened down and another roof covering, such as slate or tile, placed over the top of them. For flat roofs, felt is used as the external roof covering and is covered in a waterproof material, such as bitumen.
Slate Figure 3.19	Slate is a flat, natural substance, which is laid onto the battens with each slate tile overlapping the top of the slate in the row directly below it. The slate tiles are either nailed or hooked into place.
Tile 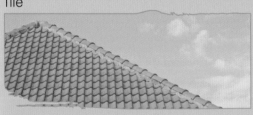 Figure 3.20	There is a huge variety of roofing tiles, made from clay, ceramics or concrete. They are designed and moulded so that they overlap with one another and are fixed to the roof in a similar way to slate tiles.
Metals  Figure 3.21	There are many different types of metal roof covering, such as corrugated sheets, flat sheets, box profile sheets or even sheets that have a tile effect. The metal is galvanised and plastic coated to provide a durable and long-lasting waterproof surface.

Table 3.5

CASE STUDY

South
Tyneside Homes

South Tyneside Council's
Housing Company

How to impress in interviews

Andrea Dickson and Gillian Jenkins sit on the interview panels for apprenticeship applications at South Tyneside Homes.

'Interviews are all about the three Ps: Preparation, Presentation and Personality.

An applicant should turn up with some knowledge about the apprenticeship programme and the company itself. For example, knowing how long it is, that they have to go to college and to work – don't say, "I was hoping you'd tell me about it"! If they've done a bit of research, it will show through and work in their favour – especially if they can explain why it is that they want to work here.

It sets them up for the interview if they come in smartly dressed. We're not marking on that, but it does show respect for the situation. It's still a formal process and, although we try to make them feel at ease as much as we possibly can, there's no getting away from the fact that they're applying for a job and it is a formal setting.

The interviews are a chance to tell the company about themselves: what they do in their spare time, what their greatest achievements have been and why. Applicants should talk about what interests them; for example, are they really interested in becoming a joiner or is that something their parents want them to do? An apprenticeship has to be something they want to do – if they have enthusiasm for the programme, then they'll fly through it. If not, it's a very long three to four years. Without that passion for it, the whole process will be a struggle; they'll come in late to work and even fail exams.

We also talk to them about any customer service experiences they've had, working in a team, project working (for example, a time you had to complete a task and what steps you took), as well as asking some questions about health and safety awareness.'

SUPPLY OF UTILITIES AND SERVICES

Most but not all dwellings and other structures are connected in some way to a wide range of utilities and services. In the majority of cities, towns and villages structures are connected to key utilities and services, such as a sewer system, potable (drinking) water, gas and electricity. This is not always the case for more remote structures, however.

Whenever construction work is carried out, whether it is on an existing structure or a new build, the supply of utilities and services or the linking up of these parts of the **infrastructure** are very important. Often they will require the services of specialist engineers from the **service provider**.

Table 3.6 outlines the main utilities and services that are provided to most structures.

Utility or service	Description
Drainage	Drainage is delivered by a range of water and sewerage companies in the UK. They are responsible for ensuring that surface water can drain away into their system.
Waste water and sewerage	Any waste water and sewage generated by the occupants of a structure needs to have the necessary pipework to link it to the main sewerage system. It is then sent to a sewage treatment works via the pipework. If there is no connection to mains sewerage, the building may have a septic tank, which is a small-scale, self-contained sewage treatment system.
Water	Each structure should be linked to the water supply that provides wholesome, potable drinking water. The pipework linking the structure to the water supply needs to be protected to ensure that backflow from any other source does not contaminate the system.
Gas	Each area has a range of different gas suppliers. This is delivered via a service pipe from the main system into the structure. Areas that do not have access to the main gas supply system use gas contained in cylinders.
Electricity	The National Grid provides electricity to a variety of different electricity suppliers. It is the National Grid that operates and maintains the cabling. There are around 28 million individual electricity customers in the UK.
Communications (telephone, data, cable)	There are several ways in which telecommunications can be linked to a structure. Traditional telephone poles hold up copper cables and not only provide telephone but also internet access to structures. In cities and many of the larger towns poles are being replaced by cables that are fibre optic and run underground. These are then linked to each individual structure.
Ducting (heating and ventilation)	Heating and ventilation engineers install and maintain duct work. The complex systems are known as HVAC. These systems can transfer air for heating or cooling of the structure. The overall system can also provide hot and cold water systems, along with ventilation.

Table 3.6

KEY TERMS

HVAC

– this is an abbreviation for 'heating, ventilation and air-conditioning'. This has been a service provided to many industrial buildings for a number of years, but it is now becoming more common in domestic dwellings, particularly new developments.

SUSTAINABILITY AND INCORPORATING SUSTAINABILITY INTO CONSTRUCTION PROJECTS

Carbon is present in all fossil fuels, such as coal or natural gas. Burning fossil fuels releases carbon dioxide, which is a greenhouse gas linked to climate change.

Energy conservation aims to reduce the amount of carbon dioxide in the atmosphere. The idea is to do this by making buildings better insulated and, at the same time, make heating appliances more efficient. It also means attempting to generate energy using renewable and/or low or zero carbon methods.

According to the government's Environment Agency, sustainable construction is all about using resources in the most efficient way. It also means cutting down on waste on site and reducing the amount of materials that have to be disposed of and put into landfill.

In order to achieve sustainable construction the Environment Agency recommends:

* reducing construction, demolition and excavation waste that needs to go to landfill

* cutting back on carbon emissions from construction transport and machinery

* responsibly sourcing materials

* cutting back on the amount of water that is wasted

* making sure construction does not have an impact on biodiversity.

Sustainable construction and incorporating it into construction projects

Recently the idea of sustainable construction has focused on ensuring that the building is not only of good quality and affordable, but also that it is efficient.

Sustainable construction also means having the least negative environmental impact. So this means minimising the use of raw materials, energy, land and water. This is not only during the construction phase but also for the lifetime of the building.

Finite and renewable resources

We all know that resources such as coal and oil will eventually run out. These are examples of finite resources.

Oil is not just used as fuel – it is in plastic, dyes, lubricants and textiles. All of these are used in the construction process.

Renewable resources are those that are produced either by moving water, the sun or the wind. They include materials that come from plants, such as biodiesel, or the oils used to make adhesives.

The construction process itself is only part of the problem. It is also the longer term impact and demands that the building will have on the environment. This is why there has been a drive towards sustainable homes and there is a Code for Sustainable Homes (an environmental assessment method for rating and certifying the performance of new homes).

KEY TERMS

Landfill

– 170 million tonnes of waste from homes and businesses are generated in England and Wales each year. Much of this has to be taken to a site to be buried.

Biodiversity

– wherever there is construction there is a danger that wildlife and plants could be disturbed or destroyed. Protecting biodiversity ensures that at risk species are conserved.

Figure 3.22 Most modern new-builds follow sustainable principles

Construction and the environment

In 2010 construction, demolition and excavation produced 20 million tonnes of waste that had to go into landfill. The construction industry is also responsible for most illegal fly tipping (illegally dumping waste). In any year the Environment Agency responds to around 350 serious pollution incidents caused as a result of construction.

Regardless of the size of the construction job, everyone working on the project is responsible for the impact they have on the environment. Good site layout, planning and management can help reduce these problems.

Sustainable construction helps to encourage this because it means managing resources in a more efficient way, reducing waste and reducing your **carbon footprint.**

Architecture and design

The Code for Sustainable Homes Rating Scheme was introduced in 2007. Many local authorities have instructed their planning departments to encourage sustainable development. This begins with the work of the architect who designs the building.

Local authorities ask that architects and building designers:

* ensure the land is safe for development – that if it is contaminated this is dealt with first

* ensure there is access to and protection of the natural environment – this helps ensure biodiversity and tries to create open spaces for local people

* reduce the negative impact on the local environment – any buildings keep noise, air, light and water pollution down to a minimum

* conserve natural resources and cut back carbon emissions – this includes use of energy, materials and water during construction and the life of the building

* ensure comfort and security – good access, close to public transport, safe parking and protection against flooding.

Figure 3.23 Sustainable developments aim to be pleasant places to live

Using locally managed resources

The construction industry imports nearly 6 million cubic metres of sawn wood each year. However there is plenty of scope to use the many millions of cubic metres of timber produced in managed forests in the UK, particularly in Scotland.

Local timber can be used for a wide variety of different construction projects:

* softwood – including pines, firs, larch and spruce – for panels, decking, fencing and internal flooring

* hardwood – including oak, chestnut, ash, beech and sycamore – for a wide variety of internal joinery.

Using local materials reduces transportation costs and time, minimises the project's carbon footprint and means that there is less chance for the materials to be damaged in transit.

Eco-friendly, sustainable manufactured products and environmentally resourced timber

There are now many suppliers that offer sustainable building materials as a green alternative. Some tiles, for example, are now made from recycled plastic bottles and stone particles.

There is now a National Green Specification database of all environmentally friendly building materials. This provides a checklist where it is possible to compare specifications of sustainable products to traditionally manufactured products, such as bricks.

Simple changes can be made, such as using timber or ethylene-based plastics instead of UPVC window frames to ensure a building uses more sustainable materials.

As we have seen, finding locally managed resources, such as timber, makes sense in terms of cost and in terms of protecting the environment. There are always alternatives to the use of traditional resources that could affect the environment.

The Timber Trade Federation produces a timber certification system. This ensures that wood products are labelled to show that they are produced in sustainable forests.

Around 80 per cent of all the softwood used in construction comes from Scandinavia or Russia. Another 15 per cent comes from the rest of Europe, or even North America. The remaining 5 per cent comes from tropical countries, and is usually sourced from sustainable forests.

Alternative methods of building

The most common type of construction is, of course, brick and blockwork. However there are plenty of other options:

* timber frame – using green oak

* insulated concrete formwork – where a polystyrene mould is filled with reinforced concrete

Figure 3.24 Window frames made from timber

Figure 3.25 Timber Certification System

* structural insulated panels – where buildings are made up of rigid building boards rather like huge sandwiches

* modular construction – this uses similar materials and techniques to standard construction, but the units are built off site and transported ready-constructed to building site where they are connected together.

Figure 3.26 Green roofing

Figure 3.27 Flooring made from cork

KEY TERMS

Biodegradable

– this material will more easily break down when it is no longer needed. This breaking down process is done by micro-organisms.

Organic

– these are natural substances, usually extracted from plants.

There are alternatives to traditional flooring and roofing, all of which are greener and more sustainable. Green roofing has become an increasing trend in recent years. Metal roofs made of steel, aluminium and copper use a high percentage of recycled material. Solar roof shingles, or solar roof laminates, while expensive, decrease the cost of electricity and related heating costs of the dwelling. Some buildings even have a waterproof membrane, which is covered with a growing medium and planted with vegetation like sedum plants. This provides additional insulation, absorbs air pollution, helps to collect and process rainwater and keeps the roof surface temperature down.

Just as roofs are becoming greener, so too are the options for flooring. The use of bamboo, eucalyptus and cork is becoming more common. A new version of linoleum has been developed with **biodegradable**, **organic** ingredients. Some buildings are also using sustainable alternatives to traditional timber floorboards and joists, and these can be coloured, stained or patterned.

An increasing trend has been for what is known as off-site manufacture (OSM). European OSM businesses, particularly those in Germany, have built over 100,000 houses. The entire house is manufactured in a factory and then assembled on site. Walls, floors, roofs, windows and doors with built-in electrics and plumbing, all arrive on a lorry. Some manufacturers even offer completely finished dwellings, including carpets and curtains. Many of these modular buildings are designed to be far more energy efficient than traditional brick and block constructions. Many come ready fitted with heat pumps, solar panels and triple-glazed windows.

Energy efficiency and incorporating it into construction projects

Energy efficiency is all about using less energy to provide the same level of output. Governments are working towards the world's energy needs by 30 per cent before 2050. This means producing more energy efficient buildings. It also means using energy efficient methods to produce materials and resources needed to construct buildings.

Building Regulations

In terms of energy conservation, the most important UK law is the Building Regulations 2010, particularly Part L. The Building Regulations:

* list the minimum efficiency requirements

* provide guidance on compliance, the main testing methods, installation and control

* cover both new dwellings and existing dwellings.

A key part of the regulations is the Standard Assessment Procedure (SAP), which measures or estimates the energy efficiency performance of buildings.

Local planning authorities also now require that all new developments generate at least 10 per cent of their energy from renewable sources. This means that each new project has to be assessed one at a time.

Energy conservation

By law, each local authority is required to reduce carbon dioxide emissions and to encourage the conservation of energy. This means that everyone has a responsibility in some way to conserve energy:

* Clients, along with building designers, are required to include energy efficient technology in the build.

* Contractors and sub-contractors have to follow these design guidelines. They also need to play a role in conserving energy and resources when working on site.

* Suppliers of products are required by law to provide information on energy in the production of their products.

In addition, new energy efficiency schemes and Building Regulations cover the energy performance of buildings. Each new build is required to have an Energy Performance Certificate. This rates a building's energy efficiency from A (which is very efficient) to G (which is very inefficient).

Some building designers have also begun to adopt other voluntary ways of attempting to protect the environment. These include BREEAM, which is an environmental assessment method, and the Code for Sustainable Homes, which is a certification of sustainability for new builds.

DID YOU KNOW?

One of the pioneers in energy efficient construction is the German manufacturer Huf Haus at www.huf-haus.com.

DID YOU KNOW?

The Energy Saving Trust has lots of information about construction. Its website is www. energysavingtrust.org.uk.

energy® saving trust

Figure 3.28 The Energy Saving Trust encourages builders to use less wasteful building techniques and more energy efficient construction

High, low and zero carbon

When we look at energy sources, we consider their environmental impact in terms of how much carbon dioxide they release. Accordingly, energy sources can be split into three different groups:

* high carbon – those that release a lot of carbon dioxide

* low carbon – those that release some carbon dioxide

* zero carbon – those that do not release any carbon dioxide.

Some examples of high carbon, low carbon and zero carbon energy sources are given in Table 3.7.

High carbon energy source	Description
Natural gas or LPG	Piped natural gas or liquid petroleum gas stored in bottles
Fuel oils	Domestic fuel oil, such as diesel
Solid fuels	Coal, coke and peat
Electricity	Generated from non-renewable sources, such as coal-fired power stations
Low carbon energy source	
Solar thermal	Panels used to capture energy from the sun to heat water
Solid fuel	Biomass such as logs, wood chips and pellets
Hydrogen fuel cells	Convert chemical energy into electrical energy
Heat pumps	Convert low temperature heat into higher temperature heat
Combined heat and power (CHP)	Generates electricity as well as heat for water and space heating
Combined cooling, heat and power (CCHP)	A variation on CHP that also provides a basic air conditioning system
Zero carbon energy	
Electricity/wind	Uses natural wind resources to generate electrical energy
Electricity/tidal	Uses wave power to generate electrical energy
Hydroelectric	Uses the natural flow of rivers and streams to generate electrical energy
Solar photovoltaic	Uses solar cells to convert light energy from the sun into electricity

Table 3.7

It is important to try to conserve non-renewable energy so that there will be sufficient fuel for the future. The idea is that finite sources of fuel should last as long as is necessary to completely replace it with renewable sources, such as wind or solar energy.

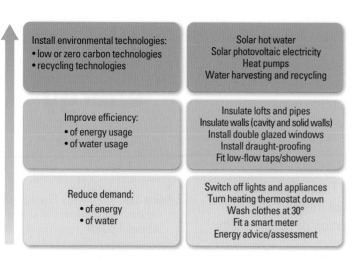

Figure 3.29 Working towards reducing carbon emissions

Alternative heating sources

There are several new ways in which we can harness the power of water, the sun and the wind to provide us with new heating sources. All of these systems are considered to be far more energy efficient than traditional heating systems, which rely on gas, oil, electricity or other fossil fuels.

Solar thermal

At the heart of this system is the solar collector, which is often referred to as a solar panel. The idea is that the collector absorbs the sun's energy, which is then converted into heat. This heat is then applied to the system's heat transfer fluid.

The system uses a differential temperature controller (DTC) that controls the system's circulating pump when solar energy is available and there is a demand for water to be heated.

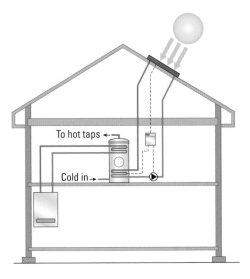

Figure 3.30 Solar thermal hot water system

In the UK, due to the lack of guaranteed solar energy, solar thermal hot water systems often have an auxiliary heat source, such as an immersion heater.

Biomass (solid fuel)

Biomass stoves burn either pellets or logs. Some have integrated hoppers that transfer pellets to the burner. Biomass boilers are available for pellets, woodchips or logs. Most of them have automated systems to clean the heat exchanger surfaces. They can provide heat for domestic hot water and space heating.

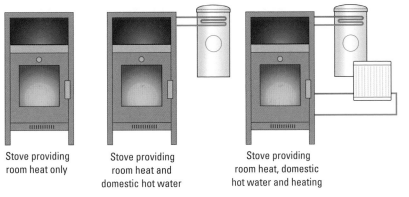

Stove providing room heat only

Stove providing room heat and domestic hot water

Stove providing room heat, domestic hot water and heating

Figure 3.31 Biomass stoves output options

Heat pumps

Heat pumps convert low temperature heat from air, ground or water sources to higher temperature heat. They can be used in ducted air or piped water **heat sink** systems.

There are a variety of different arrangements for each of the three main systems:

* Air source pumps operate at temperatures down to minus 20°C. They have units that receive incoming air through an inlet duct.

* Ground source pumps operate on **geothermal** ground heat. They use a sealed circuit collector loop, which is buried either vertically or horizontally underground.

KEY TERMS

Heat sink

– this is a heat exchanger that transfers heat from one source into a fluid, such as in refrigeration, air-conditioning or the radiator in a car.

Geothermal

– relating to the internal heat energy of the earth.

* Water source systems can be used where there is a suitable water source, such as a pond or lake.

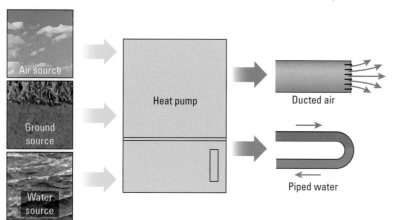

Figure 3.32 Heat pump input and output options

The heat pump system's efficiency relies on the temperature difference between the heat source and the heat sink. Special tank hot water cylinders are part of the system, giving a large surface-to-surface contact between the heating circuit water and the stored domestic hot water.

Combined heat and power (CHP) and combined cooling heat and power (CCHP) units

These are similar to heating system boilers, but they generate electricity as well as heat for hot water or space heating (or cooling). The heart of the system is an engine or gas turbine. The gas burner provides heat to the engine when there is a demand for heat. Electricity is generated along with sufficient energy to heat water and to provide space heating.

CCHP systems also incorporate the facility to cool spaces when necessary.

Wind turbines

Freestanding or building-mounted wind turbines capture the energy from wind to generate electrical energy. The wind passes across rotor blades of a turbine, which causes the hub to turn. The hub is connected by a shaft to a gearbox. This increases the speed of rotation. A high speed shaft is then connected to a generator that produces the electricity.

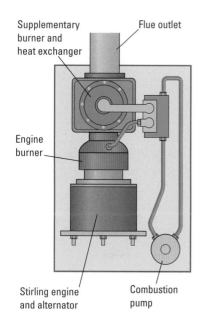

Figure 3.33 Example of a MCHP (micro combined heat and power) unit

Solar photovoltaic systems

A solar photovoltaic system uses solar cells to convert light energy from the sun into electricity. The solar cells are usually made of silicon and are semi-conductors. The sunlight hits the solar cells and photons are absorbed. This causes negatively charged electrons in the cell to detach from their atoms and flow through the cell to create electricity. The electricity is direct current (dc). The dc current is then converted by an inverter to alternating current (ac), which is the type of current used for mains electricity.

Energy ratings

Energy rating tables are used to measure the overall efficiency of a dwelling, with rating A being the most energy efficient and rating G the least energy efficient.

Alongside this is an environmental impact rating (see Fig 3.38). This measures the dwelling's impact on the environment in terms of how much carbon dioxide it produces. Again, rating A is the highest, showing it has the least impact on the environment, and rating G is the lowest.

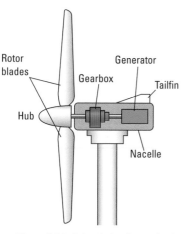

Figure 3.34 A basic horizontal axis wind turbine

A standard assessment procedure (SAP) is used to place the dwelling on the energy rating table. This will take into account:

* the date of construction, the type of construction and the location

* the heating system

* insulation (including cavity wall)

* double glazing.

The ratings are used by local authorities and other groups to assess the energy efficiency of new and old housing, and must be provided to potential purchasers when houses are sold.

Preventing heat loss

Most old buildings are under-insulated and would benefit from additional insulation, whether this is ceilings, walls or floors.

The measurement of heat loss in a building is known as the U Value. It measures how well parts of the building transfer heat. Low U Values represent high levels of insulation. U Values are becoming more important as they form the basis of energy and carbon reduction standards.

By 2016 all new housing is expected to be Net Zero Carbon. This means that the building should not be contributing to climate change.

Many of the guidelines are now part of Building Regulations (Part L). They cover:

* insulation requirements

* openings, such as doors and windows

* solar heating and other heating

* ventilation and air conditioning

* space heating controls

* lighting efficiency

* air tightness.

Building design

UK households spend £2.4bn every year just on lighting. One of the ways of tackling this cost is to use energy saving lights, but also to maximise natural lighting. For the construction industry this means:

* increased window size

* orientating building angles to make the most of sunlight – south facing windows maximise sunlight in winter and limit overheating in the summer

* considering window design by using windows with a variety of different types of opening to allow ventilation.

Solar tubes are another way of increasing light. These are small domes on the roof, which collect sunlight and then direct it through a tube (which is reflective). It is then directed through a diffuser in the ceiling to spread light into the room.

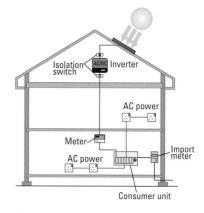

Figure 3.35 A basic solar photovoltaic system

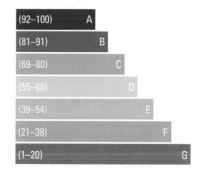

Figure 3.36 SAP energy efficiency rating table. The ranges in brackets show the percentage energy efficiency for each banding

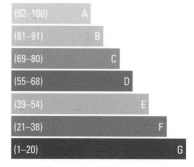

Figure 3.37 SAP environmental impact rating table

TEST YOURSELF

1. In which of the following types of buildings is a traditional strip foundation used?

   a. High rise

   b. Medium rise

   c. Low rise

   d. Industrial buildings

2. Which of the following is a reason for using a raft foundation?

   a. The subsoil is rock

   b. The subsoil is unstable

   c. The subsoil is stable

   d. The access to the site allows it

3. What holds down a floating floor?

   a. Nails and screws

   b. Adhesives

   c. Blocks

   d. Its own weight

4. What is another term for formwork?

   a. Shuttering

   b. Cavity

   c. Joist

   d. Boarding

5. What is the minimum distance the DPC should be above ground level?

   a. 50 mm

   b. 100 mm

   c. 150 mm

   d. 200 mm

6. A roof is said to be flat if it has a slope of less than how many degrees?

   a. 5

   b. 10

   c. 15

   d. 20

7. What shape is the upper part of a gable end?

   a. Rectangular

   b. Semi-circular

   c. Square

   d. Triangular

8. What do you call the horizontal timber that is placed at the top of a wall at eaves level in a roof, to hold the ends of joists or rafters?

   a. Fascia

   b. Bracings

   c. Wall plate

   d. Batten

9. What happens to the majority of construction demolition and excavation waste?

   a. It is buried on site

   b. It is burned

   c. It goes into landfill

   d. It is recycled

10. Which part of the Building Regulations 2010 requires the construction industry to consider and use energy efficiently?

   a. Part B

   b. Part D

   c. Part K

   d. Part L

Chapter 4

Unit CSA L1Occ12
ERECT AND DISMANTLE ACCESS EQUIPMENT AND WORKING PLATFORMS

LEARNING OUTCOMES

LO1/2: Know how to and be able to prepare for erecting access equipment and working platforms

LO3/4: Know how to and be able to inspect access equipment and working platform components and identify defects

LO5/6: Know how to and be able to erect and work from access equipment and working platforms

LO7/8: Know how to and be able to dismantle and store access equipment and working platform components

INTRODUCTION

The aims of this chapter are to:

* help you select appropriate access equipment and working platforms for the work to be carried out

* help you use access equipment and working platforms following health and safety guidelines

* show you how to dismantle and store access equipment and working platforms appropriately.

PREPARING FOR ERECTING ACCESS EQUIPMENT AND WORKING PLATFORMS

Painters and decorators often have to work at height to reach the tops of walls, ceilings and other awkward spaces. Access equipment and working platforms are very helpful for these tasks. However, they must be chosen, used, dismantled and stored correctly – or else accidents can occur.

Before you use access equipment and working platforms, you need to be aware of:

* the potential hazards

* relevant legislation and regulations

* instructions or guidance from the manufacturer

* any PPE you may need

* which equipment is best to use for the situation

* how to protect your working area from damage.

Hazards, health and safety and risk assessment

The main hazards of erecting and dismantling access equipment and working platforms are falls from height. Falls can be the result of:

* equipment that is faulty, damaged or broken, e.g. bent locking bars on a step ladder

* equipment that hasn't been inspected regularly

* equipment that has not been checked before use, e.g. to check that the last use did not leave any damage

* equipment that has not been set up correctly, e.g. placing a ladder on an uneven surface

* equipment that is being used for the wrong sort of job, e.g. using a ladder for heavy or lengthy work.

Other possible hazards include:

* slips and trips, e.g. from wearing inappropriate footwear, or grease on ladder rungs

* cuts and abrasions, e.g. getting your hands or fingers trapped when erecting or using equipment

* using equipment incorrectly, e.g. overreaching, standing on too high a rung.

The risks of erecting/dismantling and using access equipment are very similar, as you can see from Table 4.1 below.

Risks and hazards of erecting, using and dismantling access equipment
• Injury caused by incorrect manual handling of heavy or awkward equipment or components
• Slips and trips over components or tools
• Cuts and abrasions when operating moving parts
• Injury caused by equipment not erected correctly, e.g. collapsing
• Falls from height
• Objects falling from height, causing injury to others
• Slips when climbing
• Trips over tools on working platforms
• Cuts and abrasions when operating moving parts
• Faulty equipment causing falls or cuts and abrasions
• Incorrect use of access equipment resulting in injury

Table 4.1 Risks of erecting, using and dismantling access equipment

Hazard identification records

Hazard identification records, such as a health and safety file or hazard book, are a tool to quickly highlight common hazards on a work site or for a particular task. These not only help to reduce accidents but are also a legal requirement under the Construction (Design and Management) Regulations 2007, for projects of a certain size. In the event of an accident, the record will show which hazards on site had been identified and any steps taken to prevent the accident from happening.

Refresh your memory about hazards, health and safety and risk assessments in Chapter 1.

REED TIP

Every workplace, college or training centre is a different working environment. They may each have different outcomes from their risk assessments, and so each will have its own policies about health and safety and PPE that you should follow.

DID YOU KNOW?

Fifty per cent of accidental deaths in construction are caused by falls from height.

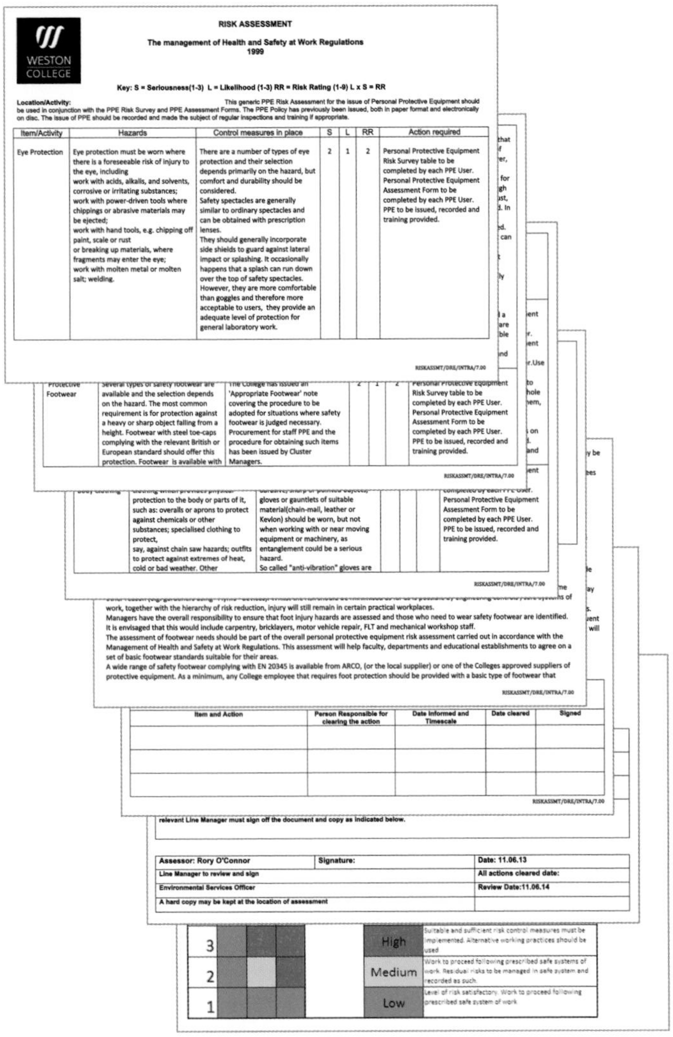

RISK ASSESSMENT

The management of Health and Safety at Work Regulations 1999

Key: S = Seriousness(1-3) L = Likelihood (1-3) RR = Risk Rating (1-9) L x S = RR

Location/Activity: This generic PPE Risk Assessment for the issue of Personal Protective Equipment should be used in conjunction with the PPE Risk Survey and PPE Assessment Forms. The PPE Policy has previously been issued, both in paper format and electronically on disc. The issue of PPE should be recorded and made the subject of regular inspections and training if appropriate.

Item/Activity	Hazards	Control measures in place	S	L	RR	Action required
Eye Protection	Eye protection must be worn where there is a foreseeable risk of injury to the eye, including work with acids, alkalis, and solvents, corrosive or irritating substances; work with power-driven tools where chippings or abrasive materials may be ejected; work with hand tools, e.g. chipping off paint, scale or rust or breaking up materials, where fragments may enter the eye; work with molten metal or molten salt; welding.	There are a number of types of eye protection and their selection depends primarily on the hazard, but comfort and durability should be considered. Safety spectacles are generally similar to ordinary spectacles and can be obtained with prescription lenses. They should generally incorporate side shields to guard against lateral impact or splashing. It occasionally happens that a splash can run down over the top of safety spectacles. However, they are more comfortable than goggles and therefore more acceptable to users, they provide an adequate level of protection for general laboratory work.	2	1	2	Personal Protective Equipment Risk Survey table to be completed by each PPE User. Personal Protective Equipment Assessment Form to be completed by each PPE User. PPE to be issued, recorded and training provided.

RISKASSMT/DRE/INTRA/7.00

Figure 4.1 A sample risk assessment

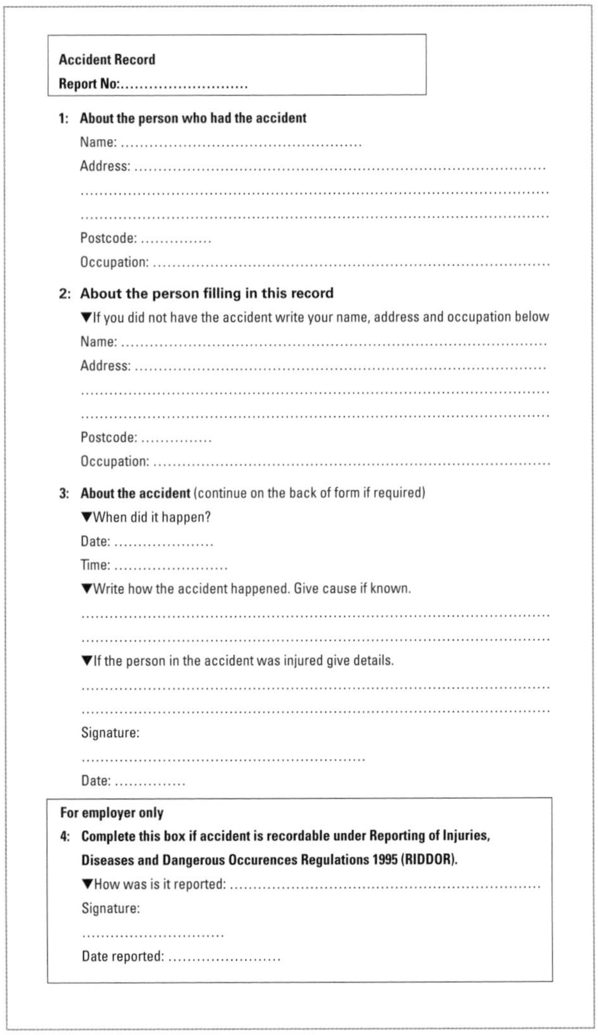

Accident Record
Report No:............................

1: About the person who had the accident

Name: ....

Address: ....

....

....

Postcode: ....

Occupation: ....

2: About the person filling in this record

▼If you did not have the accident write your name, address and occupation below

Name: ....

Address: ....

....

....

Postcode: ....

Occupation: ....

3: About the accident (continue on the back of form if required)

▼When did it happen?

Date: ....

Time: ....

▼Write how the accident happened. Give cause if known.

....

....

▼If the person in the accident was injured give details.

....

....

Signature:

....

Date: ....

For employer only

4: Complete this box if accident is recordable under Reporting of Injuries, Diseases and Dangerous Occurences Regulations 1995 (RIDDOR).

▼How was is it reported: ....

Signature:

....

Date reported: ....

Figure 4.2 A sample accident report form

PPE

If you don't wear the correct PPE when erecting or dismantling access equipment and working platforms, then the risk of accidents is higher. You may need:

- gloves to protect your hands from cuts and abrasions
- a hard hat for whenever there is a risk of head injury
- a high-vis jacket so you are visible to your colleagues and members of the public
- steel cap boots to protect your feet from any falling debris or parts of scaffolding.

The PPE you choose will also depend on the policy of your workplace or college.

More information on PPE and the laws concerning it can be found in Chapter 1.

PRACTICAL TIP

It is the responsibility of everyone on site to ensure that appropriate PPE is worn.

Sources of health and safety guidance

The Work at Height Regulations 2005

The Work at Height Regulations make it compulsory for an employer to carry out a risk assessment before any work at height is started. The starting point of the regulations is that work at height should be avoided wherever possible. Access equipment should be used if there is no other option but to work at height.

The regulations also have specific requirements for access equipment and working platforms. These can be found in the schedules at the end of the regulations, for example, *Schedule 6 Requirements for ladders* and *Schedule 3 Requirements for working platforms*. Key points from the regulations have been included throughout the rest of this chapter.

If you would like to see what the regulations look like, you can find them here: *www.legislation.gov.uk/uksi/2005/735/contents/made*. For some more information on the Work at Height Regulations, see page 4.

Approved Code of Practice (ACOP)

The Code of Practice comes out of the Construction (Design and Management) Regulations 2007 and provides useful advice and guidance for people working in the construction industry. It aims to bring health and safety into the management of construction projects. If you follow ACOP, then you are following the law that it relates to. It covers the practical requirements and general duties that must be followed on all construction sites.

Manufacturers' instructions

In the workplace, always listen to and follow directions from your employer. These will include using any safety equipment or training you are given. In addition, when working with access equipment, you must always follow the instructions that are provided by the manufacturer. These may appear on the equipment itself or may come as a separate guide on how to put together, use, dismantle and store access equipment or working platforms.

Choosing suitable access equipment and working platforms

There are a number of different types of access equipment and working platforms for various situations and uses. This may depend on the location you're working in, the height at which you're working and the length of time you'll need to use the equipment.

For example, ladders are best used for short-term work (less than 20 minutes) and only when doing light work (not carrying anything heavier than 10 kg), such as applying paint or preparing surfaces. Some equipment is better suited to use indoors, such as a step ladder. Other equipment is designed mostly to be used outside, such as scaffolding.

DID YOU KNOW?

A free pdf of ACOP is available here: *www.hse. gov.uk/pubns/priced/l144. pdf*

Access equipment and working platforms	Internal use	External use
Ladders	✓	✓
Step ladders	✓	
Mobile towers		✓
Trestle platforms	✓	
Tubular scaffolding		✓
Hop-up	✓	
Proprietary staging	✓	
Podiums	✓	

Table 4.2 Internal and external access equipment and working platforms

KEY TERMS

Prop

– the part of a step ladder that folds out and enables the ladder to be free-standing.

Rungs

– the horizontal parts of the ladder, also known as the steps.

Stiles

– the upright parts of a ladder that hold the rungs together.

Tie rods

– steel rods that sit under rungs, they support the stiles and help keep the ladder together.

In general, however, almost any access equipment can be used either inside or outside, but it depends on the size and needs of the project. For instance, if working inside a large building, you may find yourself using full tubular scaffolding, and if you were doing a small job outside, such as painting a door frame, you might use a hop-up or step ladder.

Types of access equipment and working platforms

Ladders

Ladders are one of the most common pieces of access equipment. Ladders must be leant up against something because they do not have their own **prop**, like a step ladder does. The steps of the ladder are called the **rungs**, and the long, upright parts that hold the rungs together are called the **stiles**. Ladders can be made of wood, aluminium or fibreglass. Wooden ladders are becoming less common as they are heavier and more expensive to buy.

There are different types of ladders that you may come across:

* Single ladders – these have only one section, i.e. they cannot be reduced or extended in size

* Double ladders – a type of extension ladder; they are made up of two sections that slide along each other and lock into place

* Extension ladders – an adjustable ladder with two or three sections that can be released to make the ladder longer; they can also be used as a single ladder and, when made of aluminium, they are light and portable

* Pole ladders – these are single ladders often used to access scaffolding platforms; they are made of timber and have **tie rods** under every rung

* Roof ladders – specifically designed for working on roofs, they have a hook that sits over the top of the roof to keep it stable

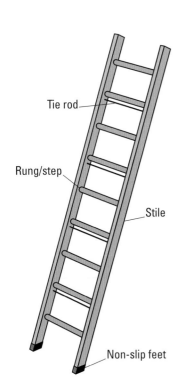

Tie rod

Rung/step

Stile

Non-slip feet

Figure 4.3 A ladder

Figure 4.4 An extension ladder

Figure 4.5 A pole ladder

Figure 4.6 A roof ladder

Step ladders and platform steps

Unlike a standard ladder, step ladders have a prop, so they can stand on their own without being rested against another surface. Step ladders are very regularly used for various construction tasks. They should only be used for quick, lightweight tasks that will be finished within about 30 minutes. A longer job will require more sturdy equipment. Like ladders, step ladders are made of wood, aluminium or fibreglass.

Platform steps are a shorter type of step ladder that has a small platform at the top and a bar or rail to hold onto. Sometimes this rail is used for hanging paint kettles.

PRACTICAL TIP

Go to the HSE website and print off their quick guide pocket card, *Top tips for ladder and step ladder safety: www.hse.gov.uk/ pubns/indg405.pdf*

DID YOU KNOW?

Platform steps are also known as swingback steps.

DID YOU KNOW?

The HSE have provided a guide on the safe use of ladders and step ladders. You can find it here: *www. hse.gov.uk/pubns/indg402. pdf*

Figure 4.7 A step ladder

Figure 4.8 A platform step ladder

Figure 4.9 A mobile tower

Mobile towers

A mobile access tower can be a safe and useful way to access work at height. They are widely used, but must be put together and used correctly, otherwise accidents can occur. Mobile towers are always constructed on lockable wheels so that they can be moved around the site without being taken apart. They are also free-standing, meaning that the scaffolding is not attached to or dependent on the building for support. Their parts are constructed of aluminium or fibreglass.

For painting and decorating, mobile towers tend to be used when there are two people working on a task, such as repairing fascia board or guttering, or applying a textured finish to a ceiling.

Trestle platforms

A trestle platform has two parts: the frame (or **trestle**) that supports the stage (or platform), and the platform itself. They are used for jobs that will likely take more than a few minutes as they are more secure than a ladder or step ladder.

A-frame trestles are shaped like the letter A and are used in pairs to support a scaffold board. Their height cannot be adjusted. Steel trestles on the other hand can be raised and lowered, and are generally considered more stable.

Figure 4.10 An A-frame trestle

Figure 4.11 A steel trestle

Proprietary staging

Proprietary staging is an attached working platform of staging boards specifically designed to help safe movement at heights. They are also known as crawling boards, lightweight stagings, and sometimes even by the brand-name 'Youngman boards'.

Proprietary staging is attached to trestles and tied in if working above 2 m. The painter and decorator would use them for spanning doorways and gaining access near the roof, e.g. when painting guttering. When working above 2 m, handrails and kickboards must also be used.

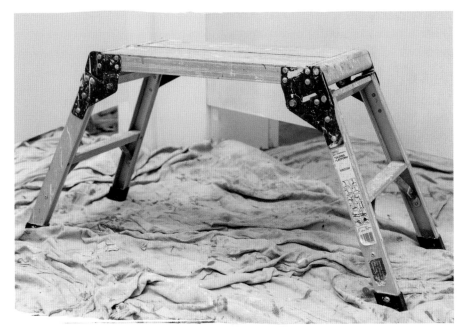

Figure 4.12 A hop-up

Figure 4.13 A podium

Podiums and hop-ups

Hop-ups and podiums are commonly used for painting and decorating. They are designed to be used for low-level access work. Hop-ups tend to be about 40–50cm in height, whereas podiums can have a platform height of up to around 1–1.5m. Podiums have 1m-high guard rails to protect the user from falling, and are similar to mobile towers in that they can be moved. Some podiums are specifically designed for working on staircases. They are a safe alternative to step ladders.

Mobile Elevated Working Platforms (MEWPs)

Even though you may not have to erect or dismantle all types of access equipment, it's possible that an employer will still expect you to use them. Some of the following MEWPs will come with training from a hire company or from your employer before you can use them, and some kinds will require you to hold a licence or card.

A MEWP is a driveable, mechanical piece of equipment that is powered by diesel or electricity. It is raised up and down by the person working at height in the basket. MEWPs come with additional risks:

* Overturning – because they are tall and narrow structures, if moved onto an uneven surface, or perhaps in extreme weather, the machine could fall over and throw the operator from the basket.

* Entrapment – if the basket were raised too high or the platform moved without checking, the operator could become stuck between the basket and a fixed structure.

* Collision – because they are a mechanical, moving object, they could accidentally hit a pedestrian, another vehicle, or overhead cables.

MEWPs should never be moved at the base while there are people on the raised platform.

PRACTICAL TIP

If you're unsure about the type of access equipment you should use, the HSE has a handy toolkit you can use at: *www.hse.gov. uk/falls/wait/wait-tool.htm*

DID YOU KNOW?

Some of these pieces of access equipment are known by different names in different parts of the country. For example, proprietary staging may just be referred to as crawling boards, and platform steps may be known as hop-ups.

Cherry picker

These are also known as boom lifts. A cherry picker is a platform that is raised vertically from the floor, but can also move forwards and backwards.

Scissor lift

A scissor lift moves only in a vertical direction, i.e. up and down, not forward and backward in the air. The platform sits on top of an accordion-like mechanism (see Fig 4.15).

See Table 1.10 on page 27 for a good summary of equipment, features and safety checks.

Figure 4.14 A cherry picker

Figure 4.15 A scissor lift

Protecting the work and its surrounding area

Tools and equipment used for erecting and dismantling access equipment need to be looked after. Any damage to components could mean that the equipment cannot be put together properly or may no longer be safe when in use.

It's not just your own work that you are protecting the area from – other site activities going on around you could also cause damage, such as other people using your equipment, site traffic, and mobile access equipment. Tools and equipment should be properly stored so that they do not create a slip or trip hazard. Leaving access equipment outside and unprotected could expose them to bad weather and damage. By keeping your tools and equipment clean and dry, you will make them perform better and last longer.

Keeping your work area tidy is always good practice. It ensures that you do not create hazards for yourself or other people on site. Any waste should be correctly disposed of.

When erecting, using or dismantling access equipment, it is a good idea to use screens, barriers or timber hoardings so that people walking by or underneath are not at risk of bumping the equipment or from being hit by falling items. Putting up notices will also help to remind others on site that you are working at height.

REED
TIP

Good communication is about listening – not just talking – and understanding the different ways people prefer to communicate.

INSPECTING ACCESS EQUIPMENT AND WORKING PLATFORM COMPONENTS AND IDENTIFYING DEFECTS

Components of access equipment and working platforms

Each of the types of access equipment listed above has specific parts and features that should be checked before using the equipment. See the table below for an explanation of these.

Component	Use
Stiles	The vertical parts of a ladder or step ladder which hold the rungs together.
Rungs	The horizontal parts of a ladder. They can be round or rectangular in shape.
Tie rods	Steel rods that sit beneath the rungs and stop the rungs on timber ladders from breaking and the stiles from separating. Tie rods should be at least under the second rung and then spaced regularly up the ladder. They should also appear under the first and fourth tread of steps.
Ropes	Two lengths of rope or cord is attached to each side of a step ladder to stop it from opening too far. However, the HSE has provided recent guidance that fixed metal stays are now preferred to ropes as they are more secure.
Pulleys	A wheel that controls the movement of a rope or cord. They are found on some types of scaffold and on rope-operated ladders.
Treads	The parts of a step ladder that you step on. Treads should be a minimum of 90 mm deep. Remember: never stand on the top step.
Hinges	Fixed to both sides of a step ladder, hinges stop the ladder from giving way.
Swingbacks	A type of step ladder that doesn't have a platform and the steps go right to the top of the stiles. It has two parts: the back frame and the front stepping part.
Locking bars	Fitted to aluminium step ladders, they hold the back frame and front steps together to prevent the ladder from collapsing. They must be fully extended and locked into place.
Non-slip inserts	Attached to the ends of the stiles. They reduce movement and slipping and can also protect the floor surface.
Scaffold boards	Made of timber and aluminium, they are used on fixed scaffolding and are the part that is walked on.
Platform staging	Made of aluminium, platforms are usually used on mobile access towers, providing a tough and non-slip surface.

Table 4.3 Components of access equipment and their use

Scaffolding

While you won't be erecting or dismantling scaffolding, you may well be using it. You will need to know how to use it safely and also how to visually inspect it and look for any faults that may need to be reported.

Tubular scaffolding

Tubular scaffolding is a structure of upright tubes (standards) and horizontal tubes (ledgers) made from either steel or aluminium. The scaffolding boards which form the working platform are supported by transoms which extend between the ledgers.

Scaffolding can be either independent (free-standing, but tied to a building) or dependent (attached to the brickwork of a building). See Fig 4.16 to help you identify the different parts of a scaffold.

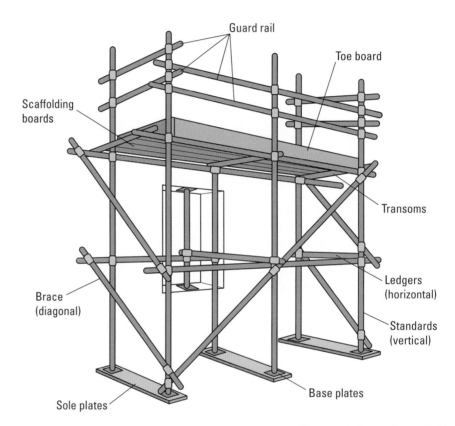

Figure 4.16 Parts of a scaffold

Figure 4.17 A universal coupler

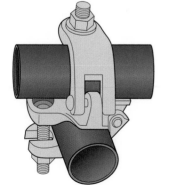

Figure 4.18 A right angle coupler

The scaffold is held together by various fittings including:

* universal couplers (Fig 4.17) which connect two tubes at right angles (one vertical, one horizontal)

* right angle couplers (Fig 4.18) which connect two tubes at right angles (both horizontal)

* swivel couplers (Fig 4.19) which connect two tubes at any angle

* sleeve couplers (Fig 4.20) which connect two tubes end to end

* base plates (Fig 4.21) which spread the load under the standards.

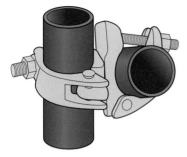

Figure 4.19 A swivel coupler

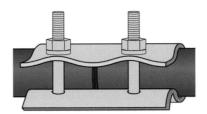

Figure 4.20 A sleeve coupler

Figure 4.21 A base plate

Slung scaffold

This is a type of dependent scaffold that is suspended from the ceiling of a building, usually in large spaces such as a theatre, factory or train station. The platforms have toe boards and guard rails all the way around so that it is safe to work above an area that is in constant use. Compare these with birdcage scaffolds in the case study on page 112.

CASE STUDY

South Tyneside Homes

South Tyneside Council's
Housing Company

Further training enhances your job prospects

Glen Richardson is a final year apprentice at South Tyneside Homes.

'You learn new skills on the job every day because every job is different. Obviously you're learning new skills in college too, but if you're given the chance to do any further training with your employer, then that's something extra you can put on your CV. It will be transferrable to other jobs too.

I've done a manual handling course on how to pick up heavy and awkward objects correctly and how to store them without injuring myself. It's definitely improved the way I work.

Even more useful was the scaffolding qualification I got. I can now erect and dismantle scaffolding, which is something you're not automatically allowed to do without the proper training. This means that I get to work on bigger jobs and buildings, and it will definitely help if I ever need to look for another job.'

Figure 4.22 A scaffolding tag

Carrying out inspections

Inspections of your access equipment should be carried out both before it is put together and once it is in use. It is essential to spot any problems or faults in the components. Inspecting equipment is an important part of ensuring accidents don't occur.

It is important not only to make sure the equipment is safe before it is used, but also while it is in use. This is because components can move around and loosen because of the weight on them, be exposed to weather when working outdoors, or get damaged while the equipment is being worked on. Even if equipment is safe for use, it must still be used correctly to avoid accidents.

Before using scaffolding, consider the following:

* Does it look safe?

* Are there any signs or tags attached to tell you whether it is unsafe or unfinished?

* Are the boards clear of debris and bulky work materials?

* Are the guardrails, scaffold boards and toe boards all in place?

* Is there a safe and suitable way of accessing the scaffold?

* Does it look complete, i.e. can you see all the parts identified in Fig 4.16?

* Are the right fittings being used?

If any faults to scaffolding have been discovered, then a tagging system is used to alert others to the problem so that the component or structure is not used by someone else. **Note:** you should *never* adjust fixed scaffolding unless you have been properly trained and are a competent, carded scaffolder.

When carrying out an inspection on scaffolding or working platforms, you should fill in an inspection report. An example of this from the HSE is shown below.

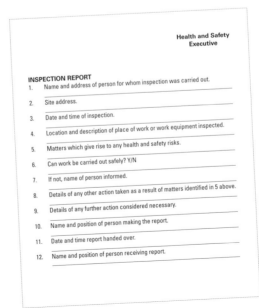

Figure 4.23 A sample inspection report

Pre-erection inspections

Mobile towers and podiums

* Check castors and wheels are swivelling freely.

* Check that there is a brake and that it is working.

Step ladders

* Check that treads, bolds, screws, and hinges are in good condition and not loose.

* Check the retaining cords and hinges are the same length and are not damaged or frayed.

* Check there are no splits or cracks in the stiles.

* Check that treads are secure and do not have any splits.

* If using an aluminium step ladder, check that stiles and treads are not warped, twisted or badly dented.

Platforms

* Check that any platforms or scaffold boards are not split.

* Check they are not warped or twisted.

* Check that boards do not have significant weaknesses, such as large knots in the wood.

Ladders

See practical task 2, *Pre-use inspection of ladders* for the correct pre-use checks.

Inspection intervals

Some access equipment and components need to be checked more often than others. The HSE provides guidance on these inspection intervals as follows.

Scaffolds and working platforms above 2 m high:

* should first be inspected after installation (being put into position) or assembly (being put together); note that mobile towers or platforms can still be moved around after they've been assembled without further inspection

* should be inspected after any exceptional circumstances which are likely to jeopardise the safety of the equipment, for example, after a major weather event such as a storm, after vandalism, or after an incident

* should be inspected at least every seven days and there should be a record of this inspection.

All other working platforms:

* should be inspected in the same way as scaffolding, except that regular inspections need only take place at suitable intervals rather than every seven days.

DID YOU KNOW?

You should never paint a wooden ladder or step ladder as it could hide any damage.

DID YOU KNOW?

If a ladder is damaged, it must be destroyed and not repaired.

PRACTICAL TIP

What does 'suitable intervals' mean? This will depend on how often the equipment is used and the conditions it is used under. For example, equipment that is used outdoors and exposed to the elements will need more frequent checks than equipment that is used indoors or used only occasionally.

DID YOU KNOW?

If you have a medical condition that causes dizziness or seizures, then you may not be fit to work at height.

Guard rails, toe boards, barriers and any other fall protection:

* should be inspected in the same way as all other working platforms.

Ladders and step ladders:

* should be inspected at suitable intervals
* should be inspected after exceptional circumstances that might affect the equipment's safety
* should be checked on each occasion before use, though a report on this inspection is not needed.

ERECTING AND WORKING FROM ACCESS EQUIPMENT AND WORKING PLATFORMS

To set up and work safely from access equipment and working platforms, you must be aware of how to:

* identify a secure base
* correctly load a working platform
* use safe manual handling techniques.

Refer back to Chapter 1, page 22 where techniques for safe lifting are covered in detail. You will need to bear these in mind when erecting and dismantling access equipment because it can at times be heavy and/or awkward to move.

The table below shows how each type of equipment should be secured, loaded and handled.

Access equipment	Securing the base	Correct loading and use	Manual handling and erecting
Ladders	• Place on firm ground, or use a board. • Place on level, clean and solid ground with good grip for ladder feet. • Tie both stiles of ladder at suitable point, preferably near the top (see Fig 4.24). • Or, if not possible, wedge against something solid, e.g. another wall. • Set up at angle of 75° (or 1m for every 4m up). • Don't rest against weak or flexible surfaces, e.g. plastic guttering.	• Keep three points of contact with ladder (two feet, one hand). • Don't do work involving both hands. • Both hands are holding on when climbing. • The ladder is close enough to the work, i.e. no overreaching. • Take one rung at a time when going up or down. • No standing on top third of the ladder, or top two or three rungs. • Avoid carrying loads over 10kg. • Never move the ladder while in use.	• Short ladders can be carried alone, holding it vertically against the shoulder, grasping a lower rung, and using other hand to hold stile avoid going near power lines or take extra care if necessary to work near them. • Long ladders should be carried by two people, one at each end, held on the shoulder. • To erect a long ladder, one person stands on bottom rung while second person takes the top rung and 'walks' down the ladder rung by rung with their hands.

Access equipment	Securing the base	Correct loading and use	Manual handling and erecting
Step ladders	• Make sure the legs are fully open. • All four legs must be in contact with ground. • Placed on a level and stable base. • Tie the step ladder if high risk work.	• Do not work side-on. • Make sure you have a handhold. • No standing on top two or three rungs (knees should be below top step). • The ladder is close enough to the work, i.e. no overreaching. • Take one rung at a time when going up or down. • Don't use to access higher levels, e.g. a roof. • Avoid carrying loads over 10 kg. • Person climbing should be facing the work. • Never move the ladder while in use.	• For set up, lean it forward a little, holding onto the stiles, then pull the back support away from the front. Make sure any locks are engaged.
Mobile towers	• Place on firm and level ground. • Brakes must be on while in use. • Surface must be strong enough to take the load at each of the four points. • Use boards underneath if needed to avoid sinking or tilting. • If using indoors, height of tower should be a base width to height ratio of 1:3.5 (but check manufacturer's guidelines). • If using outdoors, height of tower should be a base width to height ratio of 1:3 (but check manufacture guidelines).	• Do not move while people are working on the tower. • Do not move while tools, equipment and materials are on the tower. • Do not use outdoors in high winds. • For use outdoors, tie in against the structure if possible. • Be aware of overhead power lines – do not use if lines are near the tower. • Do not overreach – if you can't reach, then move the tower correctly. • To access the working platform, climb only on the ladder *inside* the tower. • Never add a ladder/step ladder to the platform for extra height.	• When moving, always push from the bottom of the tower to avoid toppling. • If you need to increase the height, the width of the base can be increased by adding outriggers to stabilise the tower (see Fig 4.26). • Anyone erecting a mobile tower must be fully trained and competent or under supervision of an experienced person.
Trestle platforms	• Set each trestle on a firm, level base. • Ensure A-frames are opened fully. • Steel trestles should be no further than 1.2 m apart. • Rest steel trestles on top of a flat scaffold board.	• Use only one working platform. • If there is a risk of falling, guard-rails, barriers and toe boards should be used. • Scaffold boards used as a platform must be the same length and thickness, and boards on an A-frame trestle should be no less than 450 mm wide. • Trestle should be stable when in use. • Access to the platform should also be safe, e.g. a securely tied ladder. • The working platform boards should be checked for splitting, twisting, warping and knots that may weaken them.	• Lift the trestle into the correct place, hold it evenly and pull both sides away from each other. Make sure all parts are opened as far as they can go.

Access equipment	Securing the base	Correct loading and use	Manual handling and erecting
Proprietary staging (crawling boards)	• Secure or tie in your platform boards with ropes into the trestles, if working at heights over 2m.	• Do not overload. • If working over 2m heights, there must be a handrail and kickboard. • Use the correct access equipment to reach your boards, e.g. a pair of steps to erect it and reach it when in use. • When using with trestles, the overhang should be no more than four times the thickness of the board.	• Proprietary staging boards are heavy and awkward to lift. You will need two people to erect or dismantle.
Podiums/ hop-ups	• If on wheels, use brakes to lock them in. Place on even ground.	• If on wheels, do not pull yourself and the podium along the working area. • Select the right height equipment so that work is conducted on the platform itself. • Do not move while people are working. • Do not move while tools, equipment and materials are on the platform. • Only one person should use at a time. • Close and lock the gate before starting work.	• Platform should be locked into place. • Handrails should be secured.

Table 4.4 Securing, loading and handling access equipment and working platforms

PRACTICAL TIP

'Footing' the ladder is the last alternative to securing the base, if it is not possible to tie the stiles or wedge it. Footing is where a second person stands on the bottom rung with both feet. It is not ideal because it does not stop the ladder from slipping sideways. When tying the ladder off initially, you will need someone to foot the ladder.

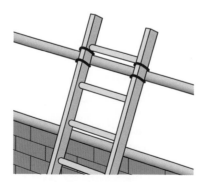

Figure 4.24 Securing a ladder at the top – for working on only. For access, a ladder must be tied 1m or 3 rungs above the working platform.

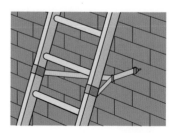

Figure 4.25 Securing a ladder at the base

Always follow the manufacturer's instructions when erecting access equipment and working platforms. Each make of equipment could be slightly different from others you have worked with before.

DISMANTLING AND STORING ACCESS EQUIPMENT AND WORKING PLATFORMS

Sequence for dismantling

Ladders

Dismantling a ladder is basically the same as erecting it, but in reverse.

1. The bottom rung should be footed.

2. Lift the ladder carefully away from the surface it is leaning on.

3. Put both hands on the stiles.

4. Walk slowly backwards while moving your hands from rung to rung.

5. Lay the ladder on the ground.

Platforms, platform steps and trestles

You can dismantle platform steps as follows:

1. Lean the steps forwards.

2. Undo the lock (if there is one).

3. Ensure the rope can move freely.

4. Move the back frame towards the front frame.

5. Lift the steps into a secure position.

Storage requirements

Ladders

Timber ladders will decay over time if stored outside. If they can't be stored under cover, then they should be covered or placed in a position that is protected from the wind and rain. Keep them away from heat sources such as boilers.

Do not hang ladders from their rungs or stiles. Instead, store horizontally on a rack, with the weight on the stiles only. They should be supported along their length so that they don't sag.

Ladders made from aluminium will corrode if store near set lime or cement.

Step ladders, trestles and platform steps

These should always be stored in an upright position in a covered area to avoid weathering. They should preferably be kept off the ground so they do not get exposed to damp.

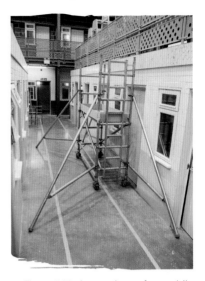

Figure 4.26 An outrigger for mobile tower base

REED TIP

Helping out on maintenance jobs around the home with your family at the weekend still counts as experience you can put on your CV or application form. Remember, however, that any work-based evidence as part of your qualification has to be countersigned by an experienced qualified operative.

CASE STUDY

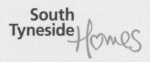

Working with a birdcage scaffold

Birdcage scaffolding is often used in buildings such as churches or theatres.

The birdcage scaffold is a type of independent scaffold with an enclosed working area so that there are no gaps for a worker to fall through. It is raised to just below the ceiling and forms a complete platform, from corner to corner, like an extra floor. It is quite expensive to erect and so tends to be used for jobs that will take a long time.

When the Hull New Theatre was being refurbished, there was a lot of painting detail on the ceiling to be restored. More than 2,600 square metres of ceiling, wall panels, balconies and box seating in the auditorium were redecorated with the use of a birdcage scaffold and a large team of painters.

As a similar alternative to birdcage scaffolding, it is possible to use a slung scaffold. This is so that it is still possible to have a congregation or audience coming into the space below during long-term inner roof and ceiling work. It can also mean faster construction times, e.g. so that the seating can be added at the same time as the ceiling work.

Figure 4.27 A birdcage scaffold

PRACTICAL TASK

1. PREPARE TO ERECT ACCESS EQUIPMENT AND WORKING PLATFORMS

OBJECTIVE

To be able to interpret guidance information, produce a hazard identification record, select and use the right PPE, and protect the work and its surrounding area from damage.

SCENARIO

You and one other person are preparing a new timber fascia for the frontage of a shop inside a shopping centre. The work can only be completed outside normal shop opening hours, therefore you will not have access to the shop itself. Due to the lack of access to a power supply, you will only be able to use hand tools.

The timber fascia is 4.5 m long and 2 m high from ground level. You will be preparing surfaces for painting. The maximum amount of time you have to complete the surface preparation is 2 hours.

STEP 1   Decide what sort of access equipment you will need to work at the highest point.

- Think about the type of work you will be doing and how long you will need to be working at height. Think about how high you will need to reach and whether you will need to move and reach your access equipment. What sorts of access equipment might be suitable?

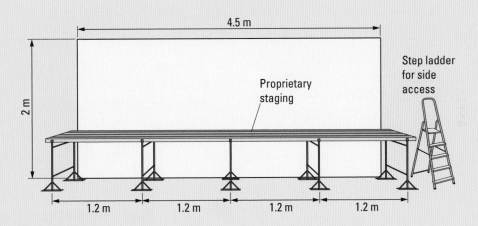

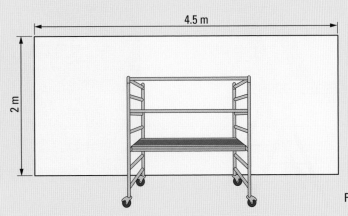

Figure 4.28 Diagram of possible working solutions for access equipment

PRACTICAL TIP

As you are working in a limited space/width, a set of steel trestles with lightweight staging platforms would be wide enough to span the whole area.

Remember that working platforms must be supported every 1.2 m. You would also require a form of access to the platform itself, e.g. a step ladder.

Because of the limited time available to complete the work, you might consider using an aluminium mobile tower which would limit the time needed to erect, dismantle and re-erect a steel trestle type of working platform.

Remember that even though you need to reach up to 2 metres, you do not need to stand above 2 metres to do this. If you would be working for more than 10–15 minutes at a time in one spot, then a step ladder would not be the best option for the entire job.

You will need something higher than a hop-up to reach the 2 m point comfortably.

PRACTICAL TIP

Your lecturer may give you a print out of a **hazard recording sheet**, or you can download a template at: *www.planetvocational.co.uk*

STEP 2 Fill out a hazard identification record.

- Think about the environment: are there likely to be other workers on site? Are there likely to be members of the public in the area?

- Think about the hazards of erecting and working with the type of access equipment you have chosen, e.g. competence of persons using the access equipment, uneven ground condition, falls from height, slips and trips, cuts and abrasions.

- Think of specific problems for the environment you're in and the equipment you've chosen, e.g. collection and storage of the equipment, security of the equipment for each separate hazard.

- For each separate hazard, what can you do to avoid or control the risk?

STEP 3 Choose your PPE.

- Using the same hazard recording sheet, consider which PPE you will need to both erect and use the access equipment you've chosen.

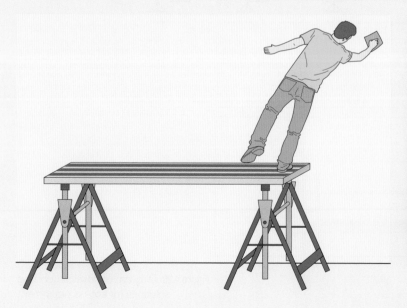

Figure 4.29 Incorrect use of access equipment

STEP 4 Look at the manufacturer's instructions for the access equipment you've chosen.

- Manufacturer's instructions can usually be found in the form of a label stuck to the equipment itself. From a hire company, the company must provide an instruction leaflet, which is in addition to the manufacturer's instruction label found on the equipment itself.

- Do you understand them? Do you need any extra pieces of PPE you haven't thought about? Is the equipment suitable for the job, e.g. does it give a maximum span and weight?

- Add any extra hazard and PPE information you've found to your hazard record.

Figure 4.30 Manufacturer's instructions

STEP 5 Protect the work and surrounding area from damage.

- Produce a sketch of the intended work area showing how you protect the work and the work area.

- Think about the working environment. Are there other operatives working on site? Are there vehicles in the area that could come into contact with your access equipment? Are there members of the public who might walk into or underneath your equipment? Is anyone at risk of falling objects from your access equipment? Will you need to put up any signs, barriers or hoardings to protect the area?

- Also consider what PPE you might need when protecting the area. You can add this to your hazard recording sheet.

DID YOU KNOW?

To remind yourself of the safety signs commonly used on construction sites and what they mean, go to page 37.

2. PRE-USE INSPECTION OF LADDERS

OBJECTIVE

To be able to inspect and record findings about the condition of two types of access ladders prior to erection and use, and select relevant PPE to be used when checking access ladders in the workplace.

TOOLS AND EQUIPMENT

A step ladder   Spanners

An extension ladder   Screwdrivers

Socket set

PPE

Ensure you select PPE appropriate to the job and site where you are working. Refer to the PPE section of Chapter 1.

STEP 1   Lay your extension ladder flat on the floor, without extending it. Open up your step ladder to its standing position.

PRACTICAL TIP

When inspecting access equipment, you will still be on site. Even though you may not be using the equipment or carrying out work tasks, you must still wear the PPE required by your college or employer, e.g. hi-vis jackets and hard hats.

STEP 2   Check for the following on your ladder:

❏ Are the stiles straight and undamaged?

❏ Are all of the feet present?

❏ Are the feet worn, damaged or caked in dirt?

❏ Are all the rungs there?

❏ Are any of the rungs bent, worn, loose or damaged?

❏ Is the ladder clean of mud, grease etc.?

❏ If you're using a purely wooden ladder, are there enough tie rods? (Note: there should be a rod for every other rung on a ladder that has wooden rungs and stiles.)

On your step ladder, check the following:

❏ Are all of the feet present?

❏ Are the feet worn, damaged or caked in dirt?

❏ Is the platform split, bent or buckled?

❏ Are the steps or treads clean of mud or grease?

STEP 3   Extend the ladder to its full length and lean it against a wall.

STEP 4   Check for the following on both your ladder and step ladder:

❏ Do the moving parts move easily?

❏ Are there any loose bolts or screws?

❏ Does the locking mechanism on the extension fully engage?

❏ Are the locking mechanisms worn or damaged?

STEP 5 Remove any dirt or grease from the ladder and tighten any loose parts.

Note that very minor adjustments are fine, but anything more serious than this, consult your supervisor. The ladder may need replacing.

PRACTICAL TIP

Remember: You should never make any alterations, remove or add anything to a ladder or other access equipment.

STEP 6 If there are any defects that you think could make the ladders unusable, you must report your concerns to the charge hand, foreman, supervisor or employer, and do not use until rectified.

Record all comments and findings using the ladder **condition checklist record**.

PRACTICAL TIP

Your lecturer may give you a print out of a **ladder condition checklist** record, or you can download a template at: *www.planetvocational. co.uk*

PRACTICAL TASK

3. ERECT, USE, DISMANTLE AND STORE AN EXTENSION LADDER

Remember to always ask yourself the following questions before using the access equipment:

- Is the access equipment of the correct *type* for the intended work?

- Have you read the manufacturer's instructions?

- Is it *fit* for purpose?

- Is it the correct *size*?

- Can you use it by yourself or do you need *help* to erect, use and dismantle the access equipment?

- Is the *grounding* level and firm?

OBJECTIVE

As part of a team of two people, erect and use an extension ladder in the recognised and safe manner, dismantle, handle and store the ladder without causing any minor or long-term damage.

TOOLS AND EQUIPMENT

A class 1 extension ladder

Ladder ties

A ladder stabilising device

PPE

Ensure you select PPE appropriate to the job and site where you are working. Refer to the PPE section of Chapter 1.

STEP 1 Place the ladder on the ground facing the intended resting position (in a safe position, away from doors etc.).

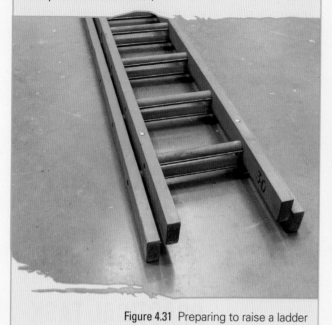

Figure 4.31 Preparing to raise a ladder

STEP 2 While another person is using their feet to stop the ladder moving, or by placing the ladder against the bottom of the wall, walk the ladder to an upright position.

Figure 4.32 Footing the ladder

STEP 3 Pull the bottom of the ladder out from the wall until you reach an angle of 75° (or a ratio of 4:1).

STEP 4 Secure (tie) both stiles of the ladder near the base, or at the top, or half way down if possible. If tying the ladder is not possible, you should use a ladder stability device, or wedge it against a wall. As a last resort, you can use another person to 'foot' the ladder.

Figure 4.33 Tying the ladder near the base

Figure 4.34 Tying the ladder at the top

Figure 4.35 Tying the ladder partway down

Figure 4.36 Ladder stability devices

PRACTICAL TIP

Remember that if you're tying a ladder at the top as pictured, that it is safe for working on, but shouldn't be used for gaining access to a roof or working platform.

PRACTICAL TIP

There are two positions for your hands when ascending and descending a ladder. You can steady yourself by moving one hand to the stile of the ladder (side) whilst the other hand holds on to the rungs as you ascend or descend. This method should be used when you are carrying small types of resources such as paint tins.

Figure 4.37 Ascending a ladder while carrying an object

STEP 5 Climb the ladder safely, always facing the rungs and maintaining three points of contact.

If you are using the ladder for access only, you should use both hands on the rungs.

STEP 6 Carry out the work you need to do on the ladder. When working on the ladder, take care not to overreach. A good guideline is to keep your belt buckle between the two stiles.

PRACTICAL TIP

Note: it is always best practice to use two people to carry long access equipment such as an extension ladder. You may not be able to see what is coming around the corner or any obstacles on site, such as doorways.

STEP 7 Carry the ladder safely.

To move the ladder to the storage area you should get help from another person to lift and carry it. If you have to move the ladder by yourself, place the ladder at approximately 75° over your shoulder, and hold the ladder with both hands. This should only be done for short distances.

Figure 4.38 Correct manual handling of a timber ladder by two people

STEP 8 Store the ladder off the ground, if possible, horizontally on at least two ladder hooks, in a dry and secure environment.

TEST YOURSELF

1. What is the biggest risk when using access equipment and working platforms?

   a. Slips

   b. Falls from height

   c. Electrocution

   d. Cuts and abrasions

2. Why might you erect a screen around your access equipment?

   a. To stop passers-by damaging your work

   b. To protect others from any falling debris

   c. To stop vehicles and passers-by from running into access equipment

   d. All of the above

3. A tie rod is:

   a. a steel bar underneath rungs on a ladder

   b. a step on a ladder

   c. a piece of cord to tie a ladder to a structure

   d. the sides of a ladder that hold the rungs

4. Which of the following is NOT part of a ladder?

   a. Rung

   b. Stiles

   c. Toe board

   d. Tread

5. What should you check mobile scaffold towers for?

   a. Wheels that spin freely

   b. Twists

   c. Knots

   d. Splits

6. What does the 1 in 4 rule mean?

   a. You should check a ladder every fourth time you use it

   b. That the ladder is at a 75° angle to the surface it leans against

   c. One in four decorators will fall off a ladder

   d. You should work on a ladder for one quarter of an hour

7. When working on a step ladder you should NOT:

   a. work side-on to the surface

   b. carry loads of more than 10 kg

   c. use it to access higher levels

   d. all of the above

8. How should ladders be stored?

   a. Upright

   b. Hanging from the rungs

   c. Laid flat on a rack

   d. Outside

9. When moving a mobile scaffold you should always:

   a. push or pull from the bottom

   b. have the wheels locked

   c. leave your tools on the platform

   d. make sure someone is still standing on the platform

10. If you spot a problem with a scaffold you should:

    a. try to fix it

    b. tell your supervisor

    c. do nothing

    d. climb up to have a closer look

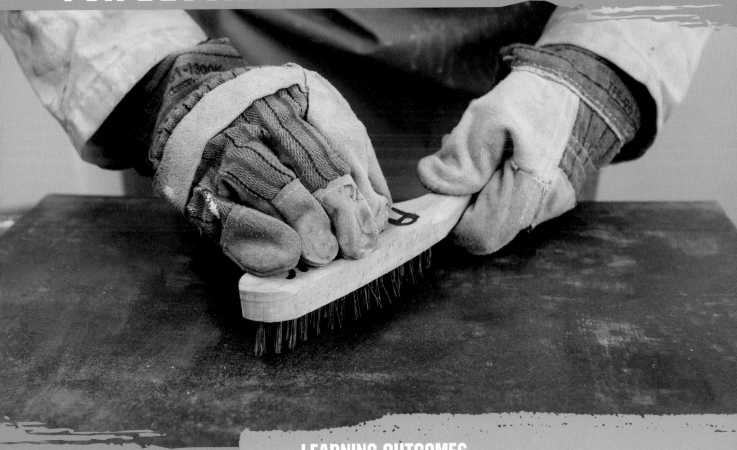

Chapter 5

UNIT CSA L10CC13

PREPARE COMMON SURFACE TYPES FOR DECORATION

LEARNING OUTCOMES

LO1/2: Know how to and be able to prepare a range of bare and previously painted and decorated surfaces to receive coatings/ covering systems

LO3/4: Know how to and be able to correct defects in common surfaces and surface coatings

LO5/6: Know how to and be able to repair and make good common surfaces

INTRODUCTION

The aims of this chapter are to:

* explain preparation methods of a range of substrates including rectifying surface defects

* help you recognise and prepare timbers and their sheet products, ferrous and non-ferrous metals, a range of trowelled finishes and plasterboard using appropriate tools and materials.

KEY TERMS

Contaminant
– a substance that pollutes the surface being prepared, such as dirt, grease, oil, rust, old paste, silicone and flakes from old coverings.

Key
– the roughness of a surface which helps a covering to adhere (stick). Lightly sanding or abrading will provide a key.

PREPARING A RANGE OF SURFACES

All surfaces will need some kind of preparation before they can be painted and decorated. If the surface is not prepared correctly – whether it is previously painted, timber, metal, brick, plastic, plastered or papered – the final finish will not look as good or last as long. Defects (such as flaking and mould) and **contaminants** (such as dirt and old paste) have to be removed, otherwise the new paint or paper will not stick to the surface. A well-prepared surface will provide a good **key** for the paint or paper to stick to.

Hazards, health and safety and risk assessment

When preparing surfaces, the main health and safety risks you may come across include:

* asthma or other respiratory complaints from breathing in contaminants, e.g. mould, dust particles, or substances such as wood preservatives or other chemicals

* getting dust or other irritants in eyes when sanding/rubbing down wood, flaking paint and metal

* chemical burns, dermatitis, and other skin problems from working with materials such as paint strippers and solvents

* inhalation of toxic fumes or old lead paint, resulting in respiratory complaints, headaches or dizziness

* fire and risk of burns from working with flammable materials such as solvents

* risk of falling from height or from falling objects (see Chapter 4 for more detailed information on working at height and using access equipment)

* electric shock or fire when working with electricity, e.g. preparing surfaces around power sockets and removing light fittings

* trip hazards, e.g. from materials and equipment lying around, dust sheets

* cuts and abrasions from using sharp equipment, such as scrapers and knives

* asbestos from old insulation and coatings.

PRACTICAL TIP

The Control of Substances Hazardous to Health (COSHH) Regulations also apply to the use of wood preservatives.

There are several precautions you should take to avoid these risks and hazards:

* wearing appropriate PPE

* not smoking near flammable materials

* making sure there is good ventilation, i.e. keeping doors and windows open

* carrying out safety checks to access equipment

* keeping a clean and tidy work area

* using washing facilities provided

* washing hands (but NOT with white spirit or other solvents), especially before eating

* switching off electricity before removing light fittings

* taping down dust sheets so you don't trip on them

* wet sanding instead of dry sanding to reduce dust

* identifying any risk of asbestos and having it removed by a licensed contractor only.

In Chapter 1 you will find more details on general health and safety issues in a construction environment.

PPE

As mentioned above, it is very important to wear the appropriate PPE when preparing surfaces, in particular, wearing gloves to protect your hands from chemicals, wearing goggles or safety glasses to protect from dust particles or flaking materials, wearing a dust mask to avoid breathing in particles and fumes, and wearing overalls to protect your skin from chemicals and solvents.

KEY TERMS

Substrate

– the substance which lies underneath the surface, such as wood, plaster, metal or brick.

Identifying surfaces

Some of the surfaces you will be working on will have been previously painted or covered. Sometimes they will be bare and the coating you put on them will be the first. Either way, it is important to know which type of surface it is (bare or previously decorated), and which type of **substrate** it is (e.g. wood, metal or plaster).

Timbers

Timbers can include hardwoods, softwoods and sheet materials. Timber is an absorbent surface and must be well prepared so that it does not take on moisture, which would cause it to rot or expand.

Softwood timbers come from fast-growing, evergreen trees and are the main type of wood used for indoor construction. They must be protected by a surface coating, but will need to be properly prepared before paint is applied. You will find softwoods used on components such as skirting boards, door and window frames, dado rails, picture rails and architraves.

Sheet materials, such as plywood, chipboard, MDF, hardboard and blockboard, must also be prepared and coated. MDF is often used for skirting boards, architraves, door frames, picture and dado rails because it is a cheaper material.

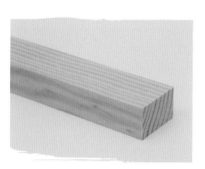

Figure 5.1 Pine

PRACTICAL TIP

Softwoods tend to be painted because of their knots and resin, and are used for work that will be hidden. If softwood is to be used outdoors, then it will need to be protected from the weather by using a wood preservative. You may come across hardwoods on external timber surfaces, which also need to be prepared in a similar way to softwoods. You will learn more about working with hardwoods at Level 2.

DID YOU KNOW?

Softwood and hardwood are not necessarily 'soft' or 'hard'. These terms refer to the cell structure of the wood: softwood has a simple structure and hardwood has a more complex one.

Types of timber sheet material

	Description
Chipboard (Fig 5.2)	This is made from a combination of flakes of wood and woodchips that have been compressed together and bonded using resin glue. It is available in many different grades, sizes and widths. It is used to make tongue and groove flooring.
Plywood (Fig 5.3)	This is made of layers of timber, which are known as veneers. The veneers are glued together with alternating grain, which gives the plywood a good deal of strength and stability.
	Plywood is graded, which helps identify where different types can be used. Each side is graded separately so you could have a high grade on one side and a lower grade on the other. If it is marked with the stamp INT then it is only to be used for interior work. This is because the plywood is not resistant to humidity or dampness. If it is marked MR it means it has medium resistance to humidity and dampness. The best external type of plywood is marked WBP, which is weather and boil proof.
	However, WBP ply can delaminate when subjected to prolonged periods of exposure to wet weather conditions so for boats marine plywood is used. This must be compliant with BS 1088 and is made to perform better in wet and humid conditions, and is resistant to fungal attack.
	Fire-retardant, moisture-resistant and pressure-resistant plywood is available, which may have been treated with chemicals to give it the required properties.
Medium density fibreboard (MDF) (Fig 5.4)	This fibreboard is made using a dry process. The fibres are bonded together with a resin adhesive. It is available in various thicknesses and sheet sizes. It is also available as ready-moulded skirting and mouldings. It is very easy to work with but should only be used internally. There are moisture-resistant versions available.
Block board (Fig 5.5)	This is a form of laminated board. Strips of wood are laminated or stuck together and then veneers are glued to form a top and bottom surface. Usually the more strips inside the 'sandwich' the higher the quality of the laminated board. Block board has strips of up to 25 mm in width. Laminboard, which is a form of block board, has strips that are less than 25 mm thick. Block board is rarely used these days.
Hardboard (Fig 5.6)	This is made from wet wood fibres being compacted at a high temperature and pressure. This is available in a number of finishes, some of which are shaped and in thicknesses of up to 6 mm. There is an oil-tempered version of hardboard, which has some moisture resistance. Hardboard is used for numerous purposes in construction. It is extensively used in exhibition work as it is easily formed around curves.

Table 5.1 Types of timber sheet material

Figure 5.2 Chipboard

Figure 5.3 Plywood

Figure 5.4 Medium density fibreboard (MDF)

Figure 5.5 Block board

Figure 5.6 Hardboard

Metal

Ferrous metals are metals that have iron content, such as cast iron, wrought iron and stainless steel. Iron and steel can rust when they come into contact with water and oxygen, e.g. when outdoors in the wind and rain. This rust, or **corrosion**, is formed by the iron content, so the more iron there is in a metal, the more rust will occur and the weaker the metal will become. Also, ferrous metals can suffer from **millscale**, a layer of metal oxides, which can flake off even when finished with paint. Ferrous metal needs to be well prepared and protected to avoid rust and flaking.

Non-ferrous metals, such as aluminium, copper, brass, bronze and zinc, do not contain any iron. They are not as strong as ferrous metals and so are usually used only for decorative purposes. When non-ferrous metals corrode, the corrosion provides a layer of protection to the metal underneath. Although non-ferrous metals do not suffer damage (i.e. rust) from corrosion as ferrous metals do, they still need to be prepared and protected from the elements. Different metals will need different preparation.

In a painting and decorating context, metal surfaces are found on radiators, pipes, handrails and balusters on staircases and outdoor balconies, gates, fireplaces, and garage doors.

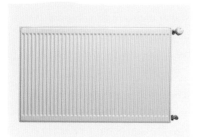

Figure 5.8 A modern radiator

Figure 5.7 Decorative wrought iron balusters

Figure 5.9 A painted fireplace

Plaster and plasterboard

Plaster and plasterboard are used on internal surfaces. Sometimes plasterboard is finished with a thin skim of plaster. They are both very absorbent materials and must be completely dry before coverings are applied.

Figure 5.10 An example of painted brickwork

PRACTICAL TIP

If you are working on buildings that are more than 100 years old, remember that they need to breathe. The materials you use should allow for this..

The two most common types of plaster are lime plaster and gypsum plaster. Lime plaster is rarely used these days, but may be found in old buildings. Plaster and plasterboard are used on ceilings, and internal and dividing walls.

Plaster can also be used externally where it is called render. Render can be made from cement and sand, lime mortar or artificial pre-mixed materials. It can take several weeks to be dry enough to paint.

Bricks and blocks

Bricks and blocks can be used on both the outside and inside of buildings. External brickwork is sometimes covered in render, and internal blockwork is usually covered with plasterboard, and then painted. Sometimes, brickwork may even be painted on directly. It is difficult to apply paint directly to bricks because they are very **porous** and absorbent.

Plastics

Plastics are often shiny and do not provide a good key for paint to adhere to. You may come across plastics when working on guttering, downpipes or radiator covers. Plastic should be degreased and given a thin coat of oil-based product to help adhesion, then a sealer, a gloss (good for a flexible surface) or eggshell that has been thinned with white spirit. This will provide a key for your top coat.

Materials

Stoppers

A stopper is a material, such as wood filler or putty, which will fill a gap or hole in a surface. It can be sanded down once dry and then primed and painted along with the rest of the surface.

KEY TERMS

Porous (material)

– something that contains tiny holes that allow water to enter or pass through it.

DID YOU KNOW?

There are three main types of brick: common/fletton bricks, which should not be painted because of their high salt content and efflorescence; engineering bricks, which cannot be painted because of their non-porous surface; and rustic/sand-faced clay bricks, which will accept paint well.

PRACTICAL TIP

Today there are alternatives to solvents. A water-based paint removes the need for paint thinners to clean your brushes. Turpentine is a greener alternative because it is made from pine tree resin; however, it is still flammable and toxic. There are also natural 'green' solvents made from citrus oil, corn and other biomass.

Solvents

Solvents, such as white spirit, acetone and turpentine, are strong and toxic chemical substances. Most types will give off fumes, so should only be used in a well-ventilated area. They are also highly flammable so should be used away from heat sources and flames. You should also avoid skin contact with solvents. Solvents are used for thinning paint (e.g. when cleaning brushes), removing grease and oil, preventing rust, and dissolving glues. They should be used with extreme care as they can damage surfaces such as furniture finishes. Because they are so toxic, solvents can also pollute soil and water, so they must be disposed of carefully in steel containers, clearly marked and transported by a recognised company. There are licensed waste disposal businesses which can deal with your hazardous waste.

Type of solvent	Uses
White spirit	Used for thinning oil-based paint, cleaning up silicone, and cleaning paint off brushes. Helps prevent rust and corrosion. Fast drying.
Methylated spirits	Used for degreasing metal surfaces, removing adhesives, and cleaning knotting solution (shellac) off brushes. Helps prevent rust and corrosion. Fast drying.
Turpentine (turps)	Used for thinning oil-based paint, making varnishes, and in furniture wax.
Acetone	Used for degreasing metal and glass. It will dissolve or melt certain types of plastic. It is an ingredient in some paints and varnishes.

Table 5.2 Solvents and their uses

Single-pack filler

Single-pack fillers are fast-drying, solvent-based wood fillers. They are usually mixed with sanding dust then used for filling gaps, knots and cracks in timber flooring. Two-pack fillers are pastes that come with an activator, which makes the paste cure.

Shellac/patent

Shellac is a resin that comes from the female lac bug, found in Asia. It can be used as a knotting solution that seals in the resin from knots in wood so that the final painted surface will not stain or discolour (see Fig 5.11). Patent is a shellac-based product used as a knotting solution. When the final coat will be light-coloured, then white knotting solution should be used, which is colourless so it won't show through the topcoats.

DID YOU KNOW?

Shellac has been used for many purposes, including waxing fruits, old vinyl records, a coating on pills, a cloth dye, and the finished coating on guitars, among many other things!

Mordant solutions

Mordant solutions are used for preparing metal surfaces such as aluminium and galvanised steel. They provide a rough finish, or key, by etching the surface so that paint will adhere more easily. Mordant solution is also known as etch primer or T-wash. It is highly toxic, so you should only work with mordant solution in a well-ventilated area, wearing a face mask.

Stabilising solution

This solvent-based solution is used on porous surfaces such as brick, old render and external masonry (stonework). It primes the surface, ready for painting, by sealing flaking and defects. While it is highly toxic (don't breathe it in or touch it), it can save a lot of time when preparing weathered surfaces.

Tools and equipment

The various tools and equipment you will need for preparing surfaces are listed in the table below.

Figure 5.11 Knotting solution on a door

Tools and equipment	Use
Scraper (Fig 5.12)	Also known as a stripping knife, the scraper is used to remove old wallpaper and flaking paint. Some scrapers have changeable blades and long handles which are good for difficult jobs, e.g. many layers of old wallpaper. With the razor edges, it is important to apply pressure evenly, otherwise the plaster underneath can be damaged.
Putty knife (Fig 5.13)	Also known as a stopping knife or glazing knife, one side of the blade is straight and the other side is curved. It is used to push putty or stopper into small holes or cracks, as well as for scraping excess putty from windows.
Chisel knife (Fig 5.14)	Similar to a scraper, but with a narrower blade, a chisel knife can be used for various surface preparation tasks such as wall scraping in hard-to-reach areas, and small filling jobs.
Knotting brush (Fig 5.15)	A knotting brush would usually be included on the lid of the knotting solution you buy. It is a short, round, brush about 1 inch wide and is used to apply the shellac or patent knotting solution.
Nail punch (Fig 5.16)	The nail punch is a metal rod used for pushing nails into a timber surface before stopping and painting so they do not stick out. The punch is usually hit with a hammer to drive the nails in.
Hot air gun (Fig 5.17)	Also known as hot air strippers, these are used for stripping off paint. They are safer to use than traditional blowtorches because they use hot air instead of a naked flame, and they are less likely to burn woodwork or crack glass. There are models that have temperature settings for extra control.
Steam stripper (Fig 5.18)	Usually powered by electricity, a steam stripper is a small water tank that heats the water like a kettle and sends steam through a hose to a plate with holes in it. The plate is then laid flat on the wallpaper and the steam seeps into the covering, which softens the paper and the glue, making it easier to scrape off.
Hammer	Hammers are used for a variety of preparation tasks, e.g. removing wire clips, picture hooks and nails sticking out of woodwork. Hammers are also used for driving in nails, either on their own or with the help of a nail punch. A scaling or chipping hammer is used for removing rust and millscale when preparing a metal surface for painting. These would tend to be used on industrial sites.
Dusting brush (Fig 5.19)	A dusting brush is used for removing dust, debris, grit or any loose and flaky material before any paint is applied. This will make sure that your finish is smooth and that no bits of debris find their way back into your paint kettle. Some painters will use a vacuum cleaner with a duster brush attachment instead.
Roller trays (Fig 5.20)	Roller trays are used for holding paint and other coatings for use with paint rollers. There is a well that holds most of the paint at the bottom and a raised, textured tray for loading the roller. They come in different sizes to suit different types of roller, and are usually made of plastic, but sometimes metal.

Tools and equipment	Use
Brushes	There are many different brush sizes and types. The filling, or bristle part, can be made of pure bristle (from the hair of wild pigs), man-made fibres (e.g. nylon), natural fibres (e.g. dried grass or plants) or mixtures of these. Synthetic bristles are best used with water-based paints and natural hair bristles are better for oil-based paints. There are some brush types that are multi-purpose. The width of brush you choose will depend on what you're painting. Wider brushes will allow you to apply paint more quickly, but you should choose a brush that is slightly narrower than the surface you're painting, e.g. a 90 mm architrave would be painted with a 75 mm brush. Brushes can also come in different shapes. Most are square-cut and are very versatile, but there are also brushes cut with a slight angle to the bristles, which make it easier to reach into corners. There are even special brushes to reach into very awkward spaces, such as behind radiators.
Paint pots/ kettles (Fig 5.21)	Also known as paint cans, a kettle is made of either metal or plastic and is used for holding the right amount of paint for a job. Paint is poured into the kettle from the bigger tin of paint. The kettle has a handle for holding onto or the handle can be used with a kettle hook so that it can be attached to ladders. They should always be cleaned thoroughly after use so that fresh paint is not contaminated with flakes of different colours.
Wire brush (Fig 5.22)	When preparing a metallic surface, you will need a wire brush to remove old flaking paint, loose rust and corrosion. They can also be used to clear loose bits from brickwork. They are made with bristles of steel or bronze. Bronze bristles will not cause any sparks, so they are the better choice for a high fire risk area. A powered rotary wire brush is a more powerful option for the same job.
Filling knife (Fig 5.23)	Similar in shape to a scraper, but of thinner and more flexible metal, a filling knife is used to apply fillers to cracks and holes. Its flexibility allows for more control when working with the filler.
Filling board (Fig 5.24)	A filling board, similar to an artist's paint palette, is used to hold and mix large amounts of fillers or stoppers. They are usually made of timber board or plastic and can have a pole attached to the base or a thumb hole to hold onto the board.
Buckets	Buckets are a useful piece of equipment for holding water and other mixtures when stripping off wallpaper and cleaning surfaces before painting.
Sponges	A large sponge is useful for applying water and other mixtures to walls when removing wallpaper.
Rubbing blocks (Fig 5.25)	Rubbing blocks come in rubber, cork or wood. They are used to hold sandpaper, making it easier to use. The paper can be simply wrapped around the block and held in place, or the block may have clips or teeth to hold onto the sandpaper.
Rollers (Figs 5.26 and 5.27)	Rollers are used to quickly apply large areas of paint on flat surfaces. A roller comes in two parts: the frame, and the sleeve, which is detachable. There are several types of roller widths and thicknesses, each designed for a different purpose, such as for painting pipes and radiators. Roller sleeves can be made of foam or sponge, lambswool in short, medium or long pile, synthetic fibres, and mohair. Short pile rollers are best for flat surfaces such as plastered walls because they give a smooth and even finish. Medium and long pile rollers are used on more uneven, rough or exterior surfaces. Synthetic sleeves are cheaper than wool and last longer, but should not be used for solvent-based paints. Lambswool sleeves are good for solvent based paints and various textures. Mohair sleeves are used for gloss or eggshell paints, and foam or sponge can be used for gloss.

Table 5.3 Tools and equipment for preparing surfaces and correcting defects

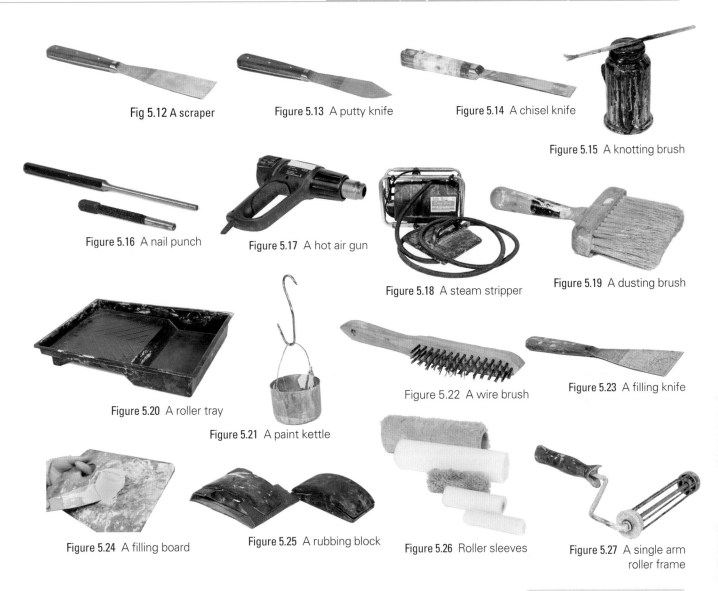

Fig 5.12 A scraper

Figure 5.13 A putty knife

Figure 5.14 A chisel knife

Figure 5.15 A knotting brush

Figure 5.16 A nail punch

Figure 5.17 A hot air gun

Figure 5.18 A steam stripper

Figure 5.19 A dusting brush

Figure 5.20 A roller tray

Figure 5.21 A paint kettle

Figure 5.22 A wire brush

Figure 5.23 A filling knife

Figure 5.24 A filling board

Figure 5.25 A rubbing block

Figure 5.26 Roller sleeves

Figure 5.27 A single arm roller frame

Protecting the work and surrounding area

Before surface preparation work is started, any furniture and belongings should be moved away from the surface, e.g. into the centre of a room, and covered with dust sheets. Fixtures, fittings and soft furnishings, such as curtains, will also need to be removed. The floor should also be carefully covered from wall to wall to ensure that no water, solvents, primers or paints can leak down into the floor covering or floorboards. Even if the carpets have been taken up, you should use dust sheets to stop old wallpaper sticking to the floor.

When working outdoors, you must still protect the area, e.g. by removing garden furniture, covering plants and laying down a tarpaulin to protect the ground.

Remember to keep your work area clean and tidy, as this will reduce any damage to your surfaces, tools and materials, either from yourself or other people living or working on site. A tidy work area is a safe work area. If you are working outdoors, the need to protect your work is even more important as bad weather may damage your surfaces and the materials you are using, e.g. when you are stripping paint and priming a surface, a wet or damp area may slow down or stop it from drying.

DID YOU KNOW?

The height of roller pile is also known as 'nap'.

PRACTICAL TIP

If you're going to be working with paint, including primers, then make sure to use a 'Wet paint' sign so that others don't touch drying paint. Otherwise you could end up having to prepare and paint the same area again, and the person who touched it won't thank you either!

PRACTICAL TIP

Don't forget that you'll need gloves, eye protection and a dust mask when disposing of toxic substances.

Waste should be disposed of appropriately, especially toxic substances such as solvents. Leaving excessive waste to pile up, such as wet wallpaper that has been scraped off, can result in damage to floor surfaces, even if dust sheets are down.

Defective areas

The defects that you are most likely to come across when preparing surfaces are listed below.

Defect	Description
Knots	Knots can be both a defect and a feature of wood. They appear where the branches were joined. Knots can give out resin that will seep through and stain the finish.
Splits	Wood may naturally contain splits in the grain, or they may occur from drying and shrinking. They can affect the strength and appearance of the wood.
Open joints	Gaps that have appeared in timber that has been previously joined together.
Resin exudation	Where residue has seeped out of a knot.
End grain	Where timber has been cut at a 90° angle to the grain – you will be able to see the rings. End grain absorbs moisture and so it should be sealed with a primer.
Corrosion	The gradual decay of metal caused by a chemical reaction with its environment, e.g. air and water. An example of corrosion would be rust on ferrous metals.
Settlement cracks	These occur as a result of gradual building movement, e.g. as a result of the soil compacting beneath the foundations. It is often noticed on ceilings and walls, around door frames and window lintels, either on the outside or inside. Most houses will have some movement in their first few years and small cracks are not usually a cause for concern.
Shrinkage cracks	These tend to affect concrete floors and walls, and often start near the corner of windows. They are a result of the ageing and drying process and can be easily spotted because they are not continuous cracks. Depending on the seriousness of the crack, they may need extra sealant so the wall stays waterproof.
Nail holes	Nail holes are commonly seen in plaster where people have hung pictures. Because they are small, they are easily repaired.
Projecting nail heads	These can be seen sticking out of plasterboard and timber where the nail is attaching the substrate to a surface. They should be punched in and filled so the surface is flat.
Indentations	These are small dips or holes in the surface caused by something bumping into it, e.g. where a door handle touches the wall behind it.
Putties	Putty around windows can decay with age and allow water to seep in. It should be repaired or replaced.
Stale paste	Sometimes wallpaper paste that has been applied in a sloppy way can leave residue on the paper surface.
Pointing	Mortar joints between bricks or blocks can become dried out and crumbly. The surface needs to be sound before primer and paint can be applied.

Table 5.4 Different types of substrate defect

Preparation processes and materials

Each surface will need a different preparation process. Use the table below to check which process you should use for each surface, and then read below to find out more about each process.

Surface type	Preparation processes used
Timber – new soft or hardwood	• Dust off surface (abrading may scratch the surface) • Punch in nails • Fill gaps and sunken nail heads • Apply knotting solution
Timber – painted	• Degrease and rinse • Fill cracks • Dry abrade • Dust down
Metal – ferrous	• Remove rust
Metal – non-ferrous	• Degrease • Abrade
Plaster/plasterboard – fresh	• Scrape to remove nibs • Dust down (do not abrade)
Plaster/plasterboard – painted	• Degrease and rinse • Abrade • Fill cracks and holes • Sand back filler • Dust down
Brickwork, blockwork, masonry and render	• Scape and brush off dirt • Scrub if there is efflorescence • Wash if mould present • Rake out if loose render • Dust down

Table 5.5 Preparation processes for different surface types

Wet and dry abrading

Abrading is the smoothing or rubbing down of a surface to get rid of any flaws. It also provides a key for the new coating to stick to, giving a smoother, better finish.

Abrasive papers are often known as sandpaper. There are different types of abrasive, and it is important to choose the correct one. An abrasive that is too fine will take more time, use more paper, and may not successfully remove all of the flaws. On the other hand, an abrasive that is too rough will not leave a smooth enough surface and scratches may be noticed in the finish. The next table shows different types of abrasives and their uses.

KEY TERMS

Abrading

– the scraping away or wearing down of a surface using friction. Also known as 'sanding' or 'rubbing down'.

Abrasive	Material	Properties	Uses
Glasspaper	Glass particles on a paper or cloth backing	Comes in Strong, Coarse, Medium and Fine grades. Tends to clog up easily, so has a short life. Can also scratch the surface too much.	Dry, hand or mechanical abrading of plaster or wood for a rough finish.
Emery	Natural emery (carborundum) attached to cloth	Used by hand, sold in sheets or narrow rolls. Used less often now due to increased use of power tools. It is also expensive.	Dry, or with a spirit lubricant for abrading metals by hand. If non-ferrous metal, just use a mordant solution to take shininess away.
Aluminium oxide	Bauxite mineral stuck to paper backing	Comes in discs, belts or sheets. Long lasting because it doesn't clog up or wear down quickly. Comes in grades of 40 to 240.	Dry, hand or mechanical abrading of wood.
Silicon carbide	Mixture of silica, coke and sand, stuck to a waterproof paper or cloth	The crystals are very sharp and long lasting, so long as they are rinsed and unclogged regularly. Comes in grades of 120 to 600. There is a self-lubricating type that does not clog.	Wet or dry, for abrading all surfaces to a very smooth finish (though not for plaster or for bare surfaces); used with mineral oil for polishing metals.

Table 5.6 Types of abrasives and their uses

Figure 5.28 Sanding with the grain

Abrasive papers come in sheets, belts, discs or rolls, depending on whether it will be used by hand or on a power tool. When choosing the right grading – how fine or coarse the paper is – the lower the number, the more coarse the paper; the higher the number, the finer the paper.

When sanding a rough surface where the flaws or debris are sticking out, use a coarse paper. When sanding down between coatings, use a medium abrasive paper. When finishing work, use a fine paper to get a smooth finish.

To reduce wastage, use only the amount of paper that you need to fit on your rubbing block, either by cutting it or folding it.

When dry abrading by hand:

* use a dry abrasive paper

* do not add any water or lubricant

* sand in the direction of the grain of the timber

* use the right grade of paper

* change paper if it becomes clogged or is not working.

When wet abrading by hand:

* wet both the surface and the abrasive

* first, sand in a circular motion (see Fig 5.29a)

* rinse out the paper to avoid the grain clogging up

* finally, sand in the longest direction of the surface (see Fig 5.29b).

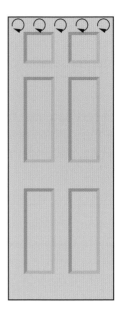

Figure 5.29a Wet sanding direction 1   Figure 5.29b Wet sanding direction 2

KEY TERMS

Knots

– a dark, resinous circle in timber where branches were joined to the tree.

Resin

– a thick, sticky substance that comes from trees and timber.

Degreasing

Painted plaster, painted wood, glazed tiles and non-ferrous metals will need to be free from any grease or oil before they can be painted. Leaving grease on the surface will reduce the adhesion of the first coat. It is best to use sugar soap or detergent and warm water to wash down the surface. For more stubborn grease, you may need to use a solvent (see Cleaning agents on page 143), e.g. on new metal.

Knotting

Bare timber often has **knots**, which occur where the branches were joined to the tree. They appear as darker areas, circular in the middle, and contain **resin** that can bleed from the knots over time. To stop the resin from coming out of the knots and staining the finished surface, a thin coat of knotting solution should be applied. If a knot is large and too resinous, it can be drilled out and plugged with another piece of wood or wood filler. Remember that knotting solution is highly flammable.

Priming

Priming is the painting of the very first coat onto a bare surface. The surface must be properly prepared before the primer is applied, otherwise it will not stick properly. There are primers designed for different types of surface, such as for wood, which will give a better result. However, a universal primer is suitable for most jobs. Some primers can also double as the undercoat, i.e. you can apply it once as the primer, and then apply it again as the undercoat. Primers should be applied by brush, or with a roller for large flat surfaces such as fresh plaster.

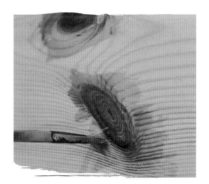

Figure 5.30 Applying knotting solution

Figure 5.31 A rotary wire brush

KEY TERMS

Scoring

– cutting or scratching through a surface, leaving small holes.

PRACTICAL TIP

When wetting in, adding a bit of detergent to the warm water will help speed up the softening of the wallpaper.
You may also find it more effective to use a wide 15-cm (6-inch) wall brush as it holds the water better, and with the use of a soap solution, such as sugar soap, it will penetrate deeper.

Stopping

Stoppers are similar to fillers, but are made from a stiffer material such as plaster or cement. They are best used for filling deep holes and gaps. Fillers are made of a smoother paste and are better for smaller jobs.

Filling

When a surface is not in good condition, e.g. if it has patches, holes or cracks, then a filler may need to be used before the surface is abraded and primed. There are different ways of filling a gap, depending on its nature and size.

Rust removal

On metal surfaces, you may notice rust or corrosion. This will need to be removed before any paint can be applied. Where there is only light rusting, it can be removed with an abrasive paper or cloth, it can be scraped away by hand using a chisel knife or 1-inch scraper, it can be scrubbed away using a wire brush, or a solvent may be used.

For more serious corrosion, a mechanical rotary wire brush will be needed. Note that anyone under the age of 18 will need to be trained before using any mechanical tools.

Raking out

Raking out is a way of preparing old render that is cracked, loose or rotting. The brick joints are raked out to ensure the same depth of all the joints before filler or new render is applied. This will also remove any loose debris. You will need a hammer and pointing chisel to rake out the joints. Once the raking out is complete, it will need to be cleaned out with water.

Wetting in

When removing old wallpaper coverings, after the paper has been scored, water must be applied to the wall using a bucket and sponge. It will seep through the holes created by the scoring, and soaks into the paper and backing, softening it and making it easier to scrape off. If working with plasterboard under the wallpaper, take care not to add too much water as it will damage the board.

Wetting in is also used before applying fillers and stoppers.

Removal of paint systems

If the existing paint is sound, then preparation need only be degreasing and spot-priming where necessary.

Where paint surfaces are peeling, flaking, blistering or cracking, then the existing paint will need to be stripped back to the bare surface. Paint can be removed either with chemicals (paint stripper) or with heat.

Paint stripper softens the old paint ready for it to be scraped off with a stripping knife. Be aware that solvent-based paint strippers are highly flammable and toxic. Use away from any sparks or naked flames, wear gloves and make sure there is good ventilation.

Paint can also be burned off using a hot air gun. The extreme heat softens the paint so it can be scraped off with a stripping knife. When working with a large, flat surface, using heat is faster and cheaper. On more delicate surfaces such as carved woodwork, glass, and flammable surfaces, it is better to use paint stripper. **Important:** if you are removing lead-based paint, you must not use heat.

Removal of wall coverings

To remove wallpaper:

1. Score the paper using a scorer or nail block to make small holes in the top coating.

2. Soak the paper with warm water to soften the paper and glue (you may need to do this more than once).

3. Allow the water to soak into the paper. You can tell when it is ready to be peeled when it is mostly dark.

4. Remove the paper using a scraper, applying even pressure so as not to damage the plaster underneath.

If the wallpaper has been painted over, you may find it difficult to remove. In this case, use a long-handled stripper with a blade to cut through the paper.

You may also need to use a steam stripper for difficult surfaces, such as those with many layers of wallpaper. Steam strippers boil water and send the steam through a hose to a plate that is placed flat on the wall. Once the plate has been applied, the paper is soft enough to be removed from that section. Be careful not to hold the plate on the wall for too long as it can damage the plaster behind. Also remember that steam is very hot – take extra care when using a steam stripper on ceilings: do not hold the plate directly above your head, and always tip the plate *away* from your body.

Primers and coating systems

Different surfaces may need different primers and coating systems, depending on the surface you are covering.

Primers can be solvent-based or water-based.

Solvent-borne primers

Primer	Description and use
Aluminium	Used especially for resinous timbers due to its good opacity and self-knotting. It is particularly good for surfaces that are likely to bleed, such as coal-tar and old bitumen-coated surfaces. Cleaned and thinned with white spirit. Darker colour means an extra undercoat may be needed for light coloured finishes. Drying time 4-6 hours; overcoat in 24 hours.
White	A wood primer for soft and hardwoods. Can be used on interior or exterior wood.
Pink	Pink primer used to be used more commonly as a timber primer because of the red lead content in old paints. Pink primer is traditionally used for soft wood (aluminium leaf primer is used for hardwoods). It doesn't affect the finished coat.

KEY TERMS

Spot-priming

– where small patches of a surface are down to the bare substrate and need to be treated with a primer.

PRACTICAL TIP

If removing vinyl wallpaper, you won't need to score it. Instead you can strip it by removing the top layer.

KEY TERMS

Opacity

– the more opaque a paint is, the harder it is to see through. Opacity is the opposite of translucency.

Primer	Description and use
Alkali resisting (ARP)	Designed for alkaline surfaces containing lime or cement (e.g. render, plaster, concrete). Thinned and cleaned using white spirit. On very porous surfaces, two coats may be needed. Drying time is 8–12 hours, but overcoating must wait 16–24 hours.
Zinc phosphate	Used for both ferrous and non-ferrous metals. It contains a rust inhibitor. Thin and clean with white spirit. Overcoat in 6–16 hours, depending on conditions.
Etch	Used for preparing non-ferrous metals to create a key for better adhesion, especially shiny metals such as zinc, aluminium etc. Thinned with butanol. Cleaned as per manufacturer's instructions. Can be used as an alternative to mordant solution. Must be applied in dry conditions. Drying time 1–4 hours; overcoat within 12–16 hours. Once mixed, must be used straight away.

Table 5.7 Solvent-borne primers

Water-borne primers

Primer	Description and use
Metal	Used for non-ferrous metal. Cleaned and thinned with water. Overcoat in 4–6 hours.
Size	A sticky glaze used to seal in porous surfaces. Traditional size is made of crushed animal bones and is usually used when paperhanging. It can also be a weak solution of wallpaper paste.
Acrylic	Can be used as primer and undercoat. Usually in white. Quick-drying, can overcoat in 2 hours, easy and cheap to thin and clean, non-toxic. Used on timber, board, paper and dry plaster. Not used on metal.
Emulsion	Can be used as a primer when watered down, mainly for use on fresh plaster where emulsion will be used as the topcoat.

Table 5.8 Water-borne primers

Coating systems

A coating system means the type of coating, the way it is applied, and the number of coatings that will be needed for a certain job. For example, when covering a fresh timber door, you would apply knotting solution, then a primer, then undercoat, then finally a gloss or eggshell finish. This would be a coating system.

KEY TERMS

VOCs (volatile organic compounds)

– a material found in many paints and coatings that helps them to dry more quickly. They evaporate into the atmosphere and are bad for the environment.

Coating system	Description and use
Solvent-borne	Also known as oil-based paints and coatings. Highly flammable. Have a high level of VOCs (volatile organic compounds).
Water-borne	Thinned and cleaned by adding water. Low fire risk. Have a low VOC content.
Preservative	Usually water-based. Help to make timber last longer by protecting it from attack by insects and mould. Can be applied by brushing, spraying, soaking and dipping.
Paper	Before painting or covering, papers can be used to line surfaces that are uneven or damaged. This can be cheaper and easier than preparing the surface as usual.

Table 5.8 Coating systems

DID YOU KNOW?

There are many new coating technologies being developed by paint manufacturers. This is in response to tighter environmental regulations and a need for products that give a better finish. For example, there is a lot of research and development in the area of low VOC paints, particularly for gloss finishes. Another new product you may come across is 'new work undercoat' and 'new work gloss' which are highly pigmented for better coverage on rough, textured or porous surfaces.

Health and safety and environmental regulations

Preparing surfaces involves particular risks to health and safety, as well as to the environment. For example, abrading materials will create a lot of dust, which can be a hazard to your eyes and respiratory health. Working with solvents brings the risk of dermatitis if your skin is not protected. These hazards, as well as cuts and abrasions, working with electricity, and working at height were all covered earlier in the chapter. There are, however, some extra risks that you must be aware of.

Asbestos

Asbestos was commonly used as insulation against heat, fire and noise. It is still found in many old buildings, but it is a very dangerous substance. Inhaling asbestos fibre can lead to serious and even deadly respiratory conditions, such as mesothelioma or lung cancer. If asbestos is discovered on site, then you must stop work immediately and inform your employer. It may only be removed by a licensed specialist. As a painter and decorator, you are most likely to find asbestos in the following materials:

* cement-based wall cladding, downpipes and gutters in warehouse type buildings

* textured coatings on ceilings and walls, such as Artex

* sprayed insulation coatings on the underside of roofs, floors, and the sides of buildings and warehouses

* insulation board on partition walls, ceiling tiles, fireproofing panels in fire doors.

Each of these carry different risk levels and need different action, e.g. from notifying the relevant authority to not attempting work on the surface at all.

Lead

Lead was also used in many products before the health risks of ingesting or inhaling it were fully understood. It was often used in making paint because it gave a bright white colour to gloss paint, helped it to harden and dry, and was flexible and 'breathable'.

PRACTICAL TIP

If you come across gutters or downpipes that you believe are made from asbestos cement you should stop work immediately, report it to your supervisor and get the necessary advice on how to deal with it.

DID YOU KNOW?

You can visit the HSE website for more detailed information on asbestos health and safety: *www.hse.gov.uk/asbestos/index.htm*

Homes built and decorated in the Victorian and post-war eras have the highest levels of lead paint. Flaking lead paint is especially risky for pregnant women and for young children whose brains and organs are still developing. It is for this reason that lead paints are no longer used for coating children's furniture and toys. Lead paint is now only allowed to be used on grade I and II listed buildings. Breathing in dust from old paintwork while abrading, or breathing in the fumes when burning old paint off, can result in lead poisoning. For this reason, when working on older buildings, it is especially important to wear a dust mask and to wash your hands before eating or drinking.

DID YOU KNOW?

You can find further guidance on the control of lead at work regulations in the approved HSE code of practice here: *www.coatings.org.uk/Coatings_Industry_Highlights/updated-lead-paint-guidelines.aspx*

Also, the British Coatings Federation publishes up-to-date guidance on working with lead paint. Go to: *www.coatings.org.uk/Coatings_Industry_Highlights/updated-lead-paint-guidelines.aspx*

CORRECTING DEFECTS IN COMMON SURFACES AND COATINGS

Figure 5.32 Efflorescence

When preparing surfaces for decoration, you must be aware of common flaws and defects in the surfaces and coatings. You will also need to know how to recognise them and how to fix them. Defects may be as a result of:

* exposure to the weather

* the surface not being prepared well previously

* incorrect application of coatings

* use of incorrect, worn or defective tools.

Common defects and the process to correct them

Efflorescence

Surfaces that contain lime or cement are known as 'chemically active'. The water-soluble salts come to the surface as it dries and ages, leaving white deposits known as efflorescence. These patches of white can appear on bricks, render and plaster. Often it will go away without any treatment, but if the surface needs to be coated, the efflorescence must be removed by dry brushing or scrubbing with a wire brush. It should not be washed because the salts will disappear in the water and only be reabsorbed into the surface.

Cissing

Cissing is where paint is not continuously joined on a surface. The paint rolls back towards itself and forms beads. Cissing occurs on smooth and shiny surfaces, so to avoid this patchy effect, surfaces must be free of grease, oil, polish or wax. They should be abraded to create a rougher texture. Before coating again, the surface must be degreased and completely dry.

Flaking or peeling

Flaking or peeling is seen when paint splits and lifts away from the surface as a result of poor adhesion. There are various possible causes:

* applying paint to damp surfaces

* applying paint to a smooth and shiny surface

* applying paint to powdery, crumbly surfaces

* thinning the paint too much

* painting when the weather is too humid, e.g. on a very cold day

* painting when the weather is too hot so the paint dries very quickly

* when surfaces expand or shrink

* where corrosion or efflorescence forms underneath the paint.

Proper preparation will avoid flaking, in particular, ensuring the surface is dry and properly sealed, using the correct primer, washing down, abrading and dusting of surfaces. If flaking has already occurred, then it can be fixed by:

1. scraping back the coating with a scraper or wire brush

2. abrading the problem areas

3. applying primer to the problem areas

4. repainting in the correct conditions.

Figure 5.33 Bittiness

Bittiness

Bittiness is the appearance of dust or grit on or below the surface of the paint. This can happen before painting, where a surface has not been cleaned and dusted off properly, or during painting where debris has attached itself to the wet surface. It can be avoided by proper preparation, i.e. ensuring the surface is clean before painting, and also by good housekeeping. Clear the area of dust and debris before you start painting.

Where bittiness has already happened, it can be fixed by lightly abrading the surface and thoroughly dusting it down before repainting.

Runs, sags and curtains

When working with too much paint on your brush or roller, the force of gravity can take over and leave you with drips of paint running down the surface. The term 'curtains' refers to a line of drips, which give the

Figure 5.34 Paint runs

ragged effect of a curtain edge. They are easily avoided by applying paint carefully and spreading it evenly across the surface. Where runs have already occurred, wash and dry the problem area, abrade it to a smooth surface, then repaint.

Mould

Mould is a type of fungus that is caused by spores in the atmosphere which grow and feed on organic matter found in various surface finishes. They often grow in damp, poorly ventilated areas, especially in old buildings. Patches of mould tend to appear in corners and behind furniture or curtains where the airflow is poor. Mould must be properly removed before paint can be applied. To fix a mouldy surface:

1. Sterilise and wash the area down with a fungicidal solution.

2. Scrape the mould off with a scraper or wire brush.

3. Allow it to dry properly.

4. Preferably wait a week to see if the mould breaks out again and needs retreating.

5. Recoat with a paint that contains a fungicide.

Figure 5.35 Patches of mould

There are a range of paints specifically designed for kitchen and bathroom use, where excessive steam and moisture occur, that reduce the chance of mould breaking out.

Materials, tools and equipment

The table below describes some extra pieces of kit that you may need to successfully remove defects from surfaces. The tools and equipment listed in Table 5.3 and the primers covered earlier will also be needed.

Materials, tools and equipment	Description and use
Sterilising fluid, fungicidal wash	Used for getting rid of mould and other growths from a surface before repainting. Often used together with a fungicidal paint to avoid mould growing back. Fungicide is poisonous – don't forget your PPE.
Stain block (proprietary and non-proprietary)	Used to both fix and avoid surface stains such as grease marks, dyes, nicotine and damp.
Barrier cream	Barrier creams can be applied before using solvents, such as methylated spirits, to protect the skin. This can be useful when using solvents for washing down, and can prevent drying out of skin by avoiding contact with the solvent.
Stiff/scrubbing brush	A stiff bristled brush used for removing rust and paint, or to remove moss or mould from rendered exterior walls.

Materials, tools and equipment	Description and use
Moisture meter (Fig 5.36)	Used to find out how much water is in the surface you are preparing, e.g. in wood or plaster, before it can be painted. The meter will give a reading either as a percentage of moisture content or on a scale of 0 to 100, with zero being dry and 100 being saturated.
Orbital sander (Fig 5.37)	An electrical tool for sanding which has abrasive paper attached to a pad. The pad moves in a circular (orbital) motion. Used for preparing and smoothing timber, metal and surfaces that have been painted before. Slower but easier to use than a belt sander (which you'd use for large areas such as floorboards). Best used on small surfaces. They produce a very fine finish.
Palm sander (Fig 5.38)	A light, handheld sander, powered by electricity. Used for dry abrading before or between coatings. Particularly helpful for fiddly surfaces such as skirting boards.
Lint-free cloths	Used for removing traces of dust before painting, and for polishing or waxing wood. They are lint-free so as not to leave any fibres behind which may show up in the finish.
Wall brush	A wide brush used for painting emulsion onto large areas and for applying water to a wall surface when removing wallpaper.

Table 5.10 Materials, tools and equipment for rectifying defects

Figure 5.36 A moisture meter

Figure 5.37 An orbital sander

Figure 5.38 A palm sander

Cleaning agents and methods to remove contamination

Solvent-based cleaners

It is very important to note that where possible you should avoid using pure solvents for tasks such as cleaning. Instead, there are a number of specially designed products that still contain the necessary solvents, but are less risky to use.

Methylated spirits are used for general cleaning of dirt. It is particularly good for removing grease and adhesives. Highly flammable, methylated spirits should not be used around naked flames or sparks and there should be no smoking nearby. It is also harmful if inhaled or if it comes into contact with the skin.

White spirit is also used for cleaning and thinning; it can be helpful in cleaning up silicone, degreasing, and cleaning paintbrushes after use with solvent-based paints. Note that it cannot be used to clean knotting solution from brushes. Both white spirit and methylated spirits are useful in preventing rust and corrosion. The advantage of using them is that they dry very quickly so that a surface can be painted straight after use.

DID YOU KNOW?

Methylated spirits is made out of alcohol, but has other ingredients added so that it cannot be drunk. It is often dyed blue or purple as a warning against consumption.

Acetone is a solvent and cleaner that can be used for removing marks from felt tip pens, crayon and permanent markers. It can be used on metal and glass and is very good at removing grease. Note that it should not be used on plastic. Acetone is highly flammable, can cause eye irritation, skin irritation or dermatitis, and breathing it in can cause headaches, dizziness, and nausea, so it should be used in a well-ventilated area.

Detergents

Instead of solvent-based cleaners, detergents can be used along with warm water to remove dirt. It must be rinsed off so there is no residue, then left to dry properly before paint can be applied.

A stronger option is to use sugar soap. It is particularly helpful in washing down paintwork before repainting, and is very good at removing nicotine stains. It can also be used to help with stripping wallpaper or removing grease. Sugar soap comes in the form of a liquid or in powder form. It can cause some skin irritation, so it's best to wear gloves when using. In powder form, be careful not to inhale it.

Health and safety risks

As we have seen, preparing surfaces involves the use of some very toxic materials, such as solvents, and exposure to various kinds of dust, fumes and other irritants. It is essential for your health and the health of those around you to:

* wear gloves

* cover your skin

* wear a dust mask

* wear safety glasses or goggles

* make sure there is good ventilation

* not smoke anywhere near flammable substances

* deal carefully with hazardous substances, especially where asbestos or lead may be present.

REPAIRING AND MAKING GOOD COMMON SURFACES

Defective areas

Timber, plaster, metal and brickwork can all suffer from the defects already listed in Table 5.4 on page 132. In order to make good these defects, you will need to be aware of the tools, equipment, processes and materials detailed below.

Tools and equipment

As well as the tools and equipment already covered, you will find the following useful for making good surfaces.

Craft knife (Fig 5.39)	Has a razor sharp, retractable, foldable or fixed blade. Useful for scoring and cutting, and scraping small bits of old paint. Often a scraper will be sufficient.
Pointing trowel (Fig 5.40)	A trowel is a bricklayer's tool used for repairing large cracks and holes in exterior walls. It spreads, levels and shapes the stopper, e.g. plaster, mortar or cement.
Wetting in brush	Used when making good render or plaster, before applying the filler, to make sure the crack doesn't dry out too quickly. A standard paintbrush will be fine for this purpose.
Hawk (Fig 5.41)	A hawk is used with a trowel to hold the filling material when repairing larger cracks in walls. It is held in the left hand (if you're right-handed), while the other hand holds the trowel.
Pole sander (Fig 5.42)	An abrasive pad is attached to the end of a pole to help with sanding in hard-to-reach, high places. Also known as a sanding pole.

Table 5.11 Tools and equipment for making good surfaces

Figure 5.40 A pointing trowel

Processes and materials

Sinking nail heads

Old surfaces will often have nails and hooks attached to them. If these are sticking out, they should either be removed (if they are not serving a purpose) or sunk in. To sink a nail head, use a nail punch and a hammer. Make sure the nail punch is covering the whole nail head, then hammer the nail in until it is **flush** with the surface. You will then need to fill the hole, sand it, prime, and finally paint. The filler and primer will help to seal the surface and stop any staining or corrosion from the nail. If the surface is a new or uncoated interior timber, then it is best to use a water-based primer that is quick-drying.

Figure 5.41 A hawk

Scraping

Scrapers can be used for a variety of tasks, such as removing nibs from a fresh plaster surface, pulling out staples, and removing wallpaper and flaking paint. There are different types of scraper available – some are sharper than others.

When working with a fresh plaster surface, be careful not to damage the flat finish. When removing wallpaper, take care to scrape evenly, otherwise you may damage the plaster underneath, which would then need further repairs.

Figure 5.42 A pole sander

KEY TERMS

Flush

– when something is completely level or even with another surface, i.e. not sticking out.

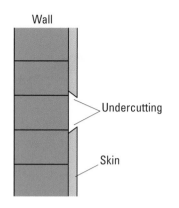

Figure 5.43 Undercutting

Raking out

Where there is loose or crumbling debris left in and around a crack or hole, it should be raked out so that you are left with a solid surface to fill and a good key for the filler to attach to. You can use a filling knife for this.

Undercutting

Where the surface is damaged and needs filling, after brushing down and raking out the crack or hole, dig into the underside of the surface that is already there. This is so there is something for the filler to hold onto. Use a knife and cut the inside surface back at an angle, leaving a wedge shape. See Fig 5.43.

Wetting in

After you have raked out and undercut a surface that is to be filled, take a wet paintbrush and use it to apply water to the crack or hole to be repaired. Lightly brush – there is no need to soak it through. This is done to stop the filler from drying out too quickly, which can lead to shrinking and, worse, falling out of the surface completely.

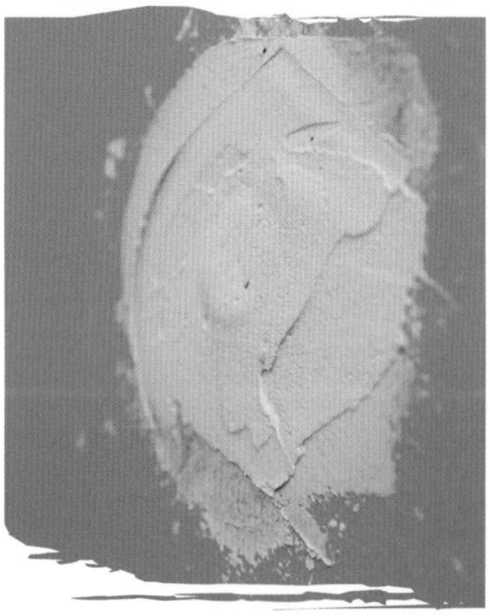

Back filling

Back filling is used on deep holes or gaps. The filler is pushed into the back of the hole and allowed to dry, and then more filler is applied in layers until the gap is flush or proud.

Proud filling

Proud filling is where the filler is pushed into the gap but is left to stand out from the main surface. This is because fillers can shrink as they dry, and you would need to fill the gap again. If, once it is dry, it is still standing proud, then it will need to be sanded back so that it is flush with the surface. See Fig 5.44.

Flush filling

Flush filling is used on small cracks or dents in the surface. The filler is applied and scraped off with a filling knife so that it is flush with the surface.

Knife filling

Knife filling is the application of filler or stopper using a filling knife. This is usually for smaller areas.

Stopping

When filling large or deep cracks and holes, a stopper will be more effective than a filler. Use a hawk to hold your mixture and a trowel to apply it. Make sure you wet in before applying the stopper.

Plaster-based stoppers, or plaster itself, would be used on internal surfaces only. When mixing these stoppers, you should only use clean water.

Cement or vinyl-based stopper is used for exterior surfaces because it is waterproof and harder wearing. You will need to prime with a sealant or stabilising solution because it is a very porous surface.

Figure 5.44 Proud filling

Products	Uses/properties									Special comments
	Interior	Exterior	Solvent-based	Water-based	Timber	Plaster	Ferrous metal	Non-ferrous metal	Brick/block-work	
Solvent-based wood fillers	x	x	x		x					
Water-based wood fillers	x	x		x	x					Easy to clean up
Linseed oil putty	x	x	x		x			x		Mainly used as glazing putty. Dries out quickly
Water-based putty	x			x	x	x			x	
Expanding foam	x	x	x				x	x	x	Good for awkward gaps, e.g. pipe entries. Also for insulating and stopping draughts
Decorator's caulk	x	x		x	x	x	x	x	x	
Silicone	x	x	x			x	x	x		A good adhesive for non-porous materials
Lightweight filler	x	x		x	x	x			x	
PVA primer/sealer	x	x		x	x	x			x	
Gypsum plaster	x			x		x	x	x	x	
Cement plaster	x	x		x		x	x	x	x	
Cement mortar	x	x		x					x	
All-purpose filler, e.g. Polyfilla	x			x		x	x	x	x	Needs to be mixed, therefore harder to use
Ready mixed filler	x			x		x	x	x	x	Easy to use

Table 5.12 Fillers and stoppers, their characteristics and uses

When using a stopper for timber, you may need to use a tinted product to match the colour of the wood as closely as possible if the wood is to be varnished.

Table 5.12 is a quick guide to the types of products that can be used on various substrates when filling or stopping. There is almost always a product for the specific job you are completing. Products exist to suit:

* interior or exterior surfaces

* wood, metals, plasters, masonry

* different budgets

* different drying times

* the size of the gaps you need to fill

* the amount of filling you need to do

* environmental considerations, e.g. solvent vs water-based.

You may find after working with various products that some are easier to work with than others, and that you may simply find a personal preference. Also bear in mind that your tutor or employer may also have their own preferences that you should follow.

Spot prime and seal

When working with a largely sound surface, you may only need to prime parts of it, e.g. a previously painted wall that has some flaky patches. In this case, you would remove the defect, by scraping or sanding it back, and then apply a primer only to the affected area. Spot priming helps to seal the surface so that contaminants won't get through or reappear on the surface, such as rust on metal surfaces.

Wet and dry abrading

After you have filled or stopped a gap, you will need to abrade the surface so that it blends in with the rest of the surface before painting. Wet and dry paper is longer lasting, and wet abrading is best when you want to achieve a very smooth finish on plaster. Abrading can be done by hand, but is faster when using a palm sander or orbital sander.

Applying caulk and sealants

Caulk is a flexible, acrylic filler. It tends not to shrink and is quick drying so it is particularly useful for filling gaps and sealing joints in skirting boards, architraves, dado rails and similar. Caulk can be applied using a silicone gun and then moulded into the right shape. It should not be sanded down afterwards. There are both paintable and non-paintable types of caulk. The acrylic type is water-based and paintable.

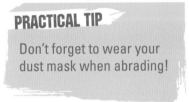

PRACTICAL TIP

Don't forget to wear your dust mask when abrading!

Figure 5.45 Caulk in a silicone gun

Silicone is also a useful sealant, often used in kitchens and bathrooms because it is waterproof, but also around external window frames. Silicone-based caulk is not paintable. It is more flexible and durable than decorator's caulk and holds up well in direct sunlight and temperature extremes.

Applying putty

Putty is used for filling dents and holes in timber, as well as for putting in glass. You may find that you need to touch up glazing putty that has started crumbling.

Before applying glazing putty to wood, the surface must be prepared, otherwise it will not stick to the surface and will fall apart quickly. When preparing the wood, abrade the surface to get rid of old paint and signs of weathering. Apply a primer (oil or water based). If the wood is new, you won't need to scrape the surface back, but will still need to prime.

Putty needs to be worked in the hands to warm it up so that it is soft enough to work with. When the putty is soft enough, use a putty knife to apply it to the wood surface, to fill the gaps, smooth the edges, and clean away any excess putty. Before you can paint the putty, you must wait at least 24 hours.

Primers used for defective areas

Remind yourself of the different types of primer in Tables 5.7 and 5.8. Remember that if you are making good a porous surface, such as render or cement mortar, then you will need a stabilising solution. Metal surfaces will need a specific metal primer, and not a universal primer. If possible, it is always better to use a primer specifically designed for that surface, e.g. when priming over timber defects, you could use a universal primer, but you may need to give it two coats if it is a very porous wood.

DID YOU KNOW?

When a product is labelled acrylic, it means that it is water-based, not solvent-based.

Figure 5.46 Applying putty

Defective areas	Suitable primers
Open joints in joinery, splits, indentations, open grained timber in softwood	Use acrylic primer or white primer
Putties	Solvent-based white primer
Holes, cracks and gaps in plaster and masonry	PVA sealant or stabilising solution
Pointing	Waterproof sealant
Stale paste	Oil-based sealer or alkali resisting primer (ARP) to stop acids from paste burning through
Rust and corrosion	Red lead primer (now only used for speciality purposes) Zinc phosphate

Table 5.13 Defective areas and suitable primers

CASE STUDY

You're always learning on the job

Sandie Webster completed her Level 1, 2 and 3 diplomas and was a gold medallist at SkillBuild. She now runs her own business (www.sandie-webster.co.uk).

'I've always wanted to do something creative. After doing my Design A-level, I worked in a showroom for a while before going on maternity leave. I wanted to learn a trade that would let me work around my kids so I started decorating. I went to college for a couple of days a week when my youngest child started school – I was the oldest on the course but it helped to have some life experience. I enjoyed it and kept at it. I had a really supportive tutor at Gainsborough College, which made a big difference.

It's all about learning on the job. You learn the theory in college but it's like starting all over again, learning about new products. I don't stick to a particular brand – the customer chooses the colours and brands they prefer. Being in business, I've learned how to speak to people. You have to validate what the customer wants instead of what you want. The customer is paying so you need to keep them happy. You learn to adapt to people at different levels.'

PRACTICAL TASK

1. PREPARE A BRICK SURFACE

OBJECTIVE

To prepare an exterior brick surface ready to receive paint.

PPE

Ensure you select PPE appropriate to the job and site conditions where you are working. Refer to the PPE section of Chapter 1.

TOOLS AND EQUIPMENT

Masonry dusting brush

Fungicidal wash

Exterior masonry filler

50 mm stripping knife

Mixing board

50 mm filling knives

STEP 1 Remove any surface contamination, such as plaster or cement splashes, using a 50 mm stripping knife.

PRACTICAL TIP

Remember that not all brick types will receive paint.

STEP 2 Apply a coat of fungicidal wash (following manufacturer's instructions) to remove any fungus/mould. Leave the wash to work as per manufacturer's instructions.

Figure 5.47 Applying fungicidal wash

PRACTICAL TIP

You may not need to use a fungicide on every brick surface you prepare, but it must be used if you can see any sign of mould. Look closely for any green covering on the wall.

STEP 3 Inspect the surface for any holes or cracks that need filling.

Figure 5.48 Holes and cracks in brick surface

Mix some exterior filler by placing the dry filler in the middle of a mixing board. Push a hole into the filler, and then (following the manufacturer's instructions on the back of the box) pour a suitable amount of water into the filler. Mix together using two 50 mm filling knives until it is the consistency of soft ice cream.

Figure 5.49 Mixing exterior filler

STEP 4 Use a filling knife to fill the surface. Apply the filler into the hole or crack using a downward action, pushing the filler in until it is completely filled to the surface. Scrape back to leave the filler flush with the surface. However, if filling a large hole, you may want to leave it standing proud.

Figure 5.50 Applying exterior filler

STEP 5 If the filler has shrunk, repeat step 4. If there are any signs of damp, you won't be able to rub it down as your abrasive paper will clog up.

Once dry, lightly abrade (rub down) the filler to match the level of the surrounding surface.

Figure 5.51 Dry filler on brick wall

Figure 5.52 Abrading the filler

PRACTICAL TASK

2. PREPARE A TIMBER WINDOW FRAME

OBJECTIVE

To prepare a bare timber window frame, sink nails and apply knotting solution, ready to receive paint.

PPE

Ensure you select PPE appropriate to the job and site conditions where you are working. Refer to the PPE section of Chapter 1.

TOOLS AND EQUIPMENT

Knotting pot/bottle (with knotting brush)	Hammer
Nail punch	Fungicidal solution (if needed)
Dusting brush	Sponge
50 mm stripping knife	Bucket

STEP 1 Remove any fungus (showing as a green coating) using a fungicidal wash. Remember to follow the manufacturer's instructions.

An alternative is to use household bleach mixed with clean water to a ratio of 50:50.

In general, brush the solution onto the surface and leave for approximately 48 hours. The solution should kill the fungus spores and get rid of any signs of fungus on the surface.

Figure 5.53 Mixing fungicidal solution

Figure 5.54 Applying fungicide to timber surface

STEP 2 Inspect the frame for any nail heads standing proud of the surface. If there are any such nails, first close the window and secure with the window catch – this will reduce the risk of the glass cracking. Then punch the nails back below the surface using a carpenter's nail punch and hammer. See Fig 5.55.

Figure 5.55 Punching in nails

STEP 3 Inspect the surface to find surface contamination, such as plaster or cement splashes. Remove contamination using a painter's 50mm stripping knife.

STEP 4 Inspect the surface for untreated knots.

Treat with a coating of a recognised knotting solution. Typically this will be brushing one or two coats of the correct type of knotting solution:

- If you will be finishing the timber with an oil-based paint system, use shellac knotting solution.

- If you will be finishing with an acrylic paint system, use white/bleached knotting solution.

Apply a coating that is slightly larger than the size of the knot itself. The timber window frame is now prepared to receive primer and undercoat, then a topcoat. Remember, you will need to abrade between these coats as the bare timber fibres will start to lift.

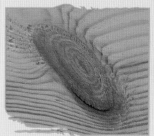

Figure 5.56 A timber knot

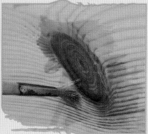

Figure 5.57 Applying knotting solution

3. REMOVE WALLPAPER FROM PLASTERED SURFACE

OBJECTIVE

To remove wallpaper to prepare a plastered wall ready to receive paint.

PPE

Ensure you select PPE appropriate to the job and site conditions where you are working. Refer to the PPE section of Chapter 1.

TOOLS AND EQUIPMENT

10cm (4-inch) wall brush

Bucket

Sponge

50mm or 75mm stripping knife

(scraper)

Working platform

Protective sheets (cotton twill)

Rubbish bags

STEP 1 Lay down protective sheets on the floor in the area you'll be working. Double them over to ensure no water seeps through to the floor covering below.

STEP 3 Fill your bucket with water. Apply water to the wallpaper using your wall brush. If needed apply water again to aid the soaking process. You will see the paper darkening as the water spreads through the scored surface.

Figure 5.59 Wetting in the wallpaper

STEP 2 Using a stripping knife, score (make cuts in) the wallpaper, without marking the wall underneath.

Figure 5.58 Scoring the wallpaper

Figure 5.60 Water soaking into paper

PRACTICAL TIP

You may find it helpful to add some detergent to the water; it can help to soften the glue. Take care not to use too much water if there is plasterboard underneath.

STEP 4 Leave water to soak for long enough to loosen the wallpaper adhesive. Once it is soft enough, hold a stripping knife at a shallow angle and push the wallpaper off the wall. Take care to keep the blade flat against the wall, otherwise you will dig holes in the plaster with the corner of the knife.

Figure 5.61 Stripping the wallpaper

STEP 5 Place all removed wallpaper in a rubbish bag and dispose of responsibly.

STEP 6 Use clean water and a sponge to wash down the wall to remove any of the wallpaper paste still on the surface.

PRACTICAL TIP

Small amounts of wallpaper can be placed in household waste, but large amounts must be taken to the local council tip or recycling centre. Old wallpaper paste is considered a dangerous chemical under COSHH.

PRACTICAL TIP

If stripping vinyl wallpaper you can pull the vinyl paper off the wall, leaving the backing paper on the wall. The backing paper can then be removed by scoring and wetting as described, or if still firmly stuck to the wall, it can be over painted with emulsion or used as lining paper. It is better practice to remove it as you cannot be sure of its adhesion.

PRACTICAL TASK

4. PREPARE FERROUS METAL SURFACES

OBJECTIVE

To prepare a ferrous metal exterior balcony ready to receive paint.

PPE

Ensure you select PPE appropriate to the job and site conditions where you are working. Refer to the PPE section of Chapter 1.

TOOLS AND EQUIPMENT

Chipping hammer	Dust pan and brush
Wire brush (hand tool)	Rubbish bag
Old paintbrush	Dust sheet
Degreaser	

STEP 1 Remove any surface contamination, such as grease or oil. Brush a coat of grease remover onto the surface, following manufacturer's instructions.

The degreaser you choose will depend on how much contamination there is – for light grease, sugar soap will be fine; for heavy duty grease you may need a solvent-based product, such as a universal degreaser.

Figure 5.62 Degreasing the surface

PRACTICAL TIP

Remember to place a dust sheet around work area to catch any falling paint and rust.

STEP 2 Wash the surface with clean water and allow it to dry. If using a water-based product, allow to dry prior to rust removal or abrading.

STEP 3 Use a chipping hammer to remove any loose areas of rust and flaking paint using a chipping motion (this is similar to the way you would use a hammer to hit a nail into timber). Remember to wear eye and hand protection as well as a dust mask.

PRACTICAL TIP

When working in small or awkward areas, you can use a stripping knife to loosen the rust and then abrade with a narrower wire brush.

STEP 4 Use the wire brush to remove any surface rust. Using a wire brush this way will also abrade (rub down) the surface.

Figure 5.63 Removing loose paint and rust with a handlheld wire brush.

STEP 5 Use a dust pan and brush to remove any dust, paint and rust particles from the metal surface. Carefully empty the dust sheet of any dust, paint or rust particles from the metal surfaces and place them in a sturdy rubbish bag and dispose of in a responsible manner (e.g. local council tip).

Re-lay the dust sheet to provide further protection around work area when applying primer, undercoat and topcoat.

PRACTICAL TASK

5. ABRADE USING A POWER TOOL

OBJECTIVE

To use an orbital sander to abrade a flat surface, such as a timber door, ready to receive paint.

TOOLS AND EQUIPMENT

Orbital sander

110V transformer (if orbital sander is 110V)

Supply of graded abrasive paper

PPE

Ensure you select PPE appropriate to the job and site conditions where you are working. Refer to the PPE section of Chapter 1.

STEP 1 Check that the orbital sander is fit for use:

- Check it is the correct type, i.e. size and voltage.

- Check the power supply type, i.e. how many volts.

- Check for any damage evident, e.g. electrical supply cable with cuts through the outer covering.

- Check for any poor repairs to the sander.

Remember, if you feel that the sander is not fit for use, do not use it and report any concerns to your supervisor immediately.

STEP 2 If the sander is rated at 110V, connect to the main supply (240V) via a 110V transformer.

Figure 5.64 110V transformer connected to main supply

STEP 3 Check that the sander has the right kind of abrasive paper attached. For a timber door, this will probably be aluminium oxide.

If you need to replace or change the paper, go to Step 7.

STEP 4 Before you turn the sander on, make sure the cable is well out of the way. Power tools can be dangerous if not used correctly – be aware of the risk of cutting through the electrical cable.

STEP 5 Standing on firm ground with your feet apart, hold the sander using both hands: with one on the handle and the other on the rest, usually found on the top towards the front. If working on a movable surface, such as a door, it is important to make sure it will not move (e.g. you could wedge it).

Figure 5.67 Correct direction to sand a timber panel door

Figure 5.65 Holding sander with cord out of the way

STEP 7 Once the paper is damaged or worn out, you will need to change the paper. Disconnect the sander from the power supply, then unclip the holding clips (holding the paper to the sander) and remove the piece of abrasive paper.

Using the old piece of paper as a template cut a new piece to the right size. Position the new paper into the end slots and re-attach using the holding clips. Reconnect the power supply and continue to abrade the surface.

STEP 6 Pass the orbital sander lightly over the surface, allowing the abrasive paper to make contact with the surface being abraded. It is good practice to sand in one direction only. When abrading timber, follow the grain.

Figure 5.68 Removing the abrasive paper

Figure 5.66 Using an orbital sander

Figure 5.69 Replacing the abrasive paper

PRACTICAL TASK

6. PREPARE A PREVIOUSLY PAINTED SURFACE

OBJECTIVE

To prepare a surface, such as a plastered wall, that has been previously painted, ready to receive a new coat of paint.

PPE

Ensure you select PPE appropriate to the job and site conditions where you are working. Refer to the PPE section of Chapter 1.

TOOLS AND EQUIPMENT

Dusting brush	Sponge	Cutting knife
Pack of tack cloths	Selection of abrasive papers	An old paintbrush
25 mm filling knife	Rubbing block	50 mm stripping knife
50 mm filling knife (two)	Caulking gun	Degreaser such as sugar soap
Mixing board	Decorator's caulk	Bucket

STEP 1 Remove any surface contamination by washing the surface down with a sponge or cloth using a proprietary cleaning material such as sugar soap, following the manufacturer's instructions.

This could typically include mixing the material with hot water in a bucket, leaving it to cool down or adding cold water. Apply to surface, working from the bottom to reduce the risk of marks showing on the wall. Wash off the cleaning material using clean water.

STEP 2 Check surface for holes, cracks, etc. (e.g. from nails or picture hooks). If there are no holes or cracks, you can proceed to Step 5 and abrade the surface.

Figure 5.71 Holes and cracks in a painted surface

Figure 5.70 Washing off surface contamination

STEP 3 If you need to use a filling product to fill any such holes or cracks, the most common type comes in a powder form.

Prepare the filler by placing the required amount of the powder on to a mixing board. Make a slight dent in the filler, pour a small amount of water into the filler and mix by folding the dry powder into the water. Continue folding the mixture until the water and powder form a paste type consistency. Using two knives can help you keep the mixture in a workable position on the board. Be careful not to add too much water as the filler will soon become unusable.

Figure 5.72 Mixing filler on a board

PRACTICAL TIP

You can also get a ready-mixed version of the powder filler, which is used in the same way, but saves you from mixing it.

STEP 4 Place some filler onto your filling knife, choosing a size of knife to suit the size of the gap you are filling. Press the filler into the hole or crack, and leave to dry.

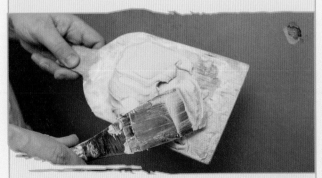

Figure 5.73 Filling a hole 1

Figure 5.74 Filling a hole 2

Figure 5.75 A hole filled level

Figure 5.76 A hole filled proud

Figure 5.77 Abrading the dried filler

PRACTICAL TIP

Your drying time will depend on the surrounding temperature and the depth of the filling material. Remember, some fillers must be filled level with the surfaces, while other types must be left standing proud of the surface to allow for shrinkage and are then abraded flush to the surface. Check which technique suits the filler you are using.

STEP 5 When the surface and any fillers are completely dry, abrade the surface using a relevant grade of abrasive paper and a rubbing block. If the surface is in a very rough condition, you will need paper at a grade of about 60–80; for a surface that needs less abrading, choose a higher grade number. For a larger surface you may wish to use a power tool.

Figure 5.78 Abrading the surface by hand

STEP 6 Use a dusting brush to remove all traces of dust. A tack cloth can also be used to remove dust, by wiping (from the top to the bottom) until the surface is free of dust.

Figure 5.79 Dusting the surface with a tack cloth

STEP 7 If the crack or joint is at a door frame or skirting board and is subject to movement, you should use decorator's caulk – a flexible filler that can be painted over.

First, rake out the crack using an old paintbrush to remove any loose particles. Use a caulking gun to force the flexible filler into the joint, slightly proud of the surface. Wipe the flexible filler using either a cloth or an old paintbrush to leave the filler level with the surface. Do not abrade the caulk; leave it to dry and then coat directly with paint.

Beware that caulk can also shrink and therefore may need to be reapplied once dry.

 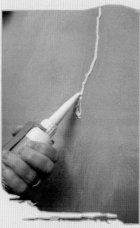

Figure 5.80 Raking out a crack   Figure 5.81 Applying flexible filler with a caulking gun

STEP 8 When the filling is dry you need to 'touch-up' the areas you've filled using a priming paint, such as thinned out emulsion. This is known as 'bringing forward'. Once the primer is dry, the surface is ready to receive its undercoat and topcoat.

Figure 5.82 Priming the filler

TEST YOURSELF

1. Which PPE should you always use when dry abrading?

   a. Overalls

   b. Dust mask

   c. Gloves

   d. All of the above

2. Which task would you use a scraper for?

   a. Removing wallpaper

   b. De-nibbing

   c. Removing flaking paint

   d. All of the above

3. Which of the following is a sheet timber material?

   a. MDF

   b. Pine

   c. Hardwood

   d. Solid wood

4. 'Wetting in' means:

   a. filling up your bucket

   b. adding water to your paint

   c. adding water to scored wallpaper

   d. washing your brushes

5. Which of the following is NOT a type of natural bristle?

   a. Badger

   b. Wild boar

   c. Horse hair

   d. Nylon

6. What is a knot?

   a. A loop in a piece of rope or string

   b. A resinous imperfection in timber

   c. Tangles in hair

   d. A unit of speed

7. If you suspect lead paint has been used, you should usually:

   a. dry abrade to remove the paint

   b. burn it off with a hot air gun

   c. seal it with an overcoat of lead-free paint

   d. replace it with more lead paint

8. To degrease a surface, you should use:

   a. sugar soap

   b. methylated sprits

   c. detergent

   d. any of the above

9. Efflorescence is:

   a. white salty deposits on brickwork

   b. where paint doesn't adhere to a surface

   c. where bits of debris get trapped under paint

   d. drips of paint from overloading the brush

10. Which of the following is NOT a type of filler?

   a. Putty

   b. Expanding foam

   c. Caulk

   d. Shellac

Chapter 6
APPLY BASIC PAINT SYSTEMS BY BRUSH AND ROLLER

LEARNING OUTCOMES

LO1/2: Know how to and be able to prepare the work area and protect the surrounding area

LO3/4: Know how to and be able to prepare materials for application, and apply water-borne and solvent-borne coatings by brush and roller

LO5/6: Know how to and be able to clean, maintain and store brushes and rollers

LO7/8: Know how to and be able to store paint materials

INTRODUCTION

The aim of this chapter is to:

* teach you how to apply water-borne and solvent-borne coatings by brush and roller.

PREPARING AND PROTECTING THE WORK AND SURROUNDING AREA

PPE

See Chapter 1 for more details about PPE. The main items of PPE you will need to protect yourself when applying paint by brush and roller are:

* overalls (to cover your skin)

* safety glasses/goggles (if in contact with solvent-based products)

* gloves (to protect from solvent-based products that may cause dermatitis).

As always, you should check the policy of your own college or workplace and follow the guidelines that they have set on use of PPE.

REED TIP

Look out for your mates. If they've forgotten to put on a piece of PPE, remind them!

Areas and items to be protected

Painters and decorators do not always work in new or empty buildings. Often, paintwork is needed in a domestic setting, such as a home, that is still in use. Or you may work in a business setting that still has items such as furniture and carpeting that need to be protected from damage. Look at the picture of a furnished room in Fig 6.1 and think about what you might need to do about each item. The following list of items will need consideration when protecting the area before preparation and painting:

* doors and windows and their furniture

* fixtures and fittings on walls and ceilings, e.g. lamp shades, smoke alarms, light switches, pictures, shelves

* flooring, e.g. boards, carpets, rugs

* furniture, e.g. tables, sofas, electrical equipment

* outdoor items, e.g. outdoor furniture, pot plants, decking.

Other factors to consider

It is not just furnishing that needs to be thought about when protecting the work and surrounding area.

Lighting

You will often come across light fittings, e.g. wall or ceiling lights. While it is safe for you to remove the lamp shades, the actual fitting should be removed by a qualified electrician. The mains power should stay turned off and the fuse removed, or use a sign warning others not to turn the power back on. Working with electricity is covered in more detail in Chapter 1, page 28.

Climate, weather, temperature

Depending on the environment you are working in, certain precautions may need to be taken to protect your work and your materials. Painting in the wrong conditions can leave you with a cracked, blistered or flaky finish.

Figure 6.1 A fully furnished room

Painting in cold

Painting in cold conditions can slow down the process. First of all, a surface such as plaster might not yet be fully dry. Each coat can take much longer to dry which in turn means you may not be able to overcoat when you are ready. The wall temperature should be above 10°C. Cold conditions can make the paint itself harder to apply.

Painting in direct sun

Painting in hot weather or direct sunlight will make your paint dry too quickly. This can leave you with uneven patches, or cracking and peeling, which you would need to re-prepare and repaint. Even if it is not a particularly warm day, the direct sun can heat a surface much higher than the air temperature. You may need to plan your work around the path of sun throughout the day, i.e. following the shade by painting the western side of the house in the morning and the eastern side in the afternoon.

Painting in wet and humid conditions

Painting outside in the rain or snow is a definite no-no as the work will be quickly ruined. However, in other humid conditions, even inside, such as bathrooms and kitchens, your paint may still be delayed from drying properly.

Painting outdoors

Outdoor work always has the added complication of being exposed to the weather. It's not always possible to avoid painting in poor weather conditions. To be able to continue work in bad weather conditions, such as wind, rain, hail and snow, you will need to protect the area. This can be done by putting up a large, tent-like structure, using a frame and some plastic sheeting. This would have the added benefit of stopping others from coming into contact with the work.

Figure 6.2 A wet paint sign

Other trades

Often your painting work will be part of a larger job, e.g. a full home renovation. This means that there will be other people working around you at different stages, from plumbers and electricians, to plasterers and tilers. It is important that when you are painting, others are aware and can avoid the area you are working in. This will prevent any damage to your finish, tins of paint knocked over, and damage to their own materials. It's a matter of both safety and practicality – any damage done to your surfaces would need to be re-prepared and painted, costing you time and money.

Having a dedicated entrance and exit from a building will make it easier for all of the trades to access the premises safely and without causing any accidents.

Public

You will sometimes be working with products that give off toxic fumes. While is it important to protect yourself from these with your own PPE, you should also remember to protect members of the general public from the same fumes.

Ventilation

Figure 6.3 An exhaust fan

Similarly, to protect yourself, your clients and the general public, when applying paint or using solvents, e.g. for thinning or cleaning, there must be somewhere for the fumes to escape. Keeping windows open or using extractor fans will help to reduce this hazard.

Dust and debris

Before you begin to paint or even open a tin of paint, it is essential that you clean and tidy the area. Preparation of the surface may have left a lot of dust and debris behind, especially if removing wallpaper or abrading the surface. If dust and debris are left around, this can not only be a trip hazard, but it may get kicked up into the air and could leave you with a poor surface finish, i.e. bittiness, which you would then have to fix.

REED TIP

Think customer service. When working in people's houses, show their space and their belongings the same respect you would expect for your own. Would you want scratches on your TV? Paint on your furniture?

Protecting the work and surrounding area from damage

Revisit Chapters 4 and 5, pages 102–103 and 131–132, to remind yourself about the need to protect your work and the surrounding area from damage caused by general work activities, contact with the public, and poor weather conditions.

Tools and equipment

There are a few extra things you will need in order to put up the right protective gear. They are described in the table below.

Tools and equipment	Description and use
Signs	When working in a public place, you should put up a sign to show that you are working. You can buy brightly coloured warning tape for this, or a simple 'wet paint' sign.
Barriers	You can use barriers to seal off your working area from other trades that are working around you, or the general public. There are lightweight, foldable work-gate barriers that have reflective panels so they can be easily seen.
Pliers	Use for removing nails.
Screwdrivers	Use for erecting signs.
Claw hammer	Use for removing nails or putting up signs.
Brushes	Use brushes to help you remove dust and debris before you paint.
Brooms	Use a broom to help you clear up the work area before you begin painting.
Shovels	Use with a broom to clear up rubbish.

Table 6.1 Tools and equipment for protecting the work and surrounding area

Protecting furnishings and fittings

Furnishings and fittings can be very expensive or even impossible to replace. Taking care of people's belongings will make a good impression on your clients.

Door furniture

Door furniture (handles, finger plates, locks, letterboxes, numbers, knockers, etc.) should be removed. Wrap the parts individually in a protective cover, e.g. newspaper or bubble wrap, then place them in a container or box along with the screws that attached them. Another option is to cover them up with masking tape, but removal is the safest and easiest way to protect them from scratches and paint spatter.

Window furniture

Window furniture (curtains, blinds, pelmets and poles) should also be removed before any work takes place. With curtains, you should carefully remove them from their pole, lay them flat, then gently fold them so as to avoid odd looking creases, and place them in a plastic bag. They should then be stored in a safe, dry place, away from the work area. When removing blinds, retract them (pull them up) first. When removing poles, rails and brackets, be sure to keep all of the small parts together.

Fixtures and fittings

Light switches and power points on walls should be covered with masking tape to avoid dust and paint spatter. If removing light coverings such as lamp shades, treat these as other furniture and put them in a safe, dry place, wrapped or covered up so they won't get covered in dust. Where there are large light coverings that cannot be removed, cover them with plastic sheeting, then tape the sheeting down. If light fittings have to be removed, an electrician should do this for you.

PRACTICAL TIP

If you're removing lots of small pieces of furniture and fittings, you may find it helpful to label the containers or boxes you put them in. This will make it quicker and easier for you to replace them all once the painting is finished.

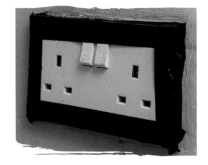

Figure 6.4 Taped up power point

Walls and ceilings may also have ventilation ducts and smoke alarms. Some of these can be unscrewed and removed, then covered and stored in a safe place. If this is not possible, use masking tape to protect them.

Other items on walls may include mirrors, pictures, shelves and ornaments. These should all be carefully removed, individually wrapped with a protective cover, e.g. bubble wrap, then stored somewhere safe, clean and dry. If it is impractical to remove shelves (along with their screws and brackets), they can be covered with plastic sheeting.

Flooring

If the carpets have not been removed, do not attempt to do this yourself. Instead cover them fully using dust sheets, polythene sheeting (for more waterproof protection), and carefully tape them down. Other surfaces such as boards, laminate or tiling should also be covered, though polythene sheeting should be enough. Rugs that are not attached to the floor should be rolled up, removed and placed somewhere safe, clean and dry.

Furniture

Furniture can include items such as chairs, tables, sofas and electrical equipment. Ideally, these should be removed from the working area. If this is not possible, bigger items can be moved into the centre of the room and carefully covered with sheeting. Plastic sheeting will stop any paint seeping through.

Outdoor items

It is easy to forget when working outside that this area should be protected too. Lawns, gardens and plants can be very sensitive to chemicals and solvents. Any portable items, such as pots and garden furniture, should be moved well out of the way and covered if they are at risk of any paint spatter. Any ground surface such as lawn or decking should be covered with sheeting.

Environmental and health and safety regulations

For the painting and decorating trade, the Environmental Protection Act 1990 (EPA) provides guidance on how materials high in VOCs, such as oil-based paints and solvents, must be disposed of safely. You will come into contact with these materials when preparing your surfaces and applying paints. Another important piece of legislation is the Control of Substances Hazardous to Health (COSHH) (2002), which you learnt about in Chapter 1, page 3.

Using masking tape

Masking tapes come in a variety of widths, strengths and adhesion for different purposes. It is used to protect surfaces, 'masking' them from the paint, as well as for attaching protective sheeting to surfaces.

Be sure to use decorator's tape (often blue) rather than household masking tape (beige), which tends to tear and pull off the paint below.

PRACTICAL TIP

Make sure that the place you are storing furniture and fittings is secure and safe from theft!

PRACTICAL TIP

Remember your safe lifting techniques when moving around heavy items of furniture.

DID YOU KNOW?

Decorator's masking tape is often blue in colour because it is easier to see where it has been applied, especially when painting light-coloured surfaces. Decorator's tape now comes in other bright colours.

Each tape has a time limit for how long it should stay on a surface before being pulled off. If you leave it for longer than this, it can be harder to remove without taking paint away or leaving residue behind.

* Exterior masking tape is designed to last in cold, hot or wet weather. It is designed to be used on the more uneven or rough surfaces that you would find outdoors.

* Interior masking tape is only designed for use indoors. It tears very easily and has low adhesion, which means it is easy to remove.

* Low tack tape is used for delicate surfaces, e.g. those that have been recently painted.

* Crepe masking tape is a stretchier tape, good for surfaces that aren't straight.

* Seven-day masking tape can remain on a surface for 7 days before the adhesive would potentially cause damage when removed. There is also 14-day tape available.

Protective sheeting

Type of protective sheeting	Description and use	Maintenance and storage
Dust sheets	Made of cotton twill, fold over once to make them thicker. Used for protecting furniture and flooring. They come in various sizes, though often 4m × 6m. They are not waterproof, so will not protect from heavy spills. Available in different thicknesses, from lightweight to heavy duty. More costly than polythene sheeting, but they are also reusable. For a more water-resistant dust sheet, you can buy cotton with a protective backing.	Shake out regularly when decorating, and then wash at the end of the job. Once clean, fold and store somewhere clean and dry so they don't suffer from mildew.
Polythene sheets	Use on their own or under dust sheets for extra protection from wet preparation. Usually cut to fit, then taped down. Can be used outdoors to protect gardens and pathways. Come in rolls of various sizes. Any paint that drips on the sheet will take longer to dry because it has no absorbency. This can also increase the risk of slip hazards.	Would usually be thrown away at the end of a job. Often used by DIYers for this reason, and for their low cost. A professional decorator would prefer cotton twill and canvas sheeting with protective backing, or to double up dust sheets when working with very messy materials.
Tarpaulin	Waterproof covers used to protect members of the public from splashes. They can be rubber-coated fabric, canvas, and coated nylon. They offer good protection from the weather and are good for use in high traffic areas.	Make sure tarpaulin is dry before rolling it up, otherwise it will get mouldy. Store in a clean, dry place.
Drop sheets	Come in both fabric and plastic. Best used outdoors to protect from rain, as well as paint and dust. The terms drop sheets and dust sheets are often used to mean the same thing.	As for dust sheets.

Table 6.2 Types of protective sheeting

PREPARING MATERIALS FOR APPLICATION

Hazards, health and safety and risk assessment

See Chapter 1 for more detailed information on identifying hazards, health and safety and risk assessment. In particular, bear in mind that when painting surfaces, you are likely to be exposed to harmful or even toxic irritants and fumes. When working with substances that may irritate your skin, avoid direct contact with the substance and cover your skin with the right PPE. When working with strong fumes, e.g. from solvent-based products, work in a well-ventilated area.

Also, refresh your memory on the hazards and regulations of working at height in Chapter 4.

Tools and equipment

Brushes and rollers

Brushes and rollers are the main tools you'll be using to apply paint. You'll recall from Chapter 5 on page 130 that brush bristles can be made from natural bristle or synthetic fibres. Brushes are made of different parts: the handle, ferrule, setting, and filling (see the diagram at Fig 6.5).

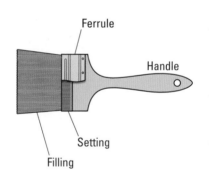

Figure 6.5 Parts of a brush

* Handles can be made of timber and plastic. Certain timber handles are treated and sealed so that water, solvent and paint are not absorbed into it.

* The ferrule joins the handle and the filling. It is often made from plated metals, but also from plastic.

* The setting is an adhesive that sticks the bristles together at the base of the brush under the ferrule.

* The filling is simply the bristles.

Rollers are used for applying paint to large, flat areas. They are faster to use than a brush, unless painting small areas, corners or irregular shapes. Rollers are made up of a frame or yoke, which can be single arm or double arm (see Figs 6.6 and 6.7), and a sleeve which slips onto the frame and is removed for easier cleaning. Sleeves can be of the following types:

* Woven fabric – resistant to shedding, needed for use on smooth surfaces, can be used with all paints, less pressure needed to apply paint.

* Mohair – goat's hair, useful for fine finishes on smooth surfaces, for use with both solvent and water-based paints.

* Sheepskin – higher in density than man-made coverings, they pick up the most paint and so do not need to be loaded as often as other rollers.

* Lambswool – the wool is attached to a man-made backing, but not as good at picking up paint as sheepskin, often used with solvent-based paints.

* Knitted – can be used on medium or rough surfaces, has high capacity for holding paint, gives fastest coverage, use with matt or satin paints, more pressure needed to apply paint.

* Foam – does not shed fibres, good for solvent-based paints but not water-based paints as it can leave an uneven finish.

Short pile is good for smooth surfaces and long pile is better for rough or uneven surfaces, as the fibres can get into the small holes. Medium pile rollers are a good all-rounder if you are dealing with a variety of surfaces.

When working on exterior surfaces, such as when painting brick or render, you will be working with both a porous surface and thicker paints. Therefore you will need to use a textured roller with long pile and a coarse wall brush so that you get into all the small holes and cracks.

Figure 6.6 Single arm or cage roller frame

When working on interior surfaces, particularly plaster, you should use a synthetic brush or a universal roller sleeve with your water-based paints.

When painting with oil-based materials inside, it is better to use a mohair roller or a pure bristle brush.

When priming metals you will need a very coarse brush that will carry thick primers such as zinc phosphate.

Figure 6.7 Double arm roller frame

Other equipment

We covered some of the equipment you need for painting in Chapter 5, e.g. paint kettles, roller trays, buckets, dust sheets and roller cages.

Paint stirrers

As the name suggests, these are used to stir paint. Paint is made up of different parts: the liquid part (water or solvent), the binding part, and the pigment or colour. In some paint types, these can become separated in the paint can and so they must be mixed thoroughly before applying them to a surface.

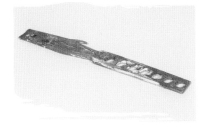

Figure 6.8 A paint stirrer

A specially designed stirrer will have small holes which allow the paint to pass through more easily.

Strainers

Paint can become contaminated with dirt, rust, dust or old flecks of dried paint that fall into the can, especially when opening. If this happens, paint will need to be strained so that it goes onto the surface smoothly and does not cause bittiness.

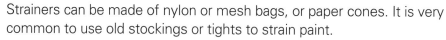

Figure 6.9 A paint strainer

Figure 6.10 A paint scuttle

PRACTICAL TIP

Not all paints should be strained or stirred. Always check the instructions on the tin.

KEY TERMS

Decant

– to pour paint from the tin to a smaller container such as a roller tray or kettle

Strainers can be made of nylon or mesh bags, or paper cones. It is very common to use old stockings or tights to strain paint.

Extension poles
Extension poles can be attached to the end of the roller handle so that you can reach high places, such as ceilings, without needing to use access equipment.

Scuttles
When painting from a height with a roller, a scuttle is used to hold paint. It looks like a rectangular bucket, with a textured inside, similar to a roller tray. Some scuttles come with hooks so they can be hung off a ladder, as you can with a paint kettle.

Stages of preparation

Opening the tin
See the practical task, *Prepare a tin of emulsion for painting* on page 190 for step-by-step instructions on how to open a tin of paint.

Stirring the paint
Most types of paint must be stirred before use, but always check the instructions on the tin. They will tell you whether the paint should be stirred or not, but never shake a tin before opening it. Some paints, such as non-drip gloss, should not be stirred, otherwise their special properties will no longer work. Use a paint stirrer, rather than any old stick, because the small holes will allow the paint to pass through and mix it more quickly.

Decanting the paint
It is rarely a good idea to work directly from the main paint tin. Often they are too big and heavy to move around while you work. They may also get contaminated with debris, or if they get tipped over, a lot of paint would be lost. Instead, it is better to **decant** your paints into a smaller container, such as a paint kettle. See the practical task, *Prepare a tin of emulsion for painting* on page 190 for step-by-step instructions on how to decant a tin of paint.

Search and strain
When opening a tin of paint that has already been used, you will need to check the condition of the paint. If a tin of oil paint has been opened before a skin may have formed. This skin will have caught any dust and debris and can be removed.

If there is any dust or debris in the paint itself, or old dried flakes of paint, it will need to be strained. You can simply add a strainer to the top of your paint kettle so that the paint passes through when decanting.

Note that not all paints should be strained. Certain primers would be affected by the straining process so that they would not be effective any more. Their special characteristics (e.g. heat resistance or fast drying time) would disappear and they would no longer work as they are designed to. Once again, as with stirring paints, always check the manufacturer's instructions on the tin.

Adjust viscosity

Viscosity means the thickness of the paint. The viscosity of paint can be changed by adding thinner to dilute it: either solvent or water depending on the type of paint. It is this part of the paint that evaporates in the drying process.

The viscosity needs to be at the right level to allow the paint to be applied easily. If a paint has been opened before, it may have changed viscosity since its first use, i.e. some of the solvent or water has evaporated, and will need to be thinned again before use.

Thinning may also be needed to help the surface better absorb the paint, e.g. adding water to emulsion as a primer for fresh plaster. This helps to seal the surface and prolong the life of the coatings.

> **KEY TERMS**
>
> **Viscosity**
>
> – the thickness or stickiness of a paint which can be adjusted adding thinner.

APPLYING COATINGS WITH BRUSH AND ROLLER

Basic paint systems and their components

Paint is made up of various different parts, depending on the type of paint and its uses. The main general ingredients of all paints are:

* pigment (the solid, colour part)

* binder (resin which makes paint stick to the surface)

* thinner (water or solvent which disappears as the paint dries).

Water-borne paint systems

Film former

Also known as the binder or resin, in water-based paints such as emulsion, the film former is made of synthetic materials such as acrylic and PVA. Its purpose is to make the paint hold together and stick to the surface.

Pigment and extender

This is the solid part of paint that gives it its colour. Its **opacity** prevents the colour of the previous paint layers showing through. Pigments can be synthetic (man-made) or natural.

> **KEY TERMS**
>
> **Opacity**
>
> – the degree to which paint is transparent or see-through. The higher the opacity, the less you can see through the paint. A thicker paint will be more opaque.

Extenders are used for giving the paint the paint more body or bulk. Adding extender to paint makes it cheaper to make, easier to apply and slows down the settling of pigment to the bottom of the tin.

Dispersant/emulsifier

Dispersant or emulsifier (also known as stabiliser and plasticiser) is added to paint to keep the particles separate and prevent them from clumping together or settling to the bottom. They are also known as plasticisers because they make the paint more elastic and help give a smooth finish.

Solvent/thinner

The solvent in a water-based paint is water. Solvents are also called thinners because they dilute or thin the paint. The purpose of the thinner is to dissolve the resin so it is the right thickness to enable easy application. It is the solvent part of paint that evaporates into the air when paint dries.

Driers

Driers are also known as hardeners or catalysts. They are added to some paints to speed up the drying process.

Additives

Additives include driers, emulsifiers, and extenders as described above. They are extra ingredients added to the basic components of paint to change the properties of the paint such as their finish, their 'spreadability' and drying time. Some paints also contain additives designed to resist mould growth, often used in moist areas such as bathrooms.

Solvent-borne paint systems

Film former

The film former in solvent-based paints has the same purpose as for water-based paints. The difference is that they are made of different resins. Older styles of paint used oil, which gave them a high degree of flexibility. Other types of binder are now more commonly used and each has properties that affect the paint's shine, strength or durability.

Pigment

Pigment in solvent-based paints has the same characteristics as for water-based paints. It is interesting to note that in the early to mid-1900s, a great deal of pigment came from lead. Its general use has been banned since 1992.

Solvent/thinner

The thinner in solvent-based paints is solvent. You can read more about the different types of solvent in Chapter 5, page 128.

Driers

Though they have the same purpose as for water-based paints, driers or hardeners can be added to solvent-based paints to create a harder or shinier finish, such as in enamel paint.

Additives

The purpose of additives is the same as for water-based paints. Oil-based paints can contain **terebine driers** – an additive that helps paint to dry in cold, damp or exposed areas.

Correct techniques for applying paint

Using the correct methods for applying paint will mean you avoid problems with the finish, such as runs, brush or roller marks, or patchiness. A high standard of finish should be what you aim for, which means that any visible defects should be avoided.

Using a brush

Loading the brush

Loading the brush is simply dipping the brush into the paint, about a third of the way up the bristles. You should then work the paint into the bristles by gently pushing the brush against the inside of the kettle, and finally tap the brush against the rim to remove excess paint. See the practical task, *Apply solvent-borne paint to a panelled door and frame* on page 192 for step-by-step instructions on how to load your brush correctly.

Some painters scrape the brush against the rim to get the brush back into shape, but this tends to remove too much paint and can leave your tin or pot in a mess. Other painters remove the excess paint by making a downward brush stroke on the surface itself, next to where they are about to start painting.

Laying on

When painting with gloss, start towards the top of the surface, painting in vertical strips using an upward stroke, and then (without reloading the brush) cross those strips horizontally. You will then need to lay off (see next page).

When brush painting large areas with emulsion, use a diagonal criss-cross motion, starting at the top of your wall or surface. This will mean that you are not left with any brush marks and will not need to lay off.

If you are using a vinyl emulsion paint, then you can lay off using an arcing motion, from side to side in a semi-circle. This will avoid runs or sags.

Figure 6.11 Loading the brush

Figure 6.12 Laying on gloss paint

Figure 6.13 Criss-cross method

Figure 6.14 Cutting in with an angled brush using a pencil grip

Cutting in

Where walls join up with ceilings, door and window frames, skirting boards, and around light switches and sockets, you will need to 'cut in' with a brush. This is because it is difficult to reach to the edge of these areas with a roller, or because one of the surfaces will be painted a different colour.

When cutting in, hold your paint brush like a pencil at the base of the brush, rather than the end of the handle. This will give you more control and help to stop your muscles getting tired.

Laying off

Because paint is a liquid, gravity can make any excess paint drip down the surface, creating runs or sags. To avoid these, you must always lay off. Laying off will also help to blend in the brush strokes so they can't be seen in the final finish.

After you've used up all the paint on your brush – when it is no longer moving smoothly along the surface – use light, upward strokes over the area you've just painted. Any paint drips and brush marks should disappear.

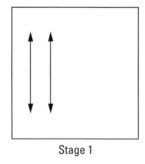
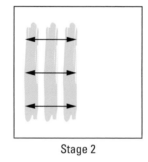
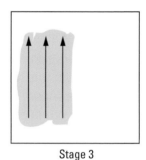

| Stage 1 | Stage 2 | Stage 3 |

Figure 6.15 Applying paint and laying off solvent-based paint

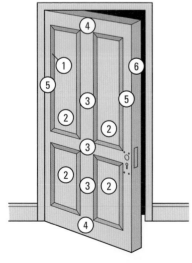

Figure 6.16 The correct order for painting a panelled door

* When painting large, flat surfaces such as walls, you are more likely to use a roller. If you do use a brush, be sure to overlap with the wet edge of the previously painted section.

* Ceilings should be painted first, followed by walls, and then any woodwork or decorative features.

* Do not lay off ceilings in one direction only – use the criss-cross method.

Painting doors

When painting a panelled door, each section is painted in a specific order so that the wet edges of the paint can be blended together. See Fig 6.16 for the correct order to use.

Flush doors, i.e. those with a flat, plain surface, should be painted in sections of around 30 cm square. Start painting from the top-right or top-left and then work in stages to keep a wet edge. See Fig 6.17.

Remember with all doors that if the door opens away from you, the hinge edge of the door must be painted too. If it opens towards you, then paint the edge with the latch.

Painting casement windows

When painting windows, you would usually work from top to bottom, then side to side. Always paint the sash bottom rail second to last, finishing with the uprights. Choosing the right size brush will depend on the size of the window frame – the bigger the frame, the wider the brush.

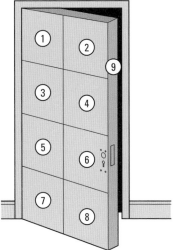

Figure 6.17 The correct order for painting a flush door

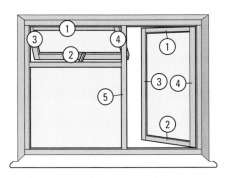

Casement window: paint opening parts before frame and interior sill

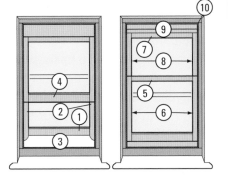

Sash window: from inside open sashes as far as they will go, paint all accessible surfaces, reverse sashes and complete painting

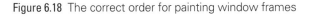

Figure 6.18 The correct order for painting window frames

Linear work

Linear work is a term for the painting of long features such as skirting boards, dado rails, architraves and cornices. It is very important that the paint on these features does not overlap with the surrounding wall, otherwise the eye will be drawn to it. These features are usually painted after the main ceiling and wall paint is applied. Painting in clean, straight lines is a skill you will acquire with practice and patience.

Figure 6.19 Adding paint to the roller tray

Using a roller

Rollers tend to be used for large, flat surfaces such as walls and ceilings. However, there are also special types of rollers designed for reaching small places, e.g. behind radiators. Remember that you will still need to cut in using a brush.

Rollers can also be used where there is some texture, such as Artex, so long as the right type of roller sleeve is used. Remind yourself about the different types of roller sleeves and their uses in Chapter 5, page 130.

When using any type of roller, you will need a tray of the right shape and size to pour your paint into. Pour your paint into the deep part of the tray – don't let it cover the higher textured part. Dip your roller into the deeper part of the tray, then roll it back and forth over the textured part of the tray to get an even coverage and remove any excess paint.

Figure 6.20 Applying paint using a roller

When applying the paint to the surface, roll up and down in diagonal motions in the shape of a W. For the same reasons as when using a brush, you should lay off in an upwards motion to make sure there are no runs or chunky patches of paint left by the edges of the roller.

Colour systems

Working with colours is part of every painter and decorator's job. The use of colour can affect our experience of a space. Colours can help express someone's personality, bring more light into a room, or even help to calm or stimulate the people in it.

Colour wheel

The colour wheel is a basic system to help us understand, describe, identify, put in order, and mix colours. There are three primary colours: red, yellow and blue. Primary colours are pure colours that cannot be made from any other colour. When each of these is mixed together, they make three more secondary colours:

* red + yellow = orange

* yellow + blue = green

* blue + red = violet.

When secondary colours are mixed, they create a tertiary colour.

* red + violet = red–violet

* red + orange = red–orange

* and so on.

In total, this makes 12 basic colours or hues. Have a look at Fig 6.21 to see how this works.

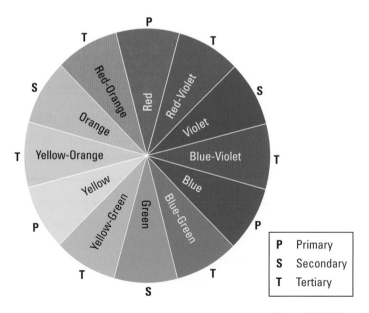

P	Primary
S	Secondary
T	Tertiary

Figure 6.21 The colour wheel

Using colour

The colours that you see in the basic colour wheel above are at their full saturation. This means that they do not have any white or black added to them; they appear at their strongest. When a hue has black added to it, this is called a 'shade' of that colour. When white is added, that hue is called a 'tint'. Look at Fig 6.22 to see the outer shades and the inner tints. The lightness or darkness of a hue is called its 'value'.

The colours from red to yellow are often described as 'warm' colours. These tend to seem closer (advancing) and more stimulating. Colours from violet to yellow–green are thought to be 'cool' colours. These seem further away (receding or retiring) and more relaxing.

Hues or colours, when seen in their purest natural state, form a natural scale or order: some are naturally light in hue (e.g. yellow), some are naturally dark (e.g. violet), and others are in between (e.g. green). This natural order of colours has been the basis for many colour theories such as in Munsell's colour theory, and is clearly seen in the colour wheel. Natural order can be seen in things that occur in nature, such as a sunset or the change of leaves in autumn.

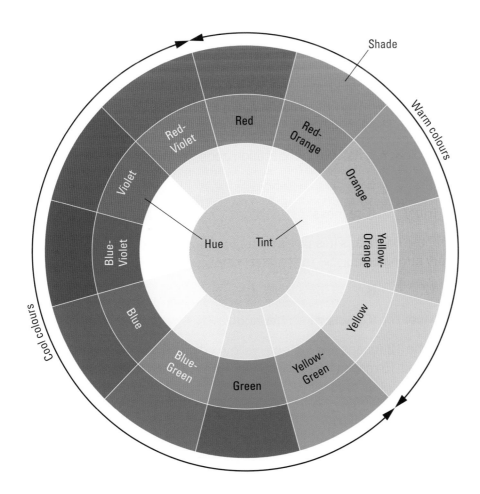

Figure 6.22 Tints and shades in the colour wheel

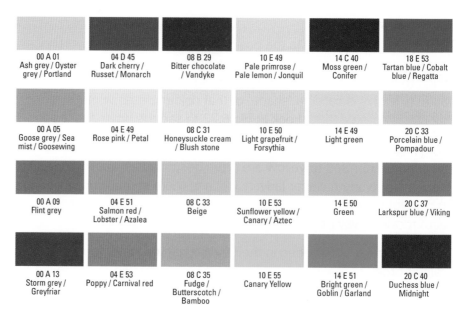

00 A 01 Ash grey / Oyster grey / Portland	04 D 45 Dark cherry / Russet / Monarch	08 B 29 Bitter chocolate / Vandyke	10 E 49 Pale primrose / Pale lemon / Jonquil	14 C 40 Moss green / Conifer	18 E 53 Tartan blue / Cobalt blue / Regatta
00 A 05 Goose grey / Sea mist / Goosewing	04 E 49 Rose pink / Petal	08 C 31 Honeysuckle cream / Blush stone	10 E 50 Light grapefruit / Forsythia	14 E 49 Light green	20 C 33 Porcelain blue / Pompadour
00 A 09 Flint grey	04 E 51 Salmon red / Lobster / Azalea	08 C 33 Beige	10 E 53 Sunflower yellow / Canary / Aztec	14 E 50 Green	20 C 37 Larkspur blue / Viking
00 A 13 Storm grey / Greyfriar	04 E 53 Poppy / Carnival red	08 C 35 Fudge / Butterscotch / Bamboo	10 E 55 Canary Yellow	14 E 51 Bright green / Goblin / Garland	20 C 40 Duchess blue / Midnight

Figure 6.23 The BS 4800 framework

BS 4800: Paint Colours for Building Purposes

The British Standards framework has a range of 122 paint colours used for building and construction work. They are often used to meet safety and legal requirements by local authorities for public buildings.

The framework is made of 5 sections labelled A to E, with A being the weakest colours and E the strongest. See Fig 6.23 to see how the colour chart is laid out. The horizontal rows are the hue rows, i.e. red, yellow, green, etc. The vertical rows show the level of grey in each colour.

Each colour has its own identification code, for example:

a) 04 E 58

(Hue) (Greyness) (Weight)

Figure 6.24 BS 4800 colour 04 E 58

Here, the 04 means it is part of the red group of colours; E means it is a very strong colour; 58 makes it a heavy colour.

b) 12 B 15

(Hue) (Greyness) (Weight)

Figure 6.25 BS 4800 colour 12 B 15

Here, the 12 means it is a green–yellow colour, B means it is quite weak, and 15 makes it very light. See Figs 6.24 and 6.25 to see what these two colours look like.

Munsell colour system

In the early 1900s, Albert H. Munsell created a system that has since been used on an international scale. Munsell's system formed the basis of the British Standards explained above. His system divides colour into three parts:

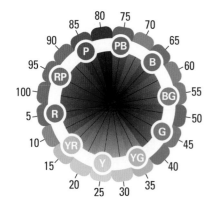

Figure 6.26 The Munsell hue circle

1. Hue: the basic colour, i.e. red, yellow, green, blue and purple, and the colours halfway in between each of these, e.g. yellow/red, green/yellow etc.

2. Value: the lightness or darkness of a colour.

3. Chroma: the greyness or purity of a colour.

On the Munsell scale, each colour appears evenly spaced to the eye, i.e. each colour is equally different to the next. Hue, value and chroma are measured by a letter or number so that a colour can be more accurately described. Colours appear differently to different people, and using a code to describe the colour means that everyone is referring to the same one.

Hue
The hues are coded as follows:

- yellow = Y
- yellow–red = YR
- red = R
- red–purple = RP

- purple = P
- purple–blue = PB
- blue = B
- blue–green = BG

- green = G
- green–yellow = GY

Each of these hues is divided into 10 sections from 1 to 10 where 5 is the purest version of the hue.

Value
Value is shown on a vertical scale of 0 to 10 where black is 0 and white is 10. Each division on the scale is a shade of grey. See Fig 6.27. The value number appears after the hue, e.g. 2R3. This would be a red that is closer to purple–red and is quite dark.

Chroma
Chroma, or a colour's purity, is shown on a horizontal scale where 0 is a neutral grey up to the purest version of the hue which can be as high as 14. Not all hues will have a chroma range this long, e.g. yellows have a greater chroma range than purples due to what the eye can physically see. The chroma number appears after the value, e.g. 5Y8/10 (see Fig 6.28).

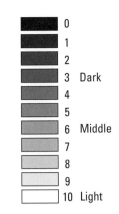

Figure 6.27 The Munsell value scale

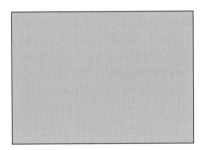

Figure 6.28 Munsell colour 5Y8/10

DID YOU KNOW?

You can visit the Munsell website for more information on the Munsell colour system: *www.munsell.com*

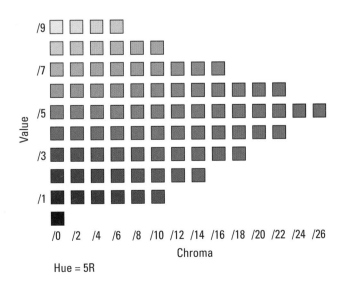

Figure 6.29 A branch of the Munsell colour tree

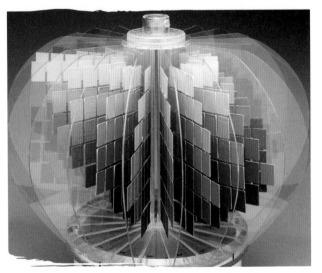

Figure 6.30 The Munsell colour tree

Possible defects after applying paint systems

Defects in your paintwork can occur if:

* paint is not applied carefully and correctly

* paint is applied in the wrong conditions (e.g. in wet weather)

* a surface has not been prepared correctly.

In the table below, there are a number of different problems or defects that can occur when you are painting, the cause of each defect and the ways to avoid or fix it.

Defects	Causes	Ways to avoid defect or fix it
Misses – areas where the paint has not been applied (Fig 6.31)	• Not taking enough care • Poor visibility/bad lighting • Undercoat is similar colour to topcoat • Wrong method of application, e.g. wrong roller type used on textured surface	• Paint more carefully, using a method to ensure you don't miss sections. • Use enough, proper lighting. • Use a different coloured undercoat. • Choose the correct tools, e.g. long pile roller. • Once dry, apply an extra coat to the whole area.
Grinning – the colour underneath the topcoat shows through (Fig 6.32)	• Trying to change colour too drastically, e.g. bright red to yellow • Applying the paint too thinly, e.g. overbrushing or overthinning the paint itself • Using the wrong colour undercoat	• Use more undercoats to mask the original colour. • Use more paint and apply it more evenly, and follow instructions for thinning on the tin. • Use an undercoat slightly lighter in colour than the topcoat. • Apply extra coats as necessary.
Runs/sags – paint is running or dripping down the surface (Fig 6.33)	• Paint has been applied too thickly or unevenly • Paint has run or dripped from mouldings, e.g. picture rails • The wet edge has started to dry and new paint applied is not blended in	• Apply evenly and not too thickly. • Avoid coating mouldings too heavily. • Plan carefully so that wet edges are minimised and not allowed to dry. • If the run is still wet, stipple with a brush to remove the run. • If it is dry, wait a few days before rubbing it down and repainting.
Excessive brushmarks/ ropiness – where brush marks can be seen in the paint finish (Fig 6.34)	• Applying paint carelessly, e.g. without laying off • Applying coat too heavily • Applying topcoat to a sloppy undercoat • Applying to undercoat that is not yet dry	• Make sure you apply paint carefully and always lay off. • Undercoats should also be applied carefully. • Make sure previous layers of paint are dry first. • If paintwork has dried, abrade the surface first, then recoat.
Paint on adjacent surfaces (Fig 6.35)	• Careless application of paint • Not using masking tape where needed	• Take extra care when painting near corners and mouldings – don't paint too close. • Use masking tape for tricky areas. • Scrape off excess, rub down and repaint.
Fat edges/wet edge build up – where an extra thick layer of paint forms along edge of painted surface (Fig 6.36)	• Accidental overpainting of a right-angled surface, e.g. a door frame	• Take extra care when painting in corners that will receive more than one coating. • Let the fat edge dry, then rub down and repaint.

Excessive bits and nibs – where small bits of dust and plaster are trapped under the paint (Fig 6.37)	• Poor preparation – plaster has not been de-nibbed before painting • An unclean surface, area or tools	• Always prepare the surface fully before painting. • Remove all dust and rubbish before painting. • Wait until the paint has dried, then de-nib or sand the area and repaint.
Irregular cutting in – an uneven appearance at edges where cutting in meets the main surface (Fig 6.38)	• Careless application when cutting in • Leaving brush marks • Cutting in not in a straight line • Overloading brush • Overreaching • Having a shaky hand	• Take care when cutting in. • Use the right amount of paint. • Cut in towards the line. • If paint touches another surface when cutting in, remove it while wet with a damp rag (water or solvent). overcoat the area to hide the problem.
Orange peel – where spray or roller coating dries with a textured finish (Fig 6.39)	• Applying paint that is too thick, i.e. needs thinning • Applying paint too thickly • Holding the spray gun too close • Setting the pressure incorrectly	• Thin paint according to instructions on the tin. • Reduce amount of paint used. • If using spray gun, set it to the right pressure. • Give the surface a complete rub down and repaint.
Roller edge marks ('tram lines') and roller skid marks – an uneven surface with small, thicker patches of paint or spatter (Fig 6.40)	• Use of wrong roller cover • Paint build up at ends of roller • Skid marks are caused by applying too much pressure to the roller, making it slide across the surface	• Choose the correct roller cover for the type of surface and paint. • Occasionally wipe off the edges of the roller into the tray. • Hold the handle firmly, but don't press too hard or force it. • Sand down and repaint affected patches.

Table 6.3 Paint defects, causes and remedies

Figure 6.31 Misses

Figure 6.32 Grinning

Figure 6.33 Runs or sags

Figure 6.34 Ropiness

Figure 6.35 Paint on adjacent surfaces

Figure 6.36 Fat edges

Figure 6.37 Bits and nibs

Figure 6.38 Irregular cutting in

Figure 6.39 Orange peel

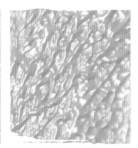
Figure 6.40 Roller edge marks

CASE STUDY

Working with colour

Kieran St Julien, a self-employed painter and decorator, says:

'Some of my customers know exactly what they want, and will tell me precisely which colours to use. Other customers need a little more help with their choices. In that case, I'll give them a colour chart and let them look through and decide. I also suggest that they may want to get some sample pots and try the colours out in the actual space.

If they need guidance about a colour scheme to use throughout the house, then I'll sit down with them and talk through the purpose of each room, such as whether it's a bathroom, a bedroom, a boy's or girl's room.

I once had a customer who chose a grey colour for their bedroom, which already had stone walls. I tried to steer them away from this, because it might feel too cold. Instead, I suggested a warmer, neutral colour. They agreed and were very pleased with the result.'

Replacing fittings and furniture

Having carefully prepared and protected your working area, once you have finished all the painting and the paint has dried:

1. Clean and remove your tools and materials (see below).
2. Make sure the area is free of dust and debris (sweep and vacuum).
3. Replace any light fittings removed.
4. Take off any remaining decorator's tape.
5. Replace window and floor coverings.
6. Uncover and put back any furniture into its original position.

REED TIP

Make sure you look after your tools or your tools won't look after you.

CLEANING, MAINTAINING AND STORING BRUSHES AND ROLLERS

As a painter and decorator, your tools are your livelihood. Treat them with care and respect and they will last a long time and serve you well. When brushes and rollers are not cleaned and stored correctly, the next time you use them, they may not give you good quality work.

Methods of cleaning

Cleaning brushes

Brushes should be cleaned immediately at the end of a job. If water-based paint is left to dry, it is no longer water soluble. Don't leave your brushes just sitting in water or solvent at the end of a job. The metal part (ferrule) can rust and the bristles can be pushed out of shape if they're resting on the bottom. It's best to use different brushes for your water-based and solvent-based paints.

To clean a brush:

1. Using the back of a knife, carefully scrape any excess paint onto a sheet of paper.

2. Grab a sheet or two of newspaper and use long brushstrokes to get rid of as much paint as you can.

3. If using **water-based paint**, wash it under clean, warm, running water.

4. Rub a bit of washing detergent or soap into the bristles and rinse until the water runs clear.

5. Once clean, flick the brush to remove excess water.

6. Gently reshape the bristles and leave the brush to dry.

7. If using **oil-based paint**, use white spirit or a brush cleaning solvent with lower emissions.

8. Pour solvent up to the top of the bristles into a small container, only just bigger than the brush, to reduce the amount of solvent you need.

9. Dip the brush into the solvent, and swirl it around to work the solvent into the bristles.

10. Once the brush is clean, remove excess solvent by flicking the brush.

11. Put a lid on the container to allow the solids to settle.

Workshop vs on site cleaning of brushes

Most brushes used for oil-based paints are kept in a brush keep (see below). However, brushes used for water-based finishes are cleaned on site, but are taken back to the compound or workshop where there is warm water to remove any dried paint.

Natural bristle brushes

Be gentle when dealing with natural bristles as they can come out of the brush more easily. When rinsing a natural bristle brush, don't use hot water, only lukewarm, as the heat can cause the ferrule to expand and the bristles to fall out. It is better to use natural bristle for oil-based paints. Synthetic brushes are best used for water-based paints.

PRACTICAL TIP

Remember the environment! Don't dispose of solvents and oil-based paints down the drain, and reduce your water and solvent use by removing as much paint from the brush as possible before rinsing. See pages 128, 168 and 187 for further advice on disposal of solvents.

PRACTICAL TIP

Don't forget to wear the right PPE when cleaning brushes and rollers in solvent.

Cleaning roller sleeves

Never leave your rollers or sleeves sitting in water or solvent at the end of a job. The frame can rust and the sleeve can be pushed out of shape. To clean a roller:

1. Scrape excess paint into your roller tray using the back of a knife or scraper.

2. Move the roller over the ribbed part of the roller tray to remove excess paint.

3. Run the roller over some sheets of newspaper, cardboard or a rag to get rid of as much paint as you can.

4. Remove the sleeve from the frame.

5. If using **water-based paint**, wash the sleeve under running water and work the paint out with your hands.

6. Rub some detergent or soap into the pile, making a good lather, then rinse until the water runs clear.

7. Squeeze as much water out of the sleeve as you can and leave it to drip dry.

8. If using oil-based paint, sit the sleeve in some clean white spirit for a short while.

9. Run the roller along a clean roller tray or scuttle.

10. Once all paint is removed, use detergent and warm water to rinse off the white spirit.

If you have used a foam roller for applying oil-based paint, then you may wish to dispose of it rather than clean it.

Storing brushes and rollers

Short-term storage

When taking short breaks from painting, e.g. overnight, it is not necessary to clean your brush or roller. However, you must take care that the paint does not dry up and harden them. Brushes and rollers can be steeped in water or solvent (depending on the paint you're using), but this is not ideal as it can bend the bristles out of shape.

Instead, wrap up your rollers in a plastic bag when leaving them overnight. Similarly, a paint brush can be wrapped in cling-film or tin foil to keep the bristles and paint wet. But remember that the solvent acetone can dissolve some plastics.

For shorter breaks, e.g. lunch breaks, you can leave the roller sleeve fully submerged in the tin of paint that you are using. This is called 'suspension'.

Long-term storage

When storing your brushes and rollers between jobs, you can use a storage tub. This will suspend your brushes in water or white spirit without having the bristles resting on the bottom and getting out of shape. The disadvantage of this method is that the water or solvent can drip out when starting your new paint work, affecting your finish.

There are also wet storage systems, known as a brush keep, which mean you can avoid having to clean your brushes after each job. The brushes are suspended not in liquid but in vapour so they can be reused straight away for the same colour. The fumes come from a pad or wick that can be topped up with fluid.

Otherwise, if you have cleaned and air dried your brushes and rollers, they can be gently moulded back into shape and then wrapped in brown paper, lint-free cloth, or the jacket or container they came in.

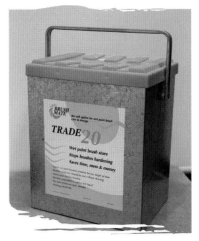

Figure 6.41 A brush keep

Environmental and safety considerations

Disposing of contaminated materials

Paints and solvents are often quite toxic and bad for the environment. Tipping solvent or paint down a drain should not be considered. Even water-based paints can damage a drainage system. Instead, you can pour your paint-contaminated water into a large bucket and leave it out to evaporate. Once the water has disappeared, you can peel off the solids and place them in the bin.

When working with paint thinners, i.e. solvents, use a small container to reduce the amount of solvent you need to use. Once it is used and dirty, you can pour it into a larger plastic container, seal it, and allow the solids to settle to the bottom. When this has happened, you can drain off the clean solvent and use it again. Once you have filled a container with paint residue, you can take it to a licensed waste disposal business or local council recycling centre which will charge to dispose of the waste for you.

> **PRACTICAL TIP**
>
> The best way of managing contaminated and toxic materials is to avoid using them in the first place. Solvent-based paints can mostly be avoided now that water-based paint technology has greatly improved.

STORING PAINT MATERIALS

Storage conditions

Water-based coatings should be stored:

* with clear labels

* on a shelf or rack off the ground

* in a storage area that is free of frost

* in a storage area with a constant temperature

* out of direct sunlight.

> **DID YOU KNOW?**
>
> Your hazardous waste must be stored safely and securely. Consider whether it can be reused. Follow the government guidance on disposal of hazardous waste.

Solvent-based coatings should be stored:

* with clear labels

* with their lids tightly sealed

* in a storage area with a constant temperature below 15°C.

Dry powder products such as sugar soap and powder fillers should be stored in an environment that is well-ventilated, low humidity, and frost-free.

Hazards of storing materials

Many of the materials you are working with can be hazardous when stored. Solvents and solvent-based coatings in particular contain volatile organic compounds (VOCs). Being volatile means that they have a high risk of fire or explosion, especially if they are stored at too high a temperature.

These materials fall under the COSHH Regulations (see Chapter 1, page 3). This means that your employer should have assessed the risks, put in place precautions and procedures, and made sure you are aware of these risks and know how to store materials safely.

You will also be working with materials that can be heavy or bulky, e.g. sacks of powdered products or large tubs of paint. When storing heavy items, place them closer to the ground to avoid awkward or heavy lifting. Remind yourself of the manual handling techniques in Chapter 1, pages 22–23.

Effects of incorrect storage

If water-based paints are stored in a very cold, frosty environment, the water part of them can freeze. This will affect the finish, even once it has defrosted.

If solvent-based paints or varnishes are stored without the lid tightly on, they may suffer from **skinning**. The paint will form a skin on the top, though this can usually be removed.

Solvent-based paints should also be inverted (turned upside-down) from time to time to stop the contents from separating or **settling**.

Storing paints incorrectly can also cause **livering**. This is where the paint has become so thick that adding a thinner to it does not work. It can sometimes happen when a paint is used past its use-by date.

If dry powders are stored in an environment that has too much moisture, they can become hard or 'set', which would leave them unusable.

CASE STUDY

The ups and downs of self-employment

Kieran St Julien, finalist in the WorldSkills UK competition 2013, says:

'I started my own business in September after spending a year at college doing my Level 1 qualification. I did consider looking for employment, but working for large companies means working away from home and my family.

I really enjoy being my own boss, picking and choosing my work, deciding when I take holidays, and not having to ask permission to go to a dentist's appointment, for example.

The downside is that if there's no work, then I have no income. January can be a difficult month because everyone is resetting, taking holidays, getting into the swing of the New Year. When you're employed, you have a guaranteed wage, but of course part of what you're earning on the job is going into your employer's pocket and not directly to you.

It was hard work to get the business up and running – it doesn't happen overnight. My biggest form of advertising is word of mouth, and while it's effective, it does take time. I've also found the internet very useful. There are lots of sites these days such as Rated People, My Builder and My Hammer. If you successfully get a job from one of these sites, then you just pay the site a small commission, somewhere between £1 and £20.'

PRACTICAL TASK

1. PREPARE A TIN OF EMULSION FOR PAINTING

OBJECTIVE

To be able to open, stir, strain and decant a tin of emulsion paint ready for application.

PPE

Ensure you select PPE appropriate to the job and site where you are working. Refer to the PPE section of Chapter 1.

TOOLS AND EQUIPMENT

Paint stock pot (paint to be used)

Paint kettle

Paint brush

Paint stirrer

Clean-up cloth

Cone strainer (or other type of paint strainer)

Paint tin opener (or old screwdriver)

STEP 1 Open tin using a recognised paint tin opener or old screwdriver.

- Place the tin on a protected surface, such as a dust sheet or newspaper, in case any paint drips from the lid when removed.

- Dust off the lid and the rim so that any dust and debris does not fall into the tin.

- Gently lever the lid off, pushing downward on the opener and working around the lid in a circle.

Figure 6.42 Opening a tin of paint

- Once the lid is loose from the tin, use both hands to lift the lid off.

Figure 6.43 Lifting the lid off

STEP 2 Hold the lid in one hand over the stock pot, and use a paint brush to wipe the inside of the paint tin lid to remove surplus paint into paint stock pot.

When finished, place the lid face up on the protected surface.

Figure 6.44 Putting surplus paint into stock pot

PRACTICAL TIP

If you don't have a paint tin opener, you can use an old screwdriver to lever the lid off a paint tin, but this not as effective and can bend the lid out of shape.

STEP 3 Using the paint stirrer, mix the paint until there is no thick paint in the bottom of the tin. Remove the stirring stick, then using a paint brush, clean off the surplus paint into the tin.

Figure 6.47 Decanting the paint

Figure 6.45 Stirring the paint

Figure 6.46 Cleaning off surplus paint

PRACTICAL TIP

It's best to use a specially designed paint stirrer because the holes allow the paint to pass through more quickly and the paint is stirred more effectively.

STEP 5 Before using the paint, thoroughly clean your paint strainer using an old paint brush and clean water. This will leave it clean and unclogged, ready for its next use.

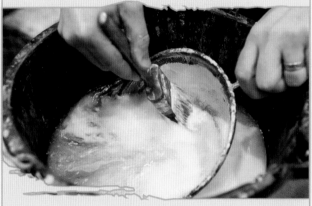

Figure 6.48 Cleaning the strainer

STEP 4 Place the strainer on top of your kettle and decant (pour) the paint very slowly through the strainer into the paint kettle:

- Pour from the back of the tin, so as not to obscure paint type details found on the front of the tin.

- Fill the paint kettle to about halfway – don't fill it – or to about the top of the bristles on your brush.

- Use a brush or rag to wipe the drips from the outside of the tin.

PRACTICAL TIP

If you're straining an oil-based paint, you may wish to use a disposable paint strainer instead of cleaning it, to reduce the amount of white spirit you are using.

2. APPLY SOLVENT-BORNE PAINT TO A PANELLED DOOR AND FRAME

OBJECTIVE

To paint a panelled door and its frame using solvent-based gloss paint; to practise loading your brush and laying off paint.

PPE

Ensure you select PPE appropriate to the job and site where you are working. Refer to the PPE section of Chapter 1.

TOOLS AND EQUIPMENT

Paint stock pot (paint to be used)

Paint kettle

Paint brush

Drop sheets (cotton twill or polythene)

STEP 1 Protect and prepare the surrounding area.

- Remove or protect any furnishings and fittings in the area, e.g. curtains, pictures.

- Lay down drop sheets to protect the floor and any coverings, taping them down so they are not a trip hazard.

- Remove, wrap and store any door furniture.

STEP 2 Wedge the door in a workable position so that it doesn't move when you're painting.

PRACTICAL TIP

You can use masking tape to protect door furniture, but removal is the better way of protecting items from damage and paint spatter.

STEP 3 Load your brush by dipping it into the paint in your paint kettle. You should cover about a third of the way up the bristles.

- Gently push the brush against the inside of the pot to work the paint into the bristles.

- Tap each side of the brush on the inside of the kettle to get rid of excess paint and to help the paint cling to the brush.

Figure 6.49 Loading the brush

PRACTICAL TIP

If you're working with a non-drip paint, do not stir it and do not remove the excess paint. It is supposed to be heavily loaded.

PRACTICAL TIP

Note that the laying on technique would be different if you were using a water-based paint. Water-based paints are designed to dry more quickly and so you would lay on and cross at the same time, i.e. the criss-cross method.

STEP 4 Apply the paint by laying on in an upward direction, making vertical stripes, then 'crossing' the coating horizontally at 90° to reduce the risk of paint runs. Finally with each brush load of paint, lay off lightly in an upward direction.

Figure 6.50 Applying paint, laying on

Figure 6.51 Applying paint, crossing

Figure 6.52 Applying paint, laying off

STEP 5 Paint the panelled door in the correct order:

- Apply paint to panels and mouldings.
- Apply paint to muntins (vertical strip between the panels).
- Apply paint to cross-rails.
- Apply paint to stiles.
- Apply paint to relevant door edge.

Figure 6.53 Painting the panels and mouldings

Figure 6.54 Painting the muntins

Figure 6.55 Painting the cross-rails

Figure 6.56 Painting the stiles

Figure 6.57 Painting the door edge

STEP 6 Apply paint to door frame by first coating the top of the frame, using horizontal brushstrokes. Next paint the left-hand side, then the right-hand side using vertical brushstrokes.

Take care not to over-apply the paint, otherwise you may end up with paint runs or curtains.

Figure 6.59b Painting the door frame 3

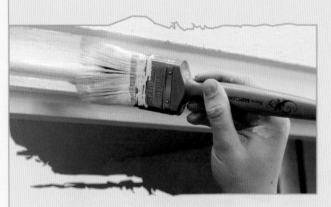

Figure 6.58 Painting the door frame 1

Figure 6.59a Painting the door frame 2

Figure 6.60 Painting the door frame 4

PRACTICAL TASK

3. APPLY WATER-BASED PAINT USING A ROLLER

OBJECTIVE

To paint a large, flat surface, such as a wall, using a roller and emulsion paint, as well as cutting in around the edges and cleaning your roller.

PPE

Ensure you select PPE appropriate to the job and site where you are working. Refer to the PPE section of Chapter 1.

TOOLS AND EQUIPMENT

Emulsion paint stock pot (paint to be used)

Paint kettle

Paint tray

Paint brush (65 mm to 10 mm size)

Paint roller sleeve and roller frame

Paint roller extension handle

Paint stirrer

Roller cleaning tool or scraper

Clean-up cloth

Brush comb or the back of a knife

Paint tin opener

Bucket (half filled with water)

Sponge

Low level working platform, such as a pair of trestles and lightweight staging or a hop-up

Drop sheets (preferably cotton twill)

STEP 1 Protect the surrounding area and prepare your paint as described in Practical tasks 1 and 2.

STEP 2 Erect your low-level working platform in one corner of the room and step up on it safely, holding your paint kettle (with the brush in it) in one hand.

STEP 3 Load up your brush, work the paint in, then tap the brush against the rim to help the paint cling to the bristles.

Apply paint by cutting in at ceiling height from left to right, taking care not to get paint onto the ceiling itself.

Be sure to move your access equipment as needed to stop you from overreaching dangerously.

Figure 6.61 Cutting in along a ceiling

STEP 4 Continue to cut in at the wall corners, then finally cut in at skirting level. It is helpful to cut in slightly onto the skirting board itself. See Figs 6.62 and 6.63.

Figure 6.62 Cutting in along the wall corners

Figure 6.63 Cutting in along skirting boards

PRACTICAL TIP

By cutting in slightly onto the top of the skirting board, the paint line will look perfectly straight even if the skirting board or plaster isn't.

STEP 5 Decant your paint from the stock pot into the deep part of your roller tray only. Load the paint roller by dipping the roller into the paint well, then roll the roller over the ridged part of the tray to remove any surplus.

Figure 6.64 Loading the roller with paint

PRACTICAL TIP

When you've finished cutting in with your paint kettle and brush, you should clean them out immediately, so they're ready for the next use. If you're planning to use them again shortly, you can cover the brush in plastic or cling-film. If using a solvent-based paint, then you can leave it in the paint itself or in a brush keep.

STEP 6 Apply paint to the wall in a 'W' pattern, then spread the paint in such a way to cover the wall without leaving any obvious 'tram line' marks from the edge of the roller where the paint has built up.

Figure 6.65 Applying paint with a roller

PRACTICAL TIP

Take care not to press the roller too hard or you could end up with skid marks where it has slid across the surface.

STEP 7 Once you have completed one section (of approximately 1 m²) you must complete another section until the entire wall is complete. This is to keep the wet edge from drying out, which could show stop lines on the wall.

1	2	3
4	5	6
7	8	9

Figure 6.66 Sequence for painting a wall with roller

STEP 8 Using the paint roller cleaning tool, a scraper or the back of a knife, remove as much of the paint as possible back into your roller tray or stock pot.

Next wash the paint from the roller by placing under clean running water and pushing the cleaning tool down the roller until as much of the paint and water is removed as possible.

Figure 6.67 Cleaning your roller

PRACTICAL TIP

Another way to clean emulsion paint off your roller tray is to leave it to dry overnight, or place it in the sun. Once dry, you can simply peel the emulsion off. If you're using a different colour next, either wash it out, use a liner, or use a different tray.

STEP 9 Hang up the roller until all water has dripped off the roller and it is in a dry condition, ready to use again.

STEP 10 Using a paint brush, remove any remaining paint found in the paint kettle and roller tray back into the paint tin (stock pot). Wash the paint kettle (and paint tray if required) using clean running water.

STEP 11 Use a brush comb or the back of a knife to remove excess paint from your cutting-in brush into your stock pot.

Wash the paint off your brush and either hang up to dry, or dry in a flat position, and arrange the brush bristles in a straight direction.

Figure 6.68 Using a brush comb

PRACTICAL TIP

Remember, if you use the same brush you used to cut in, you can save washing time.

TEST YOURSELF

1. Why should you avoid painting in direct sunlight?

   a. So you don't get sunburnt

   b. So that the paint doesn't dry too quickly

   c. Because the light is too bright

   d. Because it takes longer

2. Why should dust and debris be cleared before painting?

   a. Dust can get stuck in your paint finish, causing bittiness

   b. A dusty environment can be a respiratory hazard

   c. Debris can be a trip hazard

   d. All of the above

3. What should you do with door furniture before you start painting?

   a. Leave it on the door, but use masking tape to cover it

   b. Take it off and place it on the ground

   c. Take it off and wrap it carefully

   d. a or c

4. What is the most important disadvantage of using polythene sheeting?

   a. It is expensive

   b. It is not waterproof

   c. It requires taping down to stay in place

   d. It is disposable

5. Which part of a paint brush is called the 'ferrule'?

   a. The metal that joins the filling and the handle

   b. The handle

   c. The adhesive that sticks the bristles together

   d. Synthetic bristles

6. What type of roller sleeve would you use for a textured or rough surface?

   a. Mohair

   b. Long pile

   c. Foam

   d. Short pile

7. How much paint should you pour into your paint kettle?

   a. Fill it up to the top

   b. Fill a quarter of the kettle

   c. Fill it to about halfway

   d. Fill three-quarters of the kettle

8. What is laying off?

   a. The last paint stroke that blends in a section of paint

   b. Getting enough paint on your brush

   c. Painting in a straight line along the edges of a surface

   d. Finishing your painting for the day

9. What is the first section you should paint on a panelled door?

   a. The top

   b. The centre

   c. The sides

   d. The panels

10. What is grinning?

    a. Where the paint has run down the surface

    b. Where the colour underneath shows through

    c. Where dust and debris has become caught under the coating

    d. Where the roller edge leaves patches of thicker paint

Chapter 7

Unit CSA L1OCC15
APPLY FOUNDATION AND PLAIN PAPERS

LEARNING OUTCOMES

LO1/2: Know how to and be able to prepare the work area and protect the surrounding area

LO3/4: Know how to and be able to maintain and store tools and equipment required for applying papers

LO5/6: Know how to and be able to select and prepare adhesives required for applying papers

LO7/8: Know how to and be able to apply lining, wood ingrain and non-matching papers to walls

LO9/10: Know how to and be able to store materials

INTRODUCTION

The aims of this chapter are to:

* help you select and prepare appropriate adhesives for the papers to be applied

* help you plan, set out and apply lining and plain papers to walls.

PREPARING AND PROTECTING THE WORK AND SURROUNDING AREA

PPE

Refer to Chapter 1 for details about the PPE that is required. In particular, when applying foundation papers you will need to wear overalls and safety glasses or goggles. Your college or workplace may have additional requirements that you should follow.

Considerations when preparing the work area

When preparing an area for applying wallpaper, there are different things to consider about the space you will be working in.

* Are there any doors and windows that will need their furniture removed?

* Are there any fixtures and fittings on walls and ceilings (e.g. lamp shades, smoke alarms, light switches, pictures, shelves) that will need to be removed?

* Is there adequate access to premises?

* Are there any carpets or rugs that will need to be rolled up and stored? Floorboards that will need to be covered?

* Is the lighting strong enough to work by?

* Is the site open to the public? Will members of the public need to be protected from your work? Will you need to protect your work area from them?

* Will other trades require access to the same spaces you'll be working in?

* What climate or weather will you be working in? Is it very dry or very humid? Or are you papering a moist area, such as a bathroom?

* Is the temperature of your workspace too warm or cold for your work?

* Is there adequate ventilation, e.g. from exhaust fans or windows?

* Is there any dust and debris that needs to be removed before you begin?

A note about light fittings: While it is safe for you to remove the lamp shades, the actual fitting should be removed by a qualified electrician. The mains power should stay turned off and the fuse should be removed, or use a sign warning others not to turn the power back on. Working with electricity is covered in more detail in Chapter 1, page 28.

REED TIP

Working as a painter and decorator is about people, not just technical skills. You won't just be decorating a room, for instance, you'll be delivering a service.

Preparing the work area

Remind yourself about the use, maintenance and storage of protective sheeting in Chapter 6, page 169.

Look back at pages 167–168 to remind yourself how to protect furnishings and fittings.

Protecting the work and surrounding area from damage

Revisit Chapters 4 and 5, pages 102–103 and 131–132, to remind yourself about the need to protect your work and the surrounding area from damage. Look also at Chapter 6 pages 167–169 for the tools and equipment you will need to help you protect the area.

MAINTAINING AND STORING TOOLS AND EQUIPMENT

Table 7.1 below describes the tools and equipment you will need for applying wallpaper, what they are used for, and how to care for and maintain them.

Tools and equipment	Correct uses	Care and maintenance
Tape measure (Fig 7.1)	An essential tool for taking measurements. Usually retractable.	Keep clean and free of adhesive which can stop it from retracting properly.
Folding ruler (Fig 7.2)	A metre-long, wooden ruler that can be folded away. Used for measuring lengths and widths of an area.	
Plumb bob (Fig 7.3)	A small metallic weight attached to a line of cord, used for checking whether a wall line is vertically straight. A spirit level can also be used.	

Tools and equipment	Correct uses	Care and maintenance
Chalk and line (Fig 7.4)	Chalk is used for marking along the plumb line which then guides where to hang your first length of paper. The chalked line is held taut, then plucked so that it springs back against the wall and leaves a chalk mark. It comes in a reel (often 30 m long) and a case.	If the string begins to fray, cut off the affected section and reattach the line to the metal clip. Chalk line cartridges will need to be replaced from time to time.
Paste brush (Fig 7.5)	A brush used for applying paste to the paper. Can also be used for washing down.	Wash after use with warm, soapy water. Rinse and allow it to dry before storing.
Paste table	A folding table used for cutting, measuring and pasting papers. Also known as a pasteboard.	Keep surface and edges clean and free from adhesive as you go. A dirty surface will affect the paper you are working with.
Sponges (Fig 7.6)	Used for cleaning down your paste table regularly, wiping paste from surfaces such as door frames and skirtings, and excess paste from washable papers.	Keep your sponge clean or it will contaminate the surfaces you are trying to clean.
Bucket (Fig 7.7)	Used for mixing and keeping your paste in.	Clean after use to make sure that adhesive doesn't dry on the inside of it.
Seam roller (Fig 7.8)	Used for rolling down the edges of papers where they join, i.e. at the seams. Should only be used for non-embossed papers.	Keep roller clean and free from adhesive. Lubricate only as needed.
Paperhanging shears (Fig 7.9)	Long-bladed scissors, used for cutting lengths and trimming paper.	Must be kept sharp and clean. When cutting pre-pasted paper, wipe clean after each use. Do not scrub with abrasive paper or it will blunt the blades.
Paperhanging brush (Fig 7.10)	A wide brush of natural or synthetic bristles, used for smoothing air bubbles from paper when applied to wall or ceiling.	Avoid getting paste on the bristles. Keep clean by washing in warm, soapy water after use. Hang to dry.
Trimming knife (Fig 7.11)	Used for trimming and cutting in tight spaces or at angles. Sometimes with a retractable blade.	Keep knife edge sharp, snap off blade or replace blade as needed. A blunt blade will tear rather than cut your paper.

Table 7.1 Tools and equipment for applying papers

Figure 7.1 Tape measure

Figure 7.2 Folding ruler

Figure 7.3 Plumb bob

Figure 7.4 Chalk and line

Figure 7.5 Paste brush

Figure 7.6 Sponges

Figure 7.7 Bucket

Figure 7.8 Seam roller

Figure 7.9 Paperhanging shears

Figure 7.10 Paperhanging brush

Figure 7.11 Trimming knife

Storing tools and equipment

All of your wallpapering tools should be cleaned and dried straight after use, before being stored. Adhesive that has been left to dry will cause your tools to deteriorate. Tools should be stored in an area that:

* is dry and well-ventilated

* is secure

* has a regular temperature (not too hot, not too cold)

* is free from direct sunlight or frost.

A damp storage area can cause mildew (mould) to grow on your tools. Your metallic tools, such as shears, knives and tape measures, can also be affected by rust which will blunt your blades and cause mechanisms to stick. The damp can rot your wooden tools too.

By keeping your tools off the ground, e.g. by using shelves and hooks, you will reduce the risk of your tools getting wet or damp. Hanging your brushes up will help them to dry more quickly.

SELECTING AND PREPARING ADHESIVES FOR APPLYING PAPERS

Types of adhesive

Also known as wallpaper paste, adhesives are applied to the back of papers to stick them to the surface. There are three main types of adhesive that you will use for applying wallpapers. They each have advantages and disadvantages, so choose wisely depending on the job you're doing. See Table 7.2 below to compare the three main types.

Type of adhesive	Advantages	Disadvantages
Cellulose paste – has the highest water content of all the adhesives. It comes as a white powder in boxes and sachets and must be mixed with water just before use. It tends to be used with lightweight papers.	• Ease of application • Cheap to buy • Easy to mix • Doesn't tend to stain the wallpaper • Has a long life before application – does not rot • Contains a fungicide to stop mould growth	• Not strong enough to hold heavier papers • Not as adhesive as starch paste • Excess water content can cause paper to expand and distort • High water content can become trapped behind non-breathable papers, causing damage to plaster
Starch paste – also known as 'flour adhesive' or 'cold water paste', it is made from wheat flour. It comes in sachets to be sifted to cold water, then whisked to avoid lumps. It has less water content than cellulose paste, but more than ready-mixed.	• Can be used for lightweight to heavyweight, textured papers • Now contains a fungicide to stop mould growth and sometimes preservatives to prolong life	• More expensive than cellulose • Harder to mix • Shorter life – rots after a couple of days, so must be used fresh • Easily stains the wallpaper

Type of adhesive	Advantages	Disadvantages
Ready-mixed – a PVA-based paste that comes pre-prepared in a tub. It is thicker than the other pastes and must be diluted first.	• The most adhesive of the three types • Can be used with heavy weight papers and vinyls • Can be pasted directly onto the wall surface for some papers • Contains a fungicide to stop mould growth • Has a long life before application – does not rot	• More expensive than other pastes • Comes in larger, heavier packaging than flakes or powders • Can be too thick (hard to apply) and may need to be diluted

Table 7.2 Advantages and disadvantages of adhesives

Figure 7.12 Different types of adhesive

Factors affecting the consistency of adhesives

It is always best to follow the paper manufacturer's instructions when choosing your paste. A good rule of thumb is: the heavier the paper, the stronger the paste needs to be.

Adhesives don't always produce the same result when used under different conditions. The more consistent your paste, the better your final finish will be. Here are some factors that will affect how consistent your adhesive is and how well your adhesive works:

* Incorrect preparation – e.g. adding too much or not enough water, not leaving paste on paper long enough before applying to wall, not stirring paste enough.

* Paper type – e.g. using cellulose paste for vinyl paper which may not give immediate adhesion.

* Paper weight – e.g. using cellulose paste for a heavy paper such as woodchip.

* Surface – e.g. pasting onto an uneven surface without a lining paper, or where a porous surface absorbs the paste.

* Room/air temperature – this can affect how quickly the paste dries, e.g. a cold, damp room will cause paste to dry to slowly, and a hot room will dry the paste out more quickly, leading to dry edges.

* Shelf life – starch paste has a very limited life and shouldn't be used if it has perished.

Defects caused by incorrect consistency of adhesives

If you don't achieve the correct consistency of adhesive for the paper you're using, you risk ending up with the following defects.

Blisters

Raised pockets of air called blisters or bubbles can appear on the wallpaper. Blisters can occur if:

* the paper has not been properly brushed after application

* the wrong paste has been used

* patches of wall have been missed or pasted twice

* the lining paper underneath has not been applied correctly.

Delamination

Delamination is where the patterned or visible side of the wallpaper has come away from its backing. This can happen if the paste has soaked through the paper too much.

Stretching

If the wallpaper has been moved up the wall after it has been pasted, this can cause horizontal stretching. The paper can also stretch vertically from the weight of the paste if too much has been used, or if its consistency is too thick. The problem with stretching is that it can create gaps between the edges or seams. If the paper has a pattern, then stretching can mean the pattern no longer matches up.

Health and environmental hazards

Wear the right PPE when working with adhesives. Wallpaper adhesives should never be:

* inhaled

* ingested (eaten)

* touched with bare skin for long periods

* allowed to get into eyes.

REED TIP

If you're having trouble, always ask for help. It's better to ask and find out than to blunder on and make mistakes. By getting the help you need, you'll learn the skills properly, you'll avoid wasting time and money, and you'll have a better chance of succeeding in your future career.

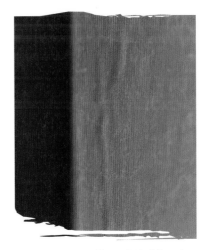

Figure 7.13 Blistering

Most wallpaper adhesives now contain a fungicide to reduce the chances of mould forming on or behind the paper. However, these can cause allergic skin rashes or conditions such as eczema.

Like many other decorating materials, leftover wallpaper adhesive should not be released into the ground or into the drains. Even though some pastes are water based, they should still not be disposed of into the water supply, particularly if it contains a fungicide. You can wait for the paste to dry out, then dispose of it as household waste.

As starch paste is made from a natural ingredient, it is not considered harmful to the environment, but bear in mind that pouring any sort of adhesive down a drain can cause it to be blocked.

APPLYING LINING, WOOD INGRAIN AND NON-MATCHING PAPERS TO WALLS

PRACTICAL TIP

Remember to always check the manufacturer's instructions on your materials. They will often contain health and safety guidance.

Hazards, health and safety

Many of the potential hazards of applying papers are the same as those for preparing surfaces and painting.

PPE

Depending on the requirements of your college or workplace, you are likely to need a number of items of PPE when applying wallpapers. In particular, you will want to have access to your:

* gloves – to avoid prolonged skin contact with adhesives

* overalls – to protect your clothes and skin

* dust mask – for when mixing adhesive powder

* eye glasses or goggles – to protect from paste and dust.

Planning the work

Before you cut any paper or apply it to the surface, there are a number of things you need to check and consider. Unless you plan ahead, you may find yourself in the middle of a job using the wrong materials, having to buy extra supplies, or having to start over again.

Check the roll:

* to read the manufacturer's instructions

* for any damage to the paper

* to see if the batch numbers are all the same

* to look at the pattern and note whether it is a **straight match** or **drop match**

* to see which way up the paper should go on the wall.

Starting and finishing point

You should always choose a starting and finishing point for your wallpapers so that the pattern matches up and that any mismatches are not too visible. Your starting point should be marked with a plumb bob and line from the top of the wall, either marking with chalk or pencil (see practical task *Measure and mark lines to hang wallpaper*, page 222).

When working with plain, un-patterned papers, it is usual to start papering next to the natural light source, i.e. the window. Use your marker line to line up the edge of the paper. You should then work around the room in a direction away from that light source so that you don't cast a shadow over the area you're papering.

Working with patterned wallpaper

When using a patterned paper on a feature such as a chimney breast (or the **focal wall**), then the paper should be aligned in the very centre of the feature or focal wall rather than to one side of your marker (see Fig 7.14). However, this may depend on the width of your focal wall: if the paper edges would end up too close to the corners, you may need to adjust your starting point. A large pattern should be centralised with a full motif appearing at the top of the wall.

The pattern on wallpaper can be either a straight match or a drop match. Fig 7.15 shows the difference between the two types.

If you are working with a straight match, you can work from the same roll of paper. But if it is a drop match, you will need to cut lengths from

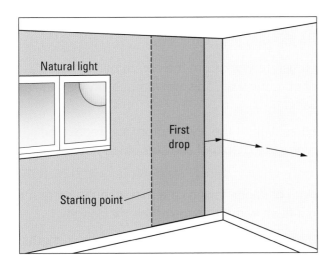

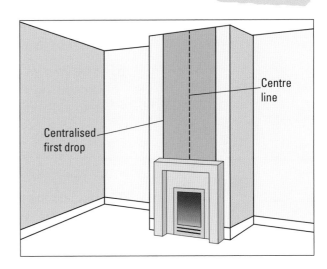

Figure 7.14 Starting points for wallpaper

Figure 7.15a A straight match

Figure 7.15b A drop match

two different rolls side by side. This will reduce waste. See the practical task *Shade, measure and cut batches of lengths of paper* on page 220 for how to cut drop match paper.

Walls, features and obstacles

Not all rooms are perfectly square and flat. Some rooms will be of different shapes, or have features such as chimney breasts, staircases, windows and doors. Most rooms will have small obstacles such as light switches and power points. These shapes, features and obstacles are not a problem, but need to be thought about when planning and applying the paper.

Papering walls

When papering a wall vertically:

1. Use the plumb line as your starting point marker.

2. Hold up the first length of pasted and folded paper.

3. Starting at the ceiling, open up the first and longest section only, taking care not to allow the rest of the folded paper to drop – the weight of the pasted paper could cause it to tear.

4. Once the first section is touching the wall, carefully slide it along the wall to align perfectly with the plumb line.

5. Use your wallpaper brush to work from the centre outwards, smoothing the paper onto the wall. This will remove any air bubbles trapped under the paper.

6. Gently allow the next section of the fold to drop, and repeat the same process until you have unfolded and smoothed down the whole length.

7. Hold up the next length of paper, taking care to match the pattern if necessary, and align it flush with the edge of the first length.

8. Use a seam roller to press down the join between the two lengths (so long as the paper is not embossed).

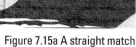

PRACTICAL TIP

When cutting around obstacles with wood ingrain paper, you cannot use a craft knife, but must instead use scissors. It is very hard to cut through the chips of wood and a knife can cause the paper to tear.

9. Press the paper into the corner edges of the ceiling and the skirting boards. You can use the back of your scissors, your wallpaper brush, or a straight edge.

10. Lift the paper back slightly, then cut along the edge mark you just made to trim the excess paper.

11. Press the paper back into place.

12. Using a wet sponge, wipe away any extra paste from both the paper and any surfaces nearby, such as the skirting boards.

You can practise your basic wallpapering skills by completing the practical task on page 226, *Apply paste and papers to walls and corners*.

Papering ceilings
When applying paper to a ceiling:

1. Find your starting point by measuring the width of one length of paper from the edge. If working with patterned paper, the centre line of the wall will be your starting point.

2. Work away from your source of natural light so you don't cast shadows on the seams.

3. If working on an irregular shaped room, hang the longest piece of wallpaper first.

4. Use a **decorator's crutch** to help you hold the folds of paper in place.

5. Align and smooth the paper, working backwards along the ceiling and unfolding as you go.

6. Continue with the next length of paper, sliding it along the ceiling to match up the edges, and pattern if necessary.

7. When you reach the edge of the ceiling, you will probably need to cut the last length to measure the space left, allowing for up to 50 mm overlap.

8. Trim the side and edges using your knife or scissors.

9. Press and smooth the edge back down, and clean the surface.

Staircases
When papering a staircase, use your plumb line to find the longest drop. You should always paper along this length first, then the stairwell, upstairs to the landing, and finally down the stairs to the hallway.

Around windows and doors
When hanging paper around a door or window frame, do as follows:

1. Hang the paper as you usually would from the ceiling edge, but allowing the paper to drop over the frame.

2. Mark the corner and edges of the frame on the paper.

3. Cut the excess paper away into the corners you've marked.

4. Smooth the paper onto the wall along the frame into the corners.

5. Trim the excess paper from the edge of the frame.

PRACTICAL TIP

Be sure to leave some overlap at the top and bottom edges of your wall – 40 to 50 mm is enough. You will trim this excess off later.

PRACTICAL TIP

Take care not to press your seam roller too hard on textured or embossed papers as this could flatten the pattern.

KEY TERMS

Decorator's crutch

– a support made of a roll of paper, some cardboard or a straight edge, used to stop your folded paper from creasing or bending when papering a ceiling.

PRACTICAL TIP

When papering on ceilings and staircases, make sure you have the right sort of stable platform to work from. It should run the entire length of the room or length of paper.

See the practical task on on page 233, *Apply papers around obstacles: recessed windows* for step-by-step instructions on how to handle this feature.

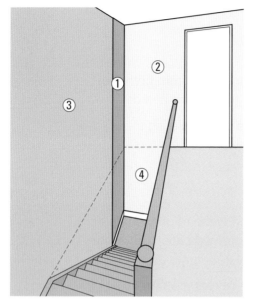

Figure 7.16 The order for papering a staircase

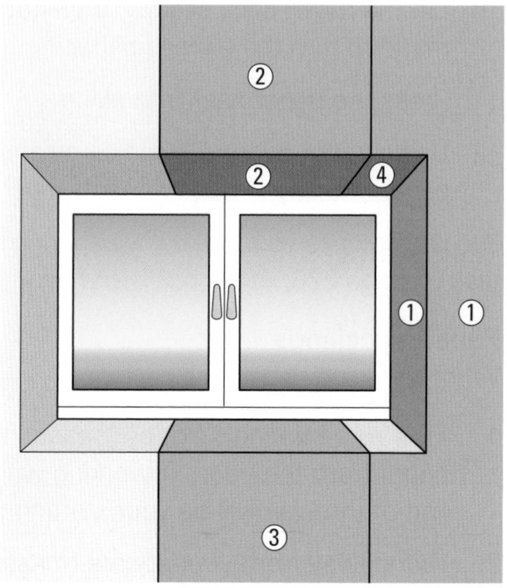

Figure 7.17 Order for applying paper to a recessed window

CASE STUDY

Learning doesn't stop with college

Kieran St Julien, who completed his Level 1 qualification at college before starting his own business, says:

'Have I acquired any new skills? Yes, absolutely. Every day you can come across something you've never seen before. But you can't always ask someone else when you're working on your own. Sometimes you just have to do a bit of problem solving.

For instance, at college we learnt how to apply wallpaper around plug sockets and light switches, but they had only ever been those ones that are quite close to the wall. One day I came across these sockets that came a good 2 inches or so out of the wall.

First of all, I just went ahead and did it how I had been taught, but of course it didn't work. Before I had another try, I had to step back, look at the problem and think carefully about how it would look and how the paper would drop. I got it right the second time around. I guess it's a mistake I'll only make once!'

Light switches and power points

When papering around light switches and power points, you will need to cut space in the paper for the fitting. See the practical task on page 232, *Apply papers around obstacles: light switches and sockets* for step-by-step instructions on how to go about this.

Prominent features

As already mentioned, when papering a strong feature or focal wall, the paper should be centralised, if you are using a pattern. This will make the room feel balanced.

Internal angles

If you were to keep papering around an internal corner without trimming it first, you would end up with wrinkles and it will not be straight. This process is also used just in case the corner is out of plumb which could mean the edges otherwise wouldn't meet.

When papering into an internal corner, do as follows:

1. Measure the width from the last length you hung into the corner. Add an extra 5–10mm to this width before you cut the paper.

2. When hanging the paper, make sure you push it well into the corner using a straight edge or similar.

3. You can then use the leftover part of the paper to start papering again on the next wall, hanging the paper right into the corner.

4. Check with a plumb bob and mark your straight line before you hang the length on the next wall.

5. Make sure you cover the overlap and take care to match up any pattern. If you are working with a patterned paper, aim for an overlap of no more than 5mm, otherwise you risk losing the pattern.

Figure 7.18 Cutting paper around a power point

PRACTICAL TIP

When working around power points, light fittings and light switches, make sure the electricity has been turned off.

PRACTICAL TIP

When working in older buildings, you may find that not all walls are the same height or width from edge to edge. When measuring your internal corners, measure near the top, the middle and bottom, adding your 5–10mm to the widest measurement.

External angles

When papering around an external angle, once again ensure you have a significant overlap (25–50mm). In the same way as you would for an internal corner, once you've papered around the corner, mark a plumb line on the next wall before applying your next section of wallpaper over the top of the overlap.

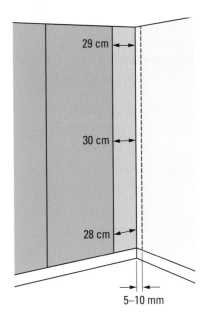

Figure 7.19 Papering around an internal corner

Calculating the quantity of paper needed

There are two ways of calculating how much paper you will need to cover an area. It is important to work this out so that there is not too much excess or wastage or not enough paper once you've started.

Girthing method

This way of measuring out the room uses the width (girth) of the wallpaper roll itself. See the practical task on page 218, *Calculate quantities of materials* for step-by-step instructions on how to use both the girthing method and area method (described below).

Note that the girthing method is not the most accurate, though it is quick and easy. You may wish to allow for an extra roll of paper in case of any miscalculations.

Area method

The area method is more precise as it uses the actual dimensions of the entire room, taking into account any areas that will not be papered, such as doors and windows.

Each wall must be measured separately or otherwise measurements taken from a drawing. The area of each wall or ceiling is calculated by multiplying the width by the height, including any doors or windows. Next, the area of each non-papered surface should have its area calculated. This amount should be subtracted from the total area of the room.

Once you have the total area that needs papering, you must find out the surface area of each roll of paper you are using. Divide this amount into the total surface area for the room. See the example calculations in the practical task on page 218 for a room with one door and one window.

Note that there can be a quite a bit of paper wastage in the wallpapering process. It is best to allow for this by adding an extra 15 to 20 per cent to the amount of paper you bring to complete a job.

Marking lines

Marking lines on your surface before you start is essential. Without a straight line to work from, you cannot achieve straight wallpaper. A marking line should be made at your starting point, but also every time you paper around an internal or external angle or corner. Remember, however, that if you are working with patterned paper, your starting point may be in the centre of a strong focal point, such as a chimney breast.

When papering vertically, you will find your marking line using a plumb bob or a spirit level. When papering horizontally, you still need to find a straight line using a spirit level.

To mark behind your plumb bob line, you can use a pencil or a chalk line with a weight attached. The chalk line is pulled away from the wall, and then released, which flicks the wall and leaves a chalk mark. To mark a

You'll be using your literacy and numeracy skills to keep accurate records, e.g. keeping track of how quickly you use the stock in your van so you don't run out, or working out how much paint or wallpaper you need to buy.

PRACTICAL TIP

Most tradespeople prefer to work in millimetres. To do this, convert all of your measurements to the same unit of measurement before you make your calculations.

line using a spirit level, simply use a pencil to draw along the straight edge of the level. For a more high-tech option, you can use a laser level to find your line. You can either attach it to the wall while you're working (although this can be awkward) or you can draw a mark underneath the laser line. There are also standalone laser lines that stand in the centre of a room and cast a horizontal line.

Application sequence for pasting paper

There are different ways that paper is pasted to the wall. Some papers come ready with their own dried adhesive, some need the paste to be applied directly to the wall, while others need the paste to be painted onto the back of the paper. Check the manufacturer's instructions before pasting your paper – they will tell you what types of paste you should use.

When applying paste to paper, remember the following:

1. Make sure you have used a dust sheet to cover the floor or any other surface you don't want to drip paste on.

2. Set up your pasting table in the middle of the room.

3. Put your paste bucket on the floor by the table, but not on the table itself, just in case it spills.

4. Put another empty bucket or box under your table to collect any paper off-cuts.

5. A third bucket filled with clean, warm water should be ready nearby for sponging off extra adhesive and for cleaning your table.

6. Lay out your length of paper with the back of the paper facing you.

7. Align the edge of the paper with the edge of your table. This will help to keep the table free of paste.

8. Take your pasting brush and apply the paste from the centre of the paper outwards. Paste the half of the length that is close to the edge.

9. Move your paper to the other edge of the table before pasting the second half. Paste as before, making sure that the entire paper surface is covered with adhesive.

10. Check that your paste has not left any brush bristles or lumps on the paper.

11. When you've pasted the section on your table, gently fold the edges of the paper into the centre (**end to centre** method) or make a **concertina fold**, ready to apply to the surface.

12. Clean your table around the edges to get rid of any paste, otherwise you might get paste on the face of your next length of paper.

If you are working with a ready-pasted paper, then the dried adhesive will need to be soaked in a trough of cold water. Place the trough on the floor by the wall that is to be covered. When it has been soaked for the time stated in the instructions, gently pull the top edge of the paper out of the water and place it on the wall as usual.

KEY TERMS

End to centre

– a way of folding paper that is simply folding each end of the paper into the centre with pasted edges together.

Concertina fold

– a way of folding paper that looks like a concertina (piano accordion). The small folds of about 35 cm are made paste-side to paste-side and face-side to face-side. They can be easily lifted and unfolded when applying the paper to the surface.

PRACTICAL TIP

Try stretching a piece of string across the top of your paste bucket so you can scrape excess paste back into the bucket. The string can also be used to rest your brush on when you're not pasting.

There are papers that require you to apply the paste directly to the wall first, and these are becoming more common. The paper has a special backing that will not expand when it is wet, whereas traditional papers need to expand, which is why they are left to soak with the paste on.

'Paste the wall' wallpaper can be a quicker and cleaner way of applying paper. Because the paper is dry, it weighs less. This reduces the possibility of tearing. Note that the wall should only be pasted one length or section at a time. If you paste the whole wall in one go, the paste will dry too quickly and the paper won't stick.

Checking the consistency of paste

If your paste is too thin, it can soak through to the face of the paper and damage it. The paste can also be messier to work with. If your paste is too thick, it will be harder to apply. The weight of the paper you're working with can also affect whether the paste is the right consistency to stick to the surface.

Always follow the manufacturer's instructions when mixing your own paste. It is better to start with too little water, and thin it gradually. You can't take excess water out of the paste!

You may need to let some pastes stand, say for 10–20 minutes, to help it achieve the right consistency. Take care not to add your adhesive to the water too quickly, as this can cause lumps.

The importance of aligning pasted edges

It is essential when folding your pasted paper that the edges are carefully aligned. This is to stop any paste getting onto the table or the face of the paper. Paste can stain and damage the decorative finish of wallpaper.

Defects

Table 7.3 below shows you the different kinds of wallpapering defects you might come across, their causes and how to avoid them.

Defect	Cause	How to avoid
Creasing (Fig 7.20)	• Uneven surfaces • Too much brushing • Not enough smoothing • Heavy-handed seam rolling	• Ensure surfaces are properly prepared. • Take care when handling, brushing, smoothing and rolling the paper.
Overlapping edges	• Over brushing • Heavy-handed seam rolling	• Use the wallpaper brush only enough to remove air bubbles and smooth the paper. • Don't push too hard with the seam roller, or avoid using a seam roller at all. • Make sure that you are applying to a plumb line.

Defect	Cause	How to avoid
Blisters or bubbles (Fig 7.21)	• Careless smoothing • Lumps in paste • Uneven pasting • Wrong adhesive • Blistering on lining paper • Incorrect soaking time	• Ensure you brush all the air bubbles out. If some will not come out, gently lift paper and smooth down again. • Remove any lumps from paste before applying to wall. • Ensure paste covers the entire back of the paper. • Always read manufacturer's instructions before choosing adhesive. • Ensure your lining paper has adhered properly before applying decorative paper. • Check that you are using the right soaking time.
Tears (Fig 7.22)	• Using thin paste • Blunt cutting tools • Careless paper handling	• Check the consistency and type of your paste. • Ensure your tools are kept clean and sharp so they cut cleanly. • Don't allow your paper folds to drop suddenly.
Polished edges	• Paste seeping through the joins • Using too much paste • Over brushing • Heavy-handed seam rolling • Too much rubbing with a rag or sponge	• Use the right type, consistency and amount of paste. • Any paste that gets on the decorative surface should be wiped clean with a warm, wet sponge. • Don't apply too much pressure to your seam roller. • Be gentle when cleaning up your paper.
Open joints (Fig 7.23)	• Poor alignment of paper • Uneven surfaces • Thin paste • Careless smoothing • Stretching the paper • Over brushing • Incorrect soaking time	• Ensure that you slide the paper so it meets the edge. • Prepare your surfaces well and/or use lining paper. • Choose and prepare your paste according to instructions. • Smooth from the centre to the edges, making sure the whole length is brushed. • Do not pull or tug at the paper as it will retract later when dry.
Loose edges/ peeling (Fig 7.24)	• Wrong paste used for paper • Not enough adhesion • Old or thin paste • Over-porous surface	• Always check the manufacturer's instructions before choosing your paste. • Mix paste as per instructions and ensure it is fresh if using starch adhesive. • Ensure surface is well prepared and/or lined.
Irregular cutting (Fig 7.25)	• Using blunt tools • Careless cutting technique	• Always keep your tools clean and sharp. • Don't rush your cutting, take care to follow your measurements and cut in a straight line.
Paste staining/ surface marking (Fig 7.26)	• Careless brushing • Dirty paste table • Wrong paste used • Paste too thin	• Align your paper edges to the table when pasting. • Wipe down your table after pasting each length. • Use the correct paste with the correct consistency.

Defect	Cause	How to avoid
Corners incorrectly negotiated	• Poor planning • Inaccurate marking of plumb line	• Make sure you have thought out your starting point, looking ahead to any obstacles or features. • Allow your plumb line to be steady before marking.
Inaccurate plumbing	• Incorrect use of tools • Not checking plumb lines frequently	• Make sure there's enough chalk on your chalk line. • Wait for the plumb line to settle before marking. • Mark lines for your starting point and when working around corners.
Dry edges (Fig 7.27)	• Not enough paste • Lack of paste • Careless brushing	• Make sure your paste goes right to the edges. • Ensure that all of the paper is covered in paste.
Delamination	• Over soaking of paper	• Follow manufacturer's instructions for correct soaking time.

Table 7.3 Defects in wall coverings

Figure 7.20 Creasing

Figure 7.21 Blisters or bubbles

Figure 7.22 Tears

Figure 7.23 Open joints

Figure 7.24 Loose edges/ peeling

Figure 7.25 Irregular cutting

Figure 7.26 Paste staining/ surface marking

Figure 7.27 Dry edges

Use of lining

Lining paper is sometimes used to improve the quality of the surface you are papering onto. If a surface is too porous, is too patchy (e.g. where there have been several holes or cracks), has a solvent-based paint on it, or has a very strong colour, then a lining paper can smooth out these problems. Because solvent-based paints have low absorbency, there might be some difficulty in getting the decorative paper to stick properly; a lining paper creates a more porous surface.

Lining paper is also sometimes used as a preparatory surface for painting on, such as when damage to a wall has not been adequately fixed. In older properties, where there has been a repair and the surface has a different porosity, a lining paper may need to be used so that the surfaces are consistent.

When applying a lining paper, you should use the cross-lining technique. This is where the lining paper is hung horizontally instead of vertically. It avoids leaving the two layers of paper with the same joins over the top of each other. Often lining paper is a different width to decorative paper so this is unlikely to occur often, but cross-lining is the safer option.

STORING MATERIALS

Refresh your memory about storing materials in Chapter 6. Here are some extra points to keep in mind when storing wallpaper materials:

* Never store rolls of paper on their ends as this will damage and crease the edges of the paper.

* Don't store rolls of paper in too high a pile or they may get squashed out of shape.

* Keep rolls of paper out of direct sunlight as this can fade the colours and patterns.

* Keep the rolls of paper on a rack and not on the floor as frost and damp can cause the paper to degrade.

PRACTICAL TASK

1. PLAN THE POSITION OF PAPER HANGINGS

OBJECTIVE

To be able to plan the position of paper hangings, find the starting and finishing point and any focal points, taking into account obstacles such as doors and windows.

TOOLS AND EQUIPMENT

Pencil and paper

Tape measure

PPE

Ensure you select PPE appropriate to the job and site conditions where you are working. Refer to the PPE section of Chapter 1.

STEP 1 In order to successfully complete a wallpapering job you must fully plan the starting and finishing points, taking into account the different elements of the room.

Take your tape measure and measure the dimensions of the room including:

- ceiling to top of skirting boards
- wall to wall
- any doors and windows
- chimney breasts or feature walls.

Make sure you take a note of each measurement.

STEP 2 Take your pencil and paper and create a rough sketch of the room, including doors and windows and any irregular shapes in the room (see Fig. 7.14 on page 207).

STEP 3 Identify whether there are any feature walls such as a chimney breast which would be a focal point.

STEP 4 If there are no noticeable feature walls, identify which wall will be your starting point by looking at where the greatest source of natural light is as you enter the room. This will tend to be the wall that your eye is first drawn to.

PRACTICAL TIP

By working around the room away from the light source, you won't cast a shadow over the area that you are papering.

PRACTICAL TASK

2. CALCULATE QUANTITIES OF MATERIALS

OBJECTIVE

To work out how much paper will be needed to complete a job by using the girthing method and the area method.

PPE

Ensure you select PPE appropriate to the job and site conditions where you are working. Refer to the PPE section of Chapter 1.

TOOLS AND EQUIPMENT

Step ladder

Pencil and paper

Tape measure

A roll of the paper you will be using

Chalk

GIRTHING METHOD

STEP 1 Take your roll of paper and, starting at one corner, place it against the wall. Make a mark of where each width ends, working your way around the room. In Fig 7.28, red chalk is shown for clarity but normally painters and decorators would use a pale chalk to avoid colour showing through the paper or transferring onto the surface.

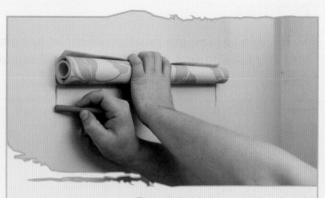

Figure 7.28 Marking widths of paper

PRACTICAL TIP

Always check the dimensions of the paper you're using before making calculations. While most wallpapers are 10 m long, and often 53 cm wide, this can vary and will affect your sums.

STEP 2 Measure the height of the room from the ceiling to the skirting boards.

Use this measurement to see how many lengths you can cut from the one roll (usually 10 m long);

e.g. if the room is 2.3 m in height, then you might get 4 lengths out of each roll of paper:

$$\frac{10\,m}{2.3\,m} = 4.34 \text{ lengths}$$

Note: You should allow for 50 mm excess at each end of the length, i.e. a total of 100 mm, so:

$$\frac{10\,m}{2.4\,m} = 4.16 \text{ lengths}$$

If the height is 3 metres, then you will get 3 lengths per roll:

$$\frac{10\,m}{3.1\,m} = 3.22 \text{ lengths}$$

STEP 3 Counting the sections you have marked around the room will tell you how many lengths you need in total.

Work out how many rolls of paper you will need for the room, for example:

No. of lengths required = 36

Height of wall from ceiling to skirting = 2.3 m

Add 100 mm (0.1 m for excess), making it 2.4 m

Length of roll = 10 m

No. of lengths per roll: $\frac{10\,m}{2.4\,m} = 4.16$ lengths (round this down to 4)

No. of rolls required: $\frac{36}{4} = 9$ rolls

AREA METHOD

STEP 1 Measure the height of the room from the ceiling to the skirting boards.

STEP 2 Measure each wall separately (or take measurements from a drawing).

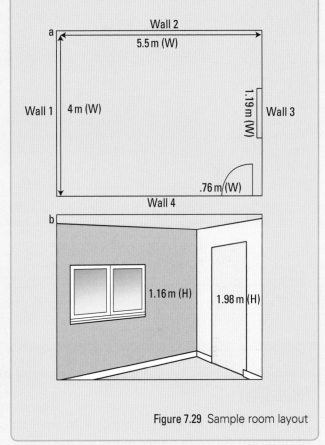

Figure 7.29 Sample room layout

STEP 3 Calculate the area by multiplying each wall by its height, e.g. using the measurements from Fig 7.29 above:

Walls 1 and 3: 2.5 m (H) × 4 m (W) = 10 m²

Walls 2 and 4: 2.5 m (H) × 5.5 m (W) = 13.75 m²

Total surface area of room: (2 × 10 m²) + (2 × 13.75 m²) = 47.5 m²

STEP 4 Measure the areas that will not need paper, such as doors and windows, e.g. using the measurements from Fig 7.29:

Door: 1.98m (H) × .76m (W) = 1.5m²

Window: 1.16m (H) × 1.19m (W) = 1.38m²

STEP 5 Subtract the non-paper areas from the overall area of the room, e.g.:

47.5m² − 1.5m² − 1.38m² = 44.62m²

The total surface area to be papered is 44.62m²

STEP 6 Calculate the surface area of the wallpaper roll you'll be using, e.g. if the roll is 10m long and 52cm wide:

Surface area of wallpaper roll: 52m × 10m = 5.2m²

PRACTICAL TIP

If using a drop match pattern paper you must allow for using more paper.

STEP 7 Calculate the number of rolls required by taking your total surface area to be papered and dividing it by the surface area of one roll of paper, e.g.:

$$\frac{44.62\,m^2}{5.2\,m^2} = 8.58 \text{ rolls of paper}$$

So, the number of rolls required here would be 9 rolls.

PRACTICAL TIP

It is best to allow for a bit of paper wastage by adding an extra 15 to 20 per cent to the amount of paper you bring to complete a job. So, in the example above, if we add 20 per cent to 8.58 rolls:

8.58/5 = 1.716

or

8.58 × 20/100 = 1.716

Total number of rolls required: 8.58 + 1.716 = 10.296, i.e. 10 rolls if rounded down.

PRACTICAL TASK

3. SHADE, MEASURE AND CUT BATCHES OF LENGTHS OF PAPER

OBJECTIVE

To shade, measure and cut batches of lengths of different types of paper ready for pasting.

PPE

Ensure you select PPE appropriate to the job and site conditions where you are working. Refer to the PPE section of Chapter 1.

TOOLS AND EQUIPMENT

Wallpapers, one roll non-matching (such as a wood ingrain or straight match) and two rolls drop match

Scissors	Dust sheet
Tape measure	Pencil
Papering table	

STEP 1 Before you cut coloured (finished) papers you must check the shade of the colour is the same. Place one opened roll of paper on the papering table. Place a second roll on top and pull it to one side of the first roll.

The colour shade should be the same when comparing both rolls.

Check the wallpaper description leaflet for batch number, code number and in some cases the name of the paper.

Figure 7.30 Checking your papers

STEP 2 Prior to working with the paper, you must measure the length of the wall from ceiling height to the top of the skirting (known as the 'drop'), and using the girthing method, work out how many drops you will need to cover the one wall.

Take a note of your measurements on a sketch or in a notepad.

PRACTICAL TIP

When calculating the area of a room, and working out your lengths of paper, you will find it easier to use the same unit of measurement, e.g. millimetres, centimetres, or metres.

Figure 7.31 Measuring height of wall

STEP 3 Place the first roll of wallpaper on the papering table and cut to the same length as the wall height. Add approximately 50 mm top and bottom for waste cutting. This piece is known as the template.

Figure 7.32 Measuring the first piece

PRACTICAL TIP

If the paper has a pattern, make sure that a full pattern motif appears at the top of the paper.

Figure 7.33 Cutting the first piece

STEP 4 For a matching paper or a straight match pattern, use the same roll and position the next piece on top of the first piece and cut to the same length.

If working with a drop match pattern paper, you will need to cut from two rolls of paper to match up the pattern.

Remember to allow extra length for any pattern match. This will be trimmed off later.

Figure 7.34 Aligning a drop match pattern

DID YOU KNOW?

When you have 4–6 lengths of paper cut and ready to paste on your table, these are collectively known as a batch of papers.

STEP 5 Repeat until you have cut enough lengths cut to cover the one wall. The number of pieces you cut will depend on the width of the surface you are covering (see practical task 4, *Measure and mark lines to hang wallpaper*).

PRACTICAL TASK

4. MEASURE AND MARK LINES TO HANG WALLPAPER

OBJECTIVE

Measure and mark lines to hang wallpaper using a plumb line or spirit level.

TOOLS AND EQUIPMENT

Tape measure	Working platform
Plumb bob or spirit level	Hammer
Pencil or chalk line	Masonry nail (see practical tip)

PPE

Ensure you select PPE appropriate to the job and site conditions where you are working. Refer to the PPE section of Chapter 1.

STEP 1 Choose a starting position that will allow you to work away from the source of natural light, usually a window (see Fig 7.14 on page 207).

STEP 2 Using a pencil or chalk, mark the starting point at ceiling height. You will need low level access equipment for this, such as a step ladder.

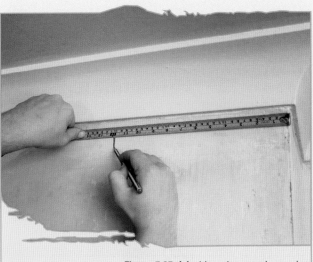

Figure 7.35 Marking the starting point

Figure 7.36 Marking the plumb line

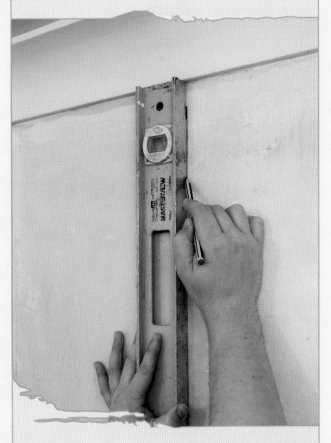

Figure 7.37 Marking the starting point with a spirit level

PRACTICAL TIP

The masonry nail is useful particularly if you are working on your own. When marking a straight line on the wall, a nail can be driven into the wall at ceiling height, the chalk line is then attached and allowed to drop down to the top of the skirting (held at this position) then pulled from the wall and allowed to hit the wall to leave a chalk mark on the wall (to obtain a true vertical line from the ceiling down the wall to the skirting).

PRACTICAL TIP

It is better to use pencil rather than chalk when you are a beginner. This is just in case you need to rehang a length of paper, as the chalk line would come off with the adhesive on the back of the paper.

STEP 3 Use a plumb line, or chalk line with a weight attached, to show true vertical. Wait for the line to stop moving, then either pluck the chalk line back or use your pencil to mark just behind the plumb line.

You can also use a spirit level. Place it in a vertical position and check that the bubble is showing plumb, then mark the wall on one side of the spirit level.

STEP 4 If there is a strong feature in the room, such as a chimney breast, you will need to measure the width and mark your line at the centre point of the feature. This is especially important when using patterned paper so that the centre of the pattern falls exactly in the middle of the focal point. This will provide a balanced effect.

When putting the paper over the centre line, first measure the width of the paper to calculate the middle point, then use this measurement to mark where the edge of the first drop should fall.

PRACTICAL TIP

Consider both the width of the chimney breast and the width of the wallpaper when deciding where to place your starting line. It may be that using the centre as your starting point will leave you with a wallpaper edge too close to the corners.

STEP 5 Mark another vertical line around the corner on the next wall. You will need this to correctly position your wallpaper again.

PRACTICAL TASK

5. SELECT AND PREPARE ADHESIVE

OBJECTIVE

To choose and prepare the appropriate adhesive, adjusting consistency for weight, atmosphere and substrate.

TOOLS AND EQUIPMENT

Bucket (with quantity markings)

Sponge

Stirring sick

Scissors

Correct type of paste

Measuring jug

PPE

Ensure you select PPE appropriate to the job and site conditions where you are working. Refer to the PPE section of Chapter 1.

STEP 1 Choose an appropriate adhesive (cellulose, starch or ready-mixed) by considering the following:

- the weight of your paper

- whether your paper is breathable

- where the paper will be hung (e.g. in a wet or dry area)

- how long the papering job will take

- whether it needs to be applied to the paper or directly to the wall.

PRACTICAL TIP

If you're applying wallpaper in a cold room, you might use a ready-mixed adhesive which will have a lower water content and therefore won't be affected by the cold atmosphere.

Another point to remember when selecting wallpaper adhesive is the surface you are working on: porous surfaces such as plaster and timber accept ready-mixed adhesive better than a water-based adhesive, which can be too easily absorbed.

STEP 2 Once you've chosen your paste, check the instructions for mixing it, e.g. how much water needs to be added.

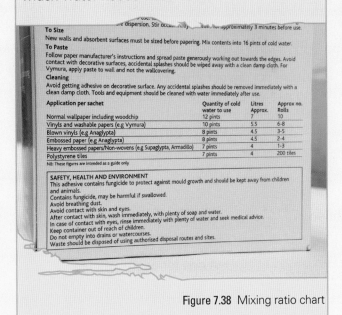

To Size

New walls and absorbent surfaces must be sized before papering. Mix contents into 16 pints of cold water.

To Paste

Follow paper manufacturer's instructions and spread paste generously working out towards the edges. Avoid contact with decorative surfaces, accidental splashes should be wiped away with a clean damp cloth. For Vymura, apply paste to wall and not the wallcovering.

Cleaning

Avoid getting adhesive on decorative surface. Any accidental splashes should be removed immediately with a clean damp cloth. Tools and equipment should be cleaned with water immediately after use.

Application per sachet	Quantity of cold water to use	Litres Approx.	Approx no. Rolls
Normal wallpaper including woodchip	12 pints	7	10
Vinyls and washable papers (e.g Vymura)	10 pints	5.5	6-8
Blown vinyls (e.g Anaglypta)	8 pints	4.5	3-5
Embossed paper (e.g Anaglypta)	8 pints	4.5	2-4
Heavy embossed papers/Non-wovens (e.g Supaglypta, Armadillo)	7 pints	4	1-3
Polystyrene tiles	7 pints	4	200 tiles

NB: These figures are intended as a guide only

SAFETY, HEALTH AND ENVIRONMENT

This adhesive contains fungicide to protect against mould growth and should be kept away from children and animals.
Contains fungicide, may be harmful if swallowed.
Avoid breathing dust.
Avoid contact with skin and eyes.
After contact with skin, wash immediately, with plenty of soap and water.
In case of contact with eyes, rinse immediately with plenty of water and seek medical advice.
Keep container out of reach of children.
Do not empty into drains or watercourses.
Waste should be disposed of using authorised disposal routes and sites.

Figure 7.38 Mixing ratio chart

STEP 3 Using a clean bucket add the correct amount of water in relation to the type of wallpaper you are working with. If the bucket does not have quantity markings, you can use a jug or even an old plastic 1-pint milk bottle (washed out first).

STEP 4 Using the stirring stick, stir the water to keep it moving before you add the cellulose powder adhesive. This will reduce the risk of lumps of paste forming.

STEP 5 Stir the mixture, following the manufacturer's instructions (usually for about 1½ minutes), then leave to stand for about 1–2 minutes. Stir the adhesive mixture again just prior to using the adhesive.

PRACTICAL TIP

Remember if you mix the adhesive as the manufacturers tell you the adhesive will act accordingly, that is the consistency will match the thickness, type and weight of the wallpaper.

STEP 6 If your adhesive is too thick, add water (small amounts at a time) until the consistency is acceptable.

If your adhesive is too thin, you will have to mix more adhesive in another bucket to a thick consistency.

Add the thin adhesive to the newly mixed (thick) adhesive, mixing together until the desired consistency is achieved. Remember that simply adding dry adhesive powder/flakes to mixed adhesive will result in lumps appearing in the adhesive.

6. APPLY PASTE AND PAPERS TO WALLS AND CORNERS

OBJECTIVE

To apply paste, fold lengths and soak wallpapers; to apply papers to wall, around corner, and trim neatly.

PPE

Ensure you select PPE appropriate to the job and site where you are working. Refer to the PPE section of Chapter 1.

TOOLS AND EQUIPMENT

Paste table/board	Cutting straight edge	Plastic rubbish bag for unwanted offcuts
Bucket of paste	Pencil	A box for useful offcuts
Stirring stick	Bucket for clean water	Wall brush (100 mm to 150 mm size)
Paperhanging brush	Sponge	Watch or clock
Scissors	Working platform	
Cleaning-up cloth	Two clean dust sheets	
Cutting knife	Paperhanger's apron	

APPLY PASTE TO PAPER

STEP 1 Position a dust sheet at the bottom of the wall you are working on. Place another dust sheet on the floor away from the work area (this dust sheet should be folded approximately 4 times, as it will be used to store pasted wallpaper ready for use).

STEP 2 Position the pasting table away from the wall to be papered. Position the bucket of paste to the right of the table if you are right-handed or to the left of the table if you are left-handed.

Figure 7.39 Setting up your paste table

STEP 3 Before you start to paste, mark the back of each length of paper, using a pencil, with numbers (1, 2 etc.) Number 1 should be the first length that you paste (and later, the first length that you hang).

STEP 4 Place one of the lengths from your batch of paper on the pasting table, face side down. Align the edge of the paper with the edge of the table furthest from you.

STEP 5 Apply paste using a wall brush size that you are comfortable with. Load the brush with paste, much like you would load a brush with emulsion paint. Apply the paste to the middle section first, then pasting away from you, paste from the middle towards to the furthest edge.

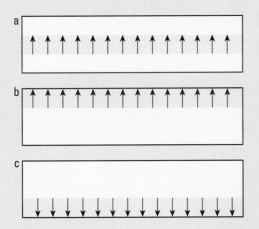

Figure 7.40 Correct sequence for applying wallpaper paste

Figure 7.41 Applying paste to furthest edge

STEP 6 Once the furthest edge is fully coated in paste, slide the paper towards you to align it to the edge closest to you. Apply your paste from the middle towards the closest edge.

Figure 7.42 Applying paste to closest edge

PRACTICAL TIP

Because you are leaning over the wallpaper, you should leave the edge nearest to you until last. This way you will not get paste over your clothing when you lean over.

STEP 7 When a length is completely pasted, you must fold the paper on to itself. This makes it easier to use and stops the paste evaporating.

If you are applying paper vertically (from ceiling height to the top of the skirting), you must fold the paper using the end-to-centre method as shown in Figure 7.43.

If you are 'crossing the wall' (applying the paper horizontally), you must fold the paper using a concertina fold, see Figure 7.44.

Figure 7.43 Wallpaper folded end to centre

Figure 7.44 A concertina fold

APPLY PAPER TO WALLS AND CORNERS

STEP 1 Taking the piece of paper you pasted first, marked number 1, carry it over to the wall area folded over your arm.

Unfold the paper from the long fold first. Position to the pre-marked vertical starting line.

At this stage do not use the paperhanging brush as you will have difficulty re-positioning the paper to the line if you need to re-place the paper.

Figure 7.45 Unfolding the paper and holding it up to the starting point

STEP 8 Using your bucket, sponge and clean water, wipe down the pasting table to make sure no paste gets on the face of your next length of paper.

STEP 9 Following the manufacturer's instructions for the correct soaking time, place the pasted paper on the folded dust sheet you placed on the floor, away from the immediate work area, and leave to soak for the recommended length of time.

STEP 2 When you are satisfied that the paper is positioned on the line, smooth out the paper using your paperhanging brush by moving across and downwards to remove any air bubbles, creases, etc.

Take care not to use too much force when smoothing the paper down to the skirting board as this could result in the paper being stretched, which might cause the paper to spring back while drying, and leave you with a mismatched pattern.

Figure 7.46 Smoothing out the paper

STEP 3 Trim the top and bottom of the length of paper in a straight line. First, run an unopened pair of scissors across the face of the paper, leaving a mark to follow.

PRACTICAL TIP

You can also use a pencil to carefully mark a line to cut along, but take care not to leave a mark.

You can also use a straight edge and cutting knife to cut the top of the paper.

Figure 7.47 Marking the cutting line

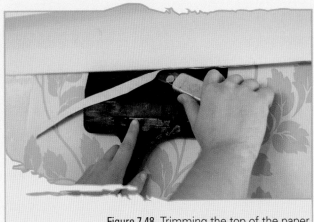

Figure 7.48 Trimming the top of the paper

STEP 4 Use a clean, damp sponge to wipe any surplus paste from the ceiling and skirting areas.

STEP 5 Position the next length (drop) of paper next to the pre-positioned paper taking care to not to leave any gaps. This is known as a butt joint. Take care to match the pattern accurately.

Figure 7.49 Positioning the second drop

STEP 6 Continue along the wall until you arrive at a corner. When you arrive at the corner, place the next piece of paper to be hung on the pasting table, folded end to end.

Measure the width of the remaining wall area to be papered – adding 5–10 mm to the width.

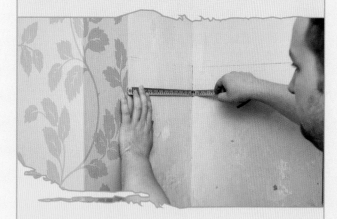

Figure 7.50 Measuring the wall to the corner

STEP 7 Mark the folded paper on the table using a pencil on the face of the paper, taking into account the extra width.

PRACTICAL TIP

A spirit level is a good tool to use as a straight edge when marking the paper on the table.

STEP 8 While the paper is still folded, carefully cut the paper along the line you have marked.

STEP 9 Offer up the paper on the wall before the corner. Hang it as usual, smoothing it out into the corner, allowing the overlap to adhere around the corner. Be careful not to get paste on your brush.

Figure 7.51 Hanging the corner piece

STEP 10 Measure the width of the remaining piece of paper you left on the papering table. Using this measurement, mark the next wall from the corner with a vertical plumb line.

Remember to allow for a poor corner (a corner where two walls meet that are not true vertical) by reducing the measured width of the wallpaper.

Figure 7.52 Marking the wall on the next corner

STEP 11   Position and smooth out the remaining cut length of paper, working from the vertical line into the corner.

Remember to take into account any pattern matches.

STEP 12   Mark and trim the paper. Smooth out any air bubbles, creases, etc.

PRACTICAL TIP

If you're working with vinyl wallpaper, where the papers overlap, you should use overlap adhesive to ensure the two pieces of paper stick to each other.

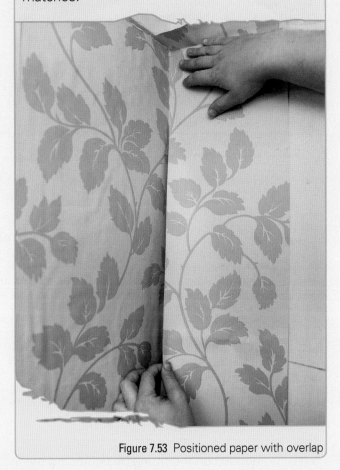

Figure 7.53 Positioned paper with overlap

PRACTICAL TASK

7. APPLY PAPERS AROUND OBSTACLES

OBJECTIVE

To apply pre-pasted papers to walls, working around light switches and power sockets; to apply paper to a recessed window

PPE

Ensure you select PPE appropriate to the job and site where you are working. Refer to the PPE section of Chapter 1.

TOOLS AND EQUIPMENT

Paperhanging brush

Scissors

Cleaning-up cloth

Cutting knife

Cutting straight edge

Pencil

Bucket for clean water

Sponge

Working platform

Plastic rubbish bag or box for offcuts

Wall brush (100mm to 150mm size)

Screwdriver

LIGHT SWITCHES AND SOCKETS

STEP 1 Turn the power off at the source, i.e. the fuse box.

Remember: the power supply to the light switch will be different to the electrical outlet so you may need to turn off more than one switch.

Figure 7.54 Isolating the power supply

STEP 2 Loosen the screws slightly so the fixing is away from the wall, but still attached.

STEP 3 Offer up the wallpaper to the wall, allowing it to fall over the light switch or electrical outlet.

Push the scissors through the middle of the wallpaper, then cut from the centre hole diagonally towards each corner of the fitting. Stop just short of the edge of the fitting.

Figure 7.55 Cutting a hole for a light switch

Figure 7.56 Hole for a light switch or power socket

STEP 4 Carefully peel the paper back and trim, leaving a few millimetres extra.

STEP 5 Press and smooth the paper behind the fitting using your paperhanging brush. Be very careful not to get any water behind the fitting.

STEP 6 Reposition the fitting by tightening the screws.

STEP 7 Remove any surplus wallpaper paste with a damp sponge, then wipe the fitting with a dry cleaning-up cloth.

STEP 8 When you have finished, reinstate the power supply.

RECESSED WINDOWS

STEP 1 Hang the paper from the ceiling over the reveal.

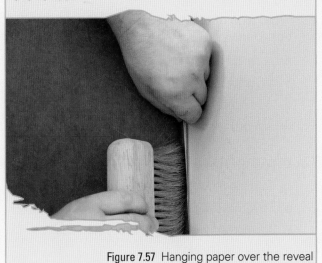

Figure 7.57 Hanging paper over the reveal

STEP 2 Cut the paper horizontally, using the top edge of the reveal as your guide.

Fold and smooth along the cut into the vertical part of the window recess. If there is a still a gap between this paper and the window, follow Steps 4 to 6.

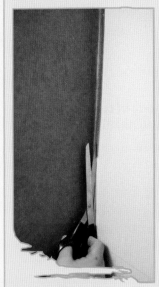 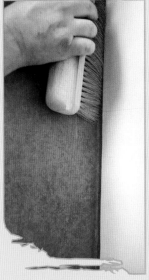

Figure 7.58 Cutting paper along the reveal

Figure 7.59 Smoothing cut paper into reveal

STEP 3 Position the next piece of wallpaper next to the first piece of paper, with no joint showing, taking into account any matching of the pattern. This should leave a small gap on the underside of the window recess, in the corner.

STEP 4 To cover the underside gap of the recess, use an offcut of paper. Take care to match up any pattern and leave an overlap of up to 50 mm. Fold and paste into the gap.

Figure 7.60 Positioning the offcut

STEP 5 Use your knife to cut through both layers of the overlapped paper and peel them off, then smooth both edges back onto the wall. This will leave an invisible gap.

STEP 6 Wipe down to remove any surplus adhesive.

PRACTICAL TIP

If you're working with vinyl wallpaper, remember to use overlap adhesive for any overlaps of the wallpaper.

TEST YOURSELF

1. What is a paperhanging brush used for?

    a. Applying paste to wallpaper

    b. Smoothing paper onto a surface

    c. Dusting off the pasting table

    d. Preparing the surface

2. What sort of tool would you use to press down the joins between paper lengths?

    a. A pasting brush

    b. A paperhanging brush

    c. A seam roller

    d. A warm, wet sponge

3. What are three advantages of using cellulose paste?

    a. Cheap, easy to mix, doesn't stain papers

    b. Good for heavy papers, can be applied direct to wall, has fungicide

    c. Does not rot, comes ready mixed, good for lightweight papers

    d. Easy to mix, can be used for heavy papers, does not rot

4. Which of the following is NOT a factor affecting the consistency of adhesives?

    a. Air temperature

    b. The bucket it's mixed in

    c. Paper weight

    d. Amount of water used

5. What defect can occur if paper has been over-soaked?

    a. Stretching

    b. Dry edges

    c. Overlapping

    d. Delamination

6. What type of pattern repeats itself horizontally?

    a. A straight match

    b. An offset match

    c. A horizontal match

    d. A drop match

7. Why should you keep a wet sponge nearby?

    a. To wipe down the pasting bench

    b. To remove excess adhesive from joins

    c. To wipe adhesive off adjacent surfaces

    d. All of the above

8. At which point of a staircase should you place your first drop?

    a. The landing

    b. The focal wall

    c. The longest drop

    d. The stairwell

9. At what time should you mark a plumb line?

    a. Before hanging each length

    b. When papering around corners

    c. b) and d)

    d. At your starting point

10. What are the two methods of calculating how much paper you will need?

    a. Girthing and Area

    b. Area and Width

    c. Perimeter and Girthing

    d. Breadth and Area

Chapter 8

CSA L10CC23
PRODUCE STANDARD DECORATIVE FINISHES

LEARNING OUTCOMES

LO1/2: Know how to and be able to prepare surfaces and produce quality ground coats for standard decorative finishes

LO3/4: Know how to and be able to produce broken colour effect using acrylic and oil-based scumbles

LO5/6: Know how to and be able to apply single colour stencils

LO7/8: Know how to and be able to form painted lines and bands

INTRODUCTION

The aims of this chapter are to:

* help you produce quality finish ground coats and apply broken colour effects

* show you how to apply standard decorative finishes of rag rolling, sponge stippling and single colour stencils.

PREPARING SURFACES AND PRODUCING QUALITY GROUND COATS

Decorative effects are used to add visual interest to a room. Some finishes are designed to look like different surface materials, such as marble, fabric, wood and other textures. They were often used in the past when these natural materials were very expensive. While these effects were particularly popular in the twentieth century due to the unavailability or cost of raw materials, there is still a need for some painters to have these skills so that older buildings can be maintained.

Before applying specialist decorative finishes, it is essential that the surface and ground coat have been well prepared.

PPE

Remind yourself in the previous chapters about the most appropriate PPE for working with paint products. In particular, when creating decorative effects you will need to protect your hands as you will be coming into close contact with paints and glazes. There are several barrier cream products available that will help to protect the skin if it comes into contact with contaminants and chemicals in paints, solvents and scumbles.

If you need to do any extra surface preparation, such as abrading, then you will also need to protect your eyes, nose and mouth.

Protecting the work and surrounding area

You should protect your working area from paint drips and spatter. This includes the floors, but also any furniture and fittings. You will probably have already laid all your dust sheets and removed fittings when preparing your surface and applying primers and undercoats. Revisit Chapter 6, page 166–169 for more information about preparing the work area.

KEY TERMS

Barrier cream

– an ointment or lotion that creates a physical barrier between the skin and substances which can cause skin infections or dermatitis.

REED TIP

If you're working on a construction site, there's no point in carrying your hard hat around – put it on your head!

Environmental and health and safety regulations

Refer back to Chapters 5 and 6 for information on the environmental, health and safety issues around working with paints, preparing surfaces, and disposal of waste. In particular, be aware that you will be working even more closely with hazardous substances: solvents and solvent-based products.

Preparation processes

In Chapter 5, you learnt about wet and dry abrading, spot priming and making good surfaces, ready to receive coatings. It is especially important when creating decorative finishes that your surface has been well prepared. If you don't have a high quality surface and ground coat finish, your decorative effects can be ruined.

Defects in decorative work

See Table 8.1 below to see the common defects in decorative work, their causes and how to avoid them.

Defect	Cause	How to avoid
Uneven colour	Small holes in the surface that have not been filled properly. This stops the top coat from spreading evenly and shows up as dark spots in the finish.	• Go over your surface carefully, looking for any indentations, cracks or holes. • Make sure that all surface imperfections have been filled with the right product. • Abrade the filled area so it is flush with the wall.
Ropiness	The ground coat has not been applied carefully, leaving misses or brush marks, not laying off, or it has been applied to a surface that is not completely dry.	• Wait for your surface and any layers of paint to dry properly. • Apply the correct type of ground coat. • Apply all primers, undercoats and ground coats carefully, making sure you lay off each time.
Sinking	The decorative coating disappears on porous surfaces, such as filler. This will leave an uneven finish for your decorative coating.	• Any patches that have been filled must be spot primed so that top coatings do not seep in or evaporate.
Bittiness	When dust or grit has appeared on or under the surface you have painted. It will make the finish look lumpy and uneven.	• Once you have finished abrading, thoroughly dust down the surface. • Keep the whole area clean as dust and debris can be kicked up and attach itself to a wet surface.

Table 8.1 Defects in decorative work

Application methods and finish

The application methods you use can affect the quality of your finish. You will need to use the right products, tools and equipment, and apply coatings correctly to avoid the defects covered in Chapter 6, pages 182–183. The decorative effect that you are trying to achieve may not work if you have not prepared your surface or applied your products correctly.

For example, brush marks will need to be removed in order to achieve the effect you want. Using a stipple brush or roller with a very fine sleeve will help make sure your ground coat is even and will remove the brush marks. When it comes to applying the specialist coat, your result will be much better.

It is important to choose your ground coat carefully. Not all paints are well suited for specialist coatings. The best types of ground coat to use are eggshell paints (either oil or water based) or something with a slight sheen such as a silk emulsion. Use a colour that is a tone lighter than the lightest part of your finish. A neutral shade is best so it does not compete with the colour of the decorative finish.

Tools and equipment

See Table 8.2 below for a description of the additional tools and equipment you will need for producing ground coats and decorative finishes. Rollers, rubbing blocks, paintbrushes, buckets, dusting brushes, paint stirrers, strainers, and kettles were all described in earlier chapters. They have the same use in applying ground coats and decorative finishes.

PRACTICAL TIP

You may also find it useful to have an old, well-worn paintbrush, known as a 'rubbing-in brush'. This can be used when applying scumbles to the surface before dragging or subtractive work, to give you a more even finish.

Tools and equipment	Description and use
Hair stipplers (Fig 8.1)	A brush made of hog hair, this is used to get rid of brush marks from oil-based paints and glazes. It is also used to create the decorative stipple finish which looks a little like suede.
Sponges (natural and synthetic) (Fig 8.2)	Used for creating a broken colour effect by either applying or removing paint using the sponge. Natural sponges produce better quality decorative finishes, though synthetic ones can also be used effectively.
Tack rags	A tack rag or tack cloth is used for cleaning dust, dirt and debris off your surface. It is 'tacky' or slightly sticky so that the dust will stick to it better.
Mohair roller	These roller covers have a short pile which is used for applying oils to surfaces. The short pile stops the oil from flicking off.
Chamois leather	Often known as a 'shammy', it is s special type of gentle and highly absorbent leather. It can be used for creating a rag-rolled effect because it is a lint-free cloth.
Lint-free cloth	Lint-free cloths are used for producing a rag-rolled effect. They are made of fabric that will not leave fibres behind on the surface.
Dragging brush (Fig 8.3)	Also known as a flogger, a dragging brush has coarse bristles that can be made of nylon, fibre or horse hair. It is used for creating a grain pattern.
Palettes (Fig 8.4)	A flat surface to place small amounts of paints on when working with stencils. They can be easily held in one hand.
Plastic pots	These are small containers to hold your decorative coatings in. The most commonly used are sign writers' pots.
Ruler	You will need a ruler to mark the central point of the area you are planning to stencil, and to make general measurements in your stencil area.
Tape measure	You will need your tape measure to pinpoint the positions for your stencil work, especially your starting, finishing and central points in the room.

Chalk and line	Similar to when working with wallpaper, when stencilling you may need to pinpoint and mark the centre of the room as your starting point, or indeed any relevant point in the room. Chalk lines are a quick way of doing this.
Pencil	Use your pencil to make light marks on the wall to help with planning where your decorative finishes will begin and end, as well as the top and bottom of the stencil to keep it in line. You must remember to clean off these marks before stencilling.
Stencil brushes (Fig 8.5)	Stencil brushes are used for applying paint through a stencil plate. They have short bristles so that excess paint can't easily get underneath the stencil plate. They come in different lengths and thicknesses.
Sponge roller	Sponges or sponge rollers can be used for applying paint to a stencil more quickly than a stencil brush. The sponge on the roller can also be used to create a dappled texture, similar to the effect you would get from using sponges for broken colour. They tend to be used when there are large areas to stencil.
Lining fitch (Fig 8.6)	A fitch is a type of fine brush used for detailed work. They come in various sizes. A lining fitch has a flat, diagonal brush end, designed for painting bands.
Straight edge (chamfered, square edge) (Fig 8.7)	You may use a straight edge when painting lines and bands on a surface. These can come with a square edge, or one that slopes or tapers off (chamfered).
Sash tool (Fig 8.8)	A sash tool is a round-headed brush. It has a long, pointed tip which makes it good for getting into small and awkward places, for cutting in and edging where precision is important. Sash tools are often used when painting lines. They come in a variety of sizes and may have either bristle or synthetic filling.
Mohair pad (Fig 8.9)	A paint pad is a rectangular, flat area attached to a handle, used for applying paint to a surface without getting the same splatter you can get from rollers. They are particularly useful for going around edges and straight lines. You can also buy replacement pads to slip onto the handle and base. The mohair on the pad gives a smooth finish.

Table 8.2 Tools and equipment for producing decorative finishes

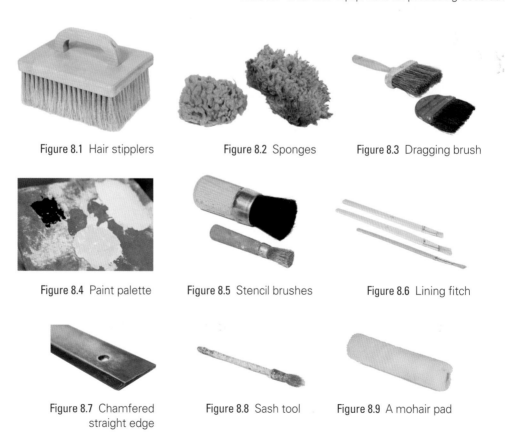

Figure 8.1 Hair stipplers

Figure 8.2 Sponges

Figure 8.3 Dragging brush

Figure 8.4 Paint palette

Figure 8.5 Stencil brushes

Figure 8.6 Lining fitch

Figure 8.7 Chamfered straight edge

Figure 8.8 Sash tool

Figure 8.9 A mohair pad

REED TIP

Try to appreciate the different strengths and weaknesses of other members of your team. It will help you to work more effectively as a group.

PRODUCING BROKEN COLOUR EFFECT USING ACRYLIC AND OIL-BASED SCUMBLES

When a decorative finish is not a solid colour on the surface, this is called a broken colour effect. More than one colour must be used to achieve the effect. Broken colour effects include dragging, sponging, and stippling. Each technique uses different tools and materials to achieve the finish. See the practical tasks beginning on page 251 for step-by-step instructions on how to achieve each effect.

Materials, tools and equipment

Glazes and scumbles

To achieve broken colour effects, you can use either an acrylic (water-based) or an oil-based scumble. A scumble is created by adding colour to a clear glaze. It can be tinted with water- or oil-based colourant or you can simply use a small amount of coloured paint. For an oil-based glaze, you would mix linseed oil and white spirit to thin it out.

A scumble will usually be opaque due to the pigment or colour that has been added. If the coating is translucent or transparent, then it will be a glaze. An acrylic scumble will be milky-white when mixed, but then dries clear.

If you are using an oil-based coating for your decorative finish and it is white, you may find that it yellows over time. Using an acrylic coating will prevent this problem, but it will not be as long lasting as an oil-based coating. Water-based coatings tend to get damaged more easily with scratches or knocks. For this reason, if producing a decorative finish on woodwork, it would be better to use an oil-based coating. Even if your ground coat is water-based, you can still use an oil-based scumble on top. Note however that you cannot use a water-based scumble over the top of an oil-based ground coat as it will not adhere to the surface and will cause cissing (where paint joins together to form beads).

Planning ahead

You should always measure up and estimate the size of your job as accurately as possible. This is so that you can make the right amount of glaze or scumble. It is better to overestimate the amount of coating you will need and be left with some over.

If you don't make enough scumble, you would have to stop the job part-way through which would affect your drying time and leave you with an obvious line between the two stages of applying the finish. Also, when mixing the colour in, it is quite difficult to get the right amount, so if you run out there is the risk that your new batch will not be exactly the same colour.

In the same way, you should plan ahead and estimate how long it will take to apply the decorative finish to the area. For instance, you wouldn't want to start the job with just half an hour until your lunch break!

Extenders and driers

Sometimes it will take a long time to achieve your effect, or you may be working on a large surface. There is a risk that your scumble or glaze could dry out, so you may need to use an extender such as glycerine or a proprietary retarding agent and add it to your water-based scumble. This will give you a longer drying time. If you need longer drying time for an oil-based scumble, you can add more linseed oil.

Sometimes you may want your finish to dry more quickly, for instance if it is very cold or if the coatings are old. You can add a drier to your oil-based scumbles to speed up the drying time.

Whether or not you use extenders or driers will depend on the conditions you are working in:

* The room temperature – a cold room may mean you need to speed up your drying time; a warm room may mean you need to slow it down.

* The thickness of your material – your scumble may be too thick or too thin for the job at hand; oil-based scumbles will stay workable for longer.

* How large the space is that you're decorating – a large space may mean you need to extend your drying time to keep the scumble workable; a small job means you may finish before the scumble dries.

* The number of layers you are applying – if you are using several colours, then you will want a faster drying time between coats.

* The number of people who are working on the same task – having more than one person working on a job will speed up your work time and may mean you do not need to use an extender.

Rag rolling

Rag rolling is an effect created by using a bunched up piece of rag, paper, chamois leather or lint-free cloth on a glaze or paint that has been applied to the surface. Your surface finish will be affected by the equipment and materials you use, e.g. using paper will give you a sharper effect than using a chamois.

It is also possible to achieve the rag rolling effect using paint rather than a scumble.

Subtractive rag rolling

When the rag touches the surface, it takes some of the scumble away (i.e. subtracts it) and leaves a textured effect that looks like crushed velvet. Subtractive rag rolling is also called 'ragging off'. The scumble or

---

KEY TERMS

Glycerine

– a chemical based liquid that has no colour or smell. It has many uses in the food and pharmaceutical industries. It is used as a thinner or extender in water-based glazes or scumbles.

Drier

– a chemical additive that will speed up the drying process when added to a paint, glaze or scumble.

PRACTICAL TIP

When rag rolling and sponge stippling, you will be in close contact with the scumble, glaze or paint. Make sure you wear gloves and some barrier cream to protect your skin.

Figure 8.10 A subtractive rag rolling effect

Figure 8.11 An additive rag rolling effect

paint is applied to the whole surface to be decorated, finishing off with a stippler to get rid of brush marks. The rag is then crumpled up and moved in different directions, lifting the glaze from parts of the surface. The rag will need to be cleaned off regularly.

Additive rag rolling

Adding your scumble or paint to the ground coat using a rag is called additive rag rolling, or 'ragging on'. The rag (or whatever material you are using) is crumpled up and dipped into the scumble or emulsion paint (though paint on its own won't give you a good finish). It should become soaked through with the coating, then wrung out and rolled into the right shape. When placing the rag onto the surface, it should be used in different directions so that the effect is random rather than accidentally creating a pattern.

Sponge stippling

Stippling creates a soft, broken colour effect. It can be done with a hog-hair stippler or a sponge.

When using a stippler, a coating is added to the ground coat, then the stippler is dabbed at the surface which removes small dots of paint. The stippler needs to be blotted from time to time to remove excess paint from the bristles. The final texture should be very even and soft, like suede, though it may vary from fine to coarse. You may get a better result by using an oil-based glaze or scumble when using a stippler.

For a more even finish, you can use the stippling process on your scumble before using a subtractive sponge effect – see practical task *Produce a sponge stippling effect* on page 253.

Using a sponge will create a more striking broken colour effect. The finish will also depend on whether a natural or synthetic sponge is used. A natural sponge will give you a more interesting and irregular effect.

If you *add* paint, scumble or glaze to the ground coat using the sponge, this is called additive sponge stippling. If you remove or *subtract a* coating from the surface, this is called subtractive sponge stippling.

This mottled look can be enhanced by using more than one colour, once each layer of coating is dry. You may even wish to use different types of sponge for the different layers. Using more than one colour can give you a marbled effect.

Bagging

Bagging is useful for hiding small surface imperfections. Similar to rag rolling or sponging, the effect is created by dabbing wet scumble with a crumpled plastic bag or cellophane. As with other techniques, it can be subtractive (removing the scumble from the surface) or additive (dabbing the scumble onto the surface). See Fig 8.12.

Dragging

Dragging creates a series of textured fine lines on your surface. It is achieved by pulling a dragging brush down through the scumble, which

Figure 8.12 Bagging effect

Figure 8.13 Dragging effect

leaves the colour of the ground coat just showing through. Dragging should only be done on a very well-prepared and smooth wall, otherwise the imperfections will show up.

Application faults and problems

Working on decorative finishes is a job that requires a lot of care. If you don't take the time to get your surface prepared, ground coat applied, coating thickness right, prepare enough coating, plan your work, and use good technique, the finished result will not look very good. Here are some problems that tend to occur when applying decorative finishes.

Loss of wet edge

As mentioned earlier, it is important to plan your work so that you don't have to stop part-way through the job. If you do, then you will lose your wet edge – the coating will start to dry at the point you stopped. This stopping and restarting point will show up in your finish. Make sure you have the time and materials to keep working the surface until a sensible stopping point, e.g. the corner of a room.

Banding/tracking

When rag rolling, bagging and sponge stippling, it is important that you overlap your work when adding or subtracting your scumble. If you don't, then you will end up with an irregular pattern in the finish. Make sure that you go over one-third of the already worked area when starting a new section.

When sponging, you can work in a circular motion to help avoid this same fault.

When stippling, make sure you work in a random pattern and not in defined sections or rows, otherwise you will see bands of colour in the finish.

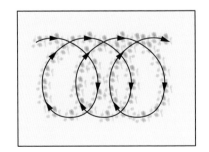

Figure 8.14 Avoiding banding or tracking

Slip/skid marks

When applying coating to your surface, it is important not to press too hard, or you might cause the roller to slide across the surface. This will leave marks and give you an imperfect starting surface to work from.

The same advice applies when using a stippler: if you press too hard or use the brush at an angle, then the bristles can splay and slip. This will leave you with lines rather than dots.

Problems with removal of masking

Before applying your decorative finishes, you may have prepared some surfaces with masking or decorator's tape. If you take the tape off too late or carelessly, then you can not only damage the decorative effect itself, but can even remove the ground coat. Both of these problems would need to be fixed and repainted. These problems can also be reduced by making sure you use the right masking product, for example a low-tack tape, so that any possible damage is minimised.

When removing the tape, roll it back onto itself, rather than away from the surface. If you try to remove it too quickly, you may take layers of coating off.

Make sure you dispose of your masking tape responsibly. Usually you would dispose of it along with your other contaminated materials at the end of a job by taking it to the local council tip or recycling service, especially if you have been working with solvent-based products.

Cleaning and storing your tools and equipment

Refresh your memory about cleaning and storing your painting tools and equipment in Chapter 6, pages 184–187. Keeping your tools clean, dry and stored appropriately will mean they last you longer and give you a better finish.

In addition, it is important to note that rags soaked in solvent should not be stored bunched up anywhere, including in your pockets, because of the risk of spontaneous combustion. Make sure you open up the rag and allow it to dry before throwing it away. Remember that you are working with solvents and solvent-based coatings, so any contaminated equipment should either be washed out or thrown out. When cleaning your tools, bear in mind the environmental guidelines and avoid pouring any scumble, glaze, paint or solvent into the drain.

If you are using a natural sponge, do take care of it – they are quite expensive.

When using a dragging brush or flogger, make sure you keep the bristles dry by wiping them on a piece of lint-free cloth as you are working. This will keep the bristles in shape.

Rollers and brushes should be cleaned and stored in the normal way, depending on the type of coatings you have used.

If using solvent-based scumbles, a chamois or lint-free cloth should be spread out for the solvents to evaporate before disposing of them. Note, however, that a chamois will no longer be soft if it has been used with a solvent-based product, so it's better to use them with water-based scumbles only.

APPLYING SINGLE COLOUR STENCILS

Stencil work is a way of decorating a room with designs and colours that may form a border, a single image, or a pattern that covers an entire surface. Because stencils can be made of almost any design, they can be a unique expression of a customer's taste and style. Stencils are an easy way of repeating a pattern consistently across a surface. For step-by-step instructions on how to create and cut out a stencil, see the practical task *Apply a single colour stencil* on page 255.

Positive and negative stencils

Positive stencils are where a design is cut out of the stencil so that the gaps are filled in which leaves the design on the wall (see Fig 8.15).

Negative stencils are where it is the *background* of a design that is cut out. When the stencil is painted over, it is the wall colour behind that forms the design (see Fig 8.16).

Figure 8.15 A positive stencil design

Figure 8.16 A negative stencil design

Planning considerations

When preparing any stencil work, it is important to think about the space you are working in. If you begin applying the design without planning first, you may end up with patterns that do not meet up around the room, nor match up as you go along. You could end up with an unbalanced look if there are gaps or irregular spaces between each motif. When you are planning your stencil work, keep in mind the following:

* Room dimensions – are the walls different sizes? How much paint will you need to complete the decorative finish for this room? Where is the central focal point of the room?

* Access requirements – will you be working up high? Down low? What access equipment and PPE will you need?

* Location of doors and windows – are the doorways or windows going to interfere with the design? Will your stencil become halved? Will it affect your starting point?

* Corners – will the design meet up well at the corners of the room? Will this affect your starting point?

* Number of repeats/connections – what is your starting point and finishing point? Are there any overlapping points in the stencil? How many times will the stencil be applied vertically and/or horizontally?

* Stencil size – how big is your stencil? If it is large, will you need to apply only part of one of the repeats?

REED TIP

A good apprentice is not just good with their hands; a good apprentice is also good at Maths and English, reliable, and shows a good attitude to work.

* Spacing – how far apart should each placement of the stencil be? Do you need to increase or reduce this space to ensure the design meets well at the corners? Is your stencil going to cover the entire wall, or just one part of it?

Marking out

Marking out your space is an essential step before you start stencilling. Each position for your stencil should be carefully marked with pencil or chalk so that the pattern will be regular and unbroken. The stencil will also need to be level all the way across the surface.

Use a chalk line to mark the area where your stencilling is to start. This will often be the central point of the wall or the focal point of the room. See Chapter 7, pages 202, 212 and 223 to remind yourself how to use a chalk line.

Depending on the design you will be stencilling, you may need to mark either horizontal or vertical lines, e.g.:

* if it is to be used as a border around the middle of the wall, then you will need to carefully mark a horizontal line that is level all the way around the room;

* if the design repeats down the wall, then you will need vertical lines marked along the wall at each point where the stencil should be placed.

Stencils may come with their own **registration marks**, or you may need to cut small Vs at the centre points of your stencils. These marks are the key to getting an accurate match up of your design.

Securing methods for stencil plates

Not all stencils will need to be fixed to the wall while you work. A smaller stencil may be simply held up against the wall. If you are using larger stencils, then you will need to attach them to the wall to avoid slipping or wrinkles in the work.

You can use a spray adhesive which will stay sticky for a while, meaning you can move it around the room until it dries. This is a quick and easy way to fix your stencils, but if the stencil is large, it may not be strong enough to hold it.

Instead, you can use masking tape or a low tack tape that will not remove any paint from your surface and will be strong enough to hold up larger stencil plates.

KEY TERMS

Registration mark

– a line, indentation, slot or notch on the edge of a stencil that is used as a marker to align different layers of a stencil or align the previous stencil with the next.

Applying your paint

See the practical task on page 255 for step-by-step instructions on how to apply single colour stencils.

Application faults

See Table 8.3 below for faults that can occur when applying stencils, their causes and how to avoid them.

Application fault	Causes	How to avoid
Creep	When too much paint has been applied over the stencil, the extra paint can bleed under the holes and blur or ruin the design.	Make sure you blot your brush or roller before applying paint to the stencil. Roll or dab the excess paint onto a paper towel or your palette first.
Smudging	Paint rubs off the stencil when it is being removed from the wall.	When removing and placing your stencils, do it carefully so that any wet paint does not touch the surface. You should also check that the paint on the stencil has dried or been wiped off before placing it on the wall again.
Paint lifting	Paint can lift off the surface when the masking tape holding the stencil on is pulled off.	Make sure you have used a low tack tape. Don't rip it off the wall, but remove it slowly and gently. This will also avoid tearing your stencil. You may consider using adhesive spray instead.
Uneven colour	When paint hasn't been applied correctly and evenly.	Keep an eye on your work and make sure all of the holes in your stencil have been filled and that you have used the same amount of paint for the whole stencil.
Bittiness	Where there is dirt or debris on the surface.	Your wall should be properly prepared before starting. Make sure the surface and the area around you is clean before starting.
Undue texture	When too much or too little paint has been applied through the stencil, e.g. if the brush or roller has been overloaded.	Blot your brush and roller each time you load it. Stencilling is usually a light effect, so less is more – you can always load your brush or roller again if needed.
Uneven weight of colour over repeats	When using more than one colour or a multi-layered stencil, the colours may have been applied more lightly or heavily between repeats of the design.	Try to use the same amount of paint for each stencil section. Start off lightly and add more paint only if you need to. If uneven weight of colour has occurred, you would need to completely redo the job.
Buckled/curled stencil plate	If your stencil has become old and worn or not cleaned and stored correctly, it can become misshapen and cause the design to be wrong or irregular.	Clean, dry and store your stencils to keep them flat for the next time you use them. You may need some extra adhesive to hold them flat against the wall, but be careful not to use too much as it can leave a residue. It may be better to cut a new stencil.

Table 8.3 Application faults

CASE STUDY

Restoring the St Pancras Renaissance Hotel

The St Pancras Renaissance Hotel was first opened in 1873 as the Midland Grand Hotel. It was designed as luxury accommodation for train travellers passing through St Pancras rail station in central London. Both the station and the hotel underwent a massive restoration project in the 2000s.

The original Victorian hotel was finished to a very high quality in a neo-Gothic style with tall decorated ceilings, murals, vibrant wallpapers and ornate stencilling with gold leaf. The hotel was closed in 1935 and later used as offices for British Rail, and sadly much of the decorative paintwork was whitewashed over. Luckily in 1967 it was protected by a Grade I listing, though it took many years for it to finally be restored to its former glory.

English Heritage helped to advise the developers in the restoration and craftspeople from all over the UK worked on undoing the damage done. They had to take back layers of emulsion and chipboard, fix the decorative finishes that were still there and copy the original colours and patterns. It was finally reopened in 2011.

Figure 8.17 Ornate stencil work in the St Pancras Renaissance Hotel

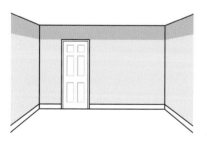

Figure 8.18 A painted line

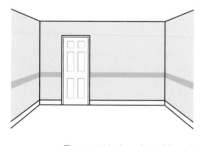

Figure 8.19 A painted band

FORMING PAINTED LINES AND BANDS

A painted line is where two sections of colour meet, often where you would expect to see a picture rail or a dado rail. You might come across them in older buildings, or in places like a hospital where there would not be an actual moulding on the wall, but where using two colours will give the impression of one. This process is essentially the same as cutting in with a brush before you fill in with a roller.

A painted band is a different colour to your ground coat and is simply designed to add interest to a room or to mimic the effect of a moulding such as a dado or picture rail.

The eye is naturally drawn to imperfections in a paint job, and so it is essential that painted lines and bands are perfectly straight, with no colour creeping over to the other side of the line, and with an even thickness all the way around the room.

Marking lines

To mark your lines and bands, use a spirit level and mark around the room with a pencil. You can also use a chalk line with one end taped to the wall. See the practical task *Paint lines and bands* on page 258 for more guidance on how to mark and paint lines and bands.

Chamfered and square-edge straight edges

Painted bands can be created with the help of a straight edge with a chamfered edge. Straight edges will often come with a square edge on one side and a chamfered one on the other.

To paint a fine band, you can hold the chamfered edge up to the wall, and using a lining fitch, run the fitch along the edge to create a thin, straight line.

Tools, equipment and materials

Most of the tools, equipment and materials you need have been covered earlier in the chapter. There are a few extra things to note:

* Water-based paints are the preferred material for painting lines and bands. This is because they dry much more quickly, allowing you to apply a neat second coat after your **dry coat**.

* Chalk can be used for marking your wall. The chalk line can be attached at one end with masking tape while the other end is held and then plucked back.

* A sash tool can be used when applying painted lines and bands. It is a round brush with a tapered end, allowing for more accurate application of paint.

Cleaning and maintaining your tools and equipment

Your sash tool, lining fitch, and mohair pad should be washed out straight after the work is finished, and then hung up to dry naturally. The brushes can be coated in a very thin grease or oil, such as Vaseline. This will stop them from drying out and will keep the bristles in shape.

Your straight edge should also be cleaned off thoroughly – if there is any paint left to dry on it, then it will no longer be straight.

PRACTICAL TIP

Today, if a painted line or band is required, it is more common to simply paint over masking tape to achieve the effect. By applying a 'dry coat' of paint to the masking tape, you will avoid any paint seeping in behind the tape, and will end up with a perfectly straight line. See the step-by-step instructions on how to do this in practical task 5, *Paint lines and bands*.

KEY TERMS

Dry coat

– applying a very light, thin coat of paint to a masking tape edge which then dries quickly before the second coat is applied.

DID YOU KNOW?

A mohair pad is used for the application of emulsion or acrylic eggshell to large areas. It is mainly used in the DIY market for painting textured woodchip or anaglypta and is used in the same way as a roller.

CASE STUDY

Making a difference

Sandie Webster has completed her Level 1, 2 and 3 diplomas and was a gold medallist at SkillBuild. She now runs her own business (www.sandie-webster.co.uk).

'At the moment, I'm painting a giant mural in a dementia assessment unit. It's a street scene down both sides of a corridor, about 12 m long. I designed it myself and drew out the shops first, before filling it in with colour. It had to be bright and not too fussy, with simple shapes. I'm learning a lot about colours from a different perspective and I can use some of the things I've learned when I'm doing normal decorating. It's taken 4 months and will be another month or so until it's finished.

I've learnt how to speak to the dementia patients, how to explain what I'm doing so they can relate to it. It can be draining but it's also nice because they're interested in what I'm doing for them. I do have to be alert, though, and not leave anything about if I have to have a break, so that nobody trips over tins or cables or walks off with something.

I was asked to do it because I did a mural at my children's school and one of the parents who works at this unit referred me to them. Word of mouth is really important. I'm pleased to have the opportunity to do something like this; it's rewarding and will really make a difference.'

Figure 8.20

PRACTICAL TASK

1. PRODUCE A RAG-ROLLING EFFECT

OBJECTIVE

To set out and prepare materials ready to produce additive and subtractive rag-rolling effects, using a coloured water-based paint.

PPE

Ensure you select PPE appropriate to the job and site where you are working. Refer to the PPE section of Chapter 1.

TOOLS AND EQUIPMENT

Paint kettles

Coloured emulsion paint

White emulsion paint

Cotton lint-free rags

Latex gloves

Stirring stick

Selection of paintbrushes

Sample boards

Paint tray

Stippling brush

Bucket of water

RAGGING ON (ADDITIVE)

STEP 1   Paint a sample board in the ground colour of your choice. This must dry completely before applying your second colour.

STEP 2   Using the same ground colour in a clean paint kettle, add a small amount of white emulsion to create a second, lighter tint. If necessary, thin the mixed colour to the consistency of soft ice cream. Remember the mixed emulsion must be dust free or your effect will be ruined.

Figure 8.21 Mixing second colour with emulsion

STEP 3   Soak a lint-free rag in clean water then squeeze it out until all the surplus water is removed, leaving the rag just damp. This is so the rag will not pick up too much of the second colour or act like a sponge. The rag itself should be about 250–300 mm square.

Figure 8.22 Soaking the rag with water

STEP 4   Place some of the second colour into a paint tray and load up the rag by soaking it in the second colour. Squeeze out any surplus paint. Remember to wear latex gloves for protection.

Figure 8.23 Soaking the rag with emulsion

STEP 5 Lightly hold the rag in a crumpled position and roll in a random pattern over the sample board, crossing over the previously rag-rolled section.

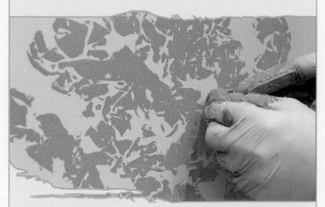

Figure 8.24 Applying rag in random pattern

The effect will be better if you apply the colour lightly, using very little pressure. Re-soak the rag when all or almost all of the coloured emulsion is used up.

RAGGING OFF (SUBTRACTIVE)

To create a subtractive rag rolling effect, you should follow Steps 1 to 3 above, then carry out the following.

STEP 6 Using a paintbrush, apply a coat of the second colour to the surface being used. Do not be concerned with any brush marks at this stage.

STEP 7 Using a stippling brush, bounce onto the surface at 90° to even out any brush marks.

Figure 8.25 Evening out the surface with a stippling brush

STEP 8 Using a damp lint-free rag, roll the surface as shown in Step 5 (ragging on). Take care not to repeat the effect in straight lines, as this is not the accepted finished result.

Figure 8.26 Ragging off

PRACTICAL TIP

To create these effects using oil-based products, follow the same technique. However, remember that using oil-based materials brings extra issues of health and safety, such as fumes, smell, extra drying times, and the risk of spontaneous combustion of a bunched up wet rag.

Also bear in mind that you can use an oil-based scumble over the top of a water-based ground coat, but you cannot do the reverse.

PRACTICAL TASK

2. PRODUCE A SPONGE STIPPLING EFFECT

OBJECTIVE

To set out and prepare materials ready to produce a sponge stippling effect, using a coloured acrylic scumble glaze.

PPE

Ensure you select PPE appropriate to the job and site where you are working. Refer to the PPE section of Chapter 1.

TOOLS AND EQUIPMENT

Paint kettles	Sample boards
Natural sea sponges	Flat paint tray
Latex gloves	Coloured emulsions
Stirring sticks	Acrylic scumble glaze
Paint stippling brush	

STEP 1 Paint a sample board in the ground colour of your choice and allow it to dry.

STEP 2 Using a small amount of a coloured emulsion, mix with a clear acrylic glaze to produce the scumble you need. Adding small amounts of colour at a time will ensure you don't make your scumble too dark or bright.

Figure 8.27 Mixing the scumble

STEP 3 Decant (pour) a small amount of the acrylic scumble into a small flat paint tray. You could also use a paint tin lid.

STEP 4 Lightly dip a damp sea sponge into the scumble.

PRACTICAL TIP

If you would like to create a more interesting look, you can use another colour once the first scumble has dried.

STEP 5 Using the coated sea sponge, dab the surface very lightly to create the desired pattern.

Remember to dab the sponge randomly, in such a way that you leave gaps between the pattern.

Figure 8.28 Dabbing scumble on surface with sponge

STEP 6 Revisit the pattern you have produced in Step 5 and join up the pattern by dabbing between the original patterns to create a design that completely covers the sample board.

Figure 8.29 Finishing the sponge pattern

PRACTICAL TASK

3. PRODUCE A DRAGGING EFFECT

OBJECTIVE

To set out, prepare materials and produce a dragging effect, using a solvent-based scumble on a timber surface.

PPE

Ensure you select PPE appropriate to the job and site where you are working. Refer to the PPE section of Chapter 1.

TOOLS AND EQUIPMENT

Oil-based glaze

Oil-based colourant or paint

Dragging brush

Rubbing-in brush (a well-used brush) or small roller

Cleaning rags

STEP 1 Prepare the surface to receive the effect, making sure that it has a very smooth finish.

STEP 2 Mix a solvent-based transparent glaze and white spirit in a ratio of 2:1. Add a small amount of the chosen colour to tint the glaze to make your scumble. Solvent-based paints can be used for this purpose.

Figure 8.30 Applying scumble to the surface

STEP 3 Using either a small roller or a worn brush (rubbing-in brush) apply a coat of scumble to the surface. Only coat an area that you can complete in about five minutes: after this time period the scumble will start to become unworkable.

STEP 4 Starting at the top of the work area, hold your dragging brush at a shallow angle. In one long stroke, drag the brush down to the bottom of the area you are working on. See Fig 8.31.

Remember to apply a small amount of scumble to the dragging brush prior to use (priming), otherwise it will lift off too much of the scumble.

Figure 8.31 Dragging the brush downwards at a shallow angle

STEP 5 Continue to apply the scumble to other sections of the work area and create the effect until the job is complete.

Figure 8.32 The dragging effect

PRACTICAL TIP

A worn rubbing-in brush is used to create a more even effect when applying your scumble.

PRACTICAL TIP

Remember: if using masking tape to mask off areas, take care not to over-apply the glaze to the masking tape as this will result in the tape lifting from the surface.

STEP 6 You will have areas where the brush cannot be dragged using a downward motion due to the angle, therefore at the bottom of each pass, turn the brush 90° and drag in an upward direction to meet the existing dragging pattern.

PRACTICAL TASK

4. APPLY A SINGLE COLOUR STENCIL

OBJECTIVE

To set out, prepare materials and apply a single colour stencil.

PPE

Ensure you select PPE appropriate to the job and site where you are working. Refer to the PPE section of Chapter 1.

TOOLS AND EQUIPMENT

Masking tape	Tracing paper	Working platform
Pencil	Stencil card	Small palette
Chalk	Paper towel	Stencil brushes
Cutting knife	Tape measure	Emulsion paint (different to ground colour)
Cutting mat	Spirit level	
Filling knife	Clean-up rags	

STEP 1 Choose the design that you will be using and produce a copy. This can be achieved by the use of a photocopier or by cutting out the design from a book or magazine, for example.

STEP 2 Place the design copy on a flat surface; use masking tape to stop the design from moving. Place a piece of tracing paper over the design, again securing with masking tape.

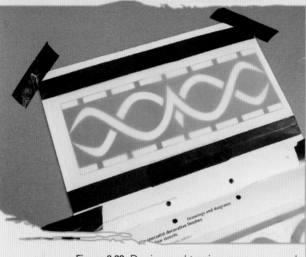

Figure 8.33 Design and tracing paper secured

STEP 3 Use a pencil to trace the design onto the tracing paper, being careful to trace all the design in detail.

Figure 8.34 Tracing the design

STEP 4 Turn the design tracing over and rub over the design details using a pencil or a piece of dust free chalk.

STEP 5 Place and secure the design copy pencil/chalk side down onto a piece of stencil card. Both the design and the stencil card must be laid on top of a flat surface.

STEP 6 With a pencil, trace (transfer) the design onto the stencil card.

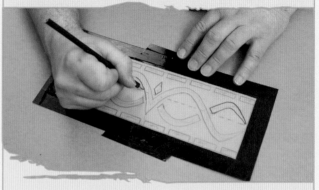

Figure 8.35 Tracing design onto stencil card

STEP 7 Place the stencil card onto a cutting mat. Cut out the transferred design with a sharp cutting knife.

The design must be positioned correctly otherwise you will have problems later on when placing the stencil in the correct position on the surface to be decorated.

Figure 8.36 Cutting out the stencil

STEP 8 Place and secure the stencil with masking tape in the desired position using a light pencil mark as a guide. You can use a spirit level and a tape measure to mark the correct position and ensure it's straight.

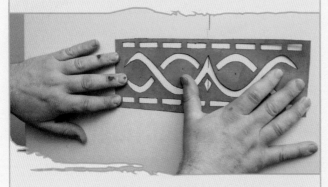

Figure 8.37 Positioning stencil on the surface

STEP 9 Place a small amount of the required stencil paint into a small palette. You can use emulsion for this.

STEP 10 Dip an appropriately sized stencil brush into the stencil paint. (The size of your brush will depend on the size and detail of your stencil.) To do this, lightly touch the paint with the tip of the brush in an upright position, at 90° to the paint.

Do not load the brush up with too much paint as this will result in a poor finish and could seep through behind the stencil.

Figure 8.38 Dipping stencil brush into the paint

STEP 11 Using the coated stencil brush, lightly tap the surface behind the secured stencil using short, sharp strokes (at 90° to the surface).

Continue to load the brush and coat the stencil card until the whole design has been transferred to the surface.

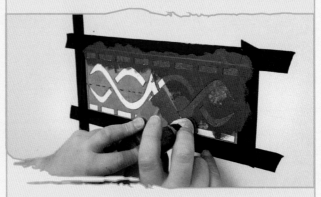

Figure 8.39 Applying paint to the stencil

If the stencil card is not sitting flat on the surface, you can use a piece of paper towel secured to a filling knife to push the card flat.

Figure 8.40 Keeping the stencil flat on the wall

When transferring the design you can also secure the stencil across the top edge using a piece of masking tape in the form of a hinge – this can help you check if all the design has been transferred by lifting the stencil card away from the surface, without the need to reposition it back onto the surface.

STEP 12 Wipe excess paint from the stencil so that the edge stays clean. Most stencils are on a waterproof membrane but they can get distorted if not hung to dry and stored flat in between card or heavy duty paper. Make sure that the stencil is completely dry otherwise it will stick to the surface.

Figure 8.41 Cleaning the stencil

PRACTICAL TASK

5. PAINT LINES AND BANDS

OBJECTIVE

To set out and paint lines and bands.

PPE

Ensure you select PPE appropriate to the job and site where you are working. Refer to the PPE section of Chapter 1.

TOOLS AND EQUIPMENT

Paint kettle

Water-based paint

Spirit level

Various paintbrushes

Decorators' low-tack masking tape

Pencil

Tape measure

PAINTING LINES

STEP 1 Decide where on the wall you intend to paint the line. Mark the surface with a single line using a pencil and spirit level. The line must be horizontal all the way around.

Figure 8.42 Marking the wall

PRACTICAL TIP

Do not assume that if you measure up from a point (e.g. a skirting board), mark the wall, then repeat using the same measurement at the other end of the wall that the line will be horizontal. This is because most skirtings will have suffered from shrinkage and movement, resulting in the skirting not being truly horizontal. Also, it may be that the floor is not completely flat.

STEP 2 Place the paint to be used in a paint kettle. Ensure it is not too thin or it might run.

Load-up a small paintbrush or lining fitch. You might find it useful to use a high-quality angled paintbrush for greater accuracy.

STEP 3 Apply the paint just below the line. Work the brush up to the line taking care not to push the brush over the line – this is called cutting in.

Reload the brush and continue until you have produced a line that follows the pencil mark all the way around the room.

Figure 8.43 Applying paint to the line

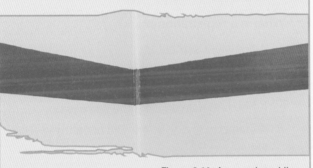

Figure 8.44 A completed line

ALTERNATIVE METHOD

You can often produce better (and faster) results by using masking tape.

Carefully place the tape above the pencil line, then apply a 'dry coat' of paint just over the edge where the masking tape meets the wall. To dry coat, when you load the brush, wipe most of it back into the paint kettle, then lightly coat the masking tape.

Work your way around the room with the dry coat on the tape edge. By the time you come back to your starting point, the thin layer of paint will have dried.

When you get back to your starting point, add a normal thickness of emulsion in the same manner, all the way around the room.

Remove the tape gently and you should be left with a perfect straight line. It is best to remove the tape while the paint is still wet, otherwise a skin can form and pull off some of the coating.

Figure 8.45 Dry coating onto masking tape

PAINTING BANDS

To produce a wider painted line (known as banding) you use the process described in Steps 1, 2 and 3 above, but marking the top line first, measuring and marking the bottom line second, thus producing a band on the surface.

Once your band is marked out, fill it in carefully with paint using the cutting in technique and making sure you don't go over the lines. Choose the size of your brush with consideration of the width of the band you are painting.

Figure 8.46 Marking top and bottom lines to produce a band

You can also use the alternative method of using masking tape to achieve a straight line, except that you will need to apply two lines of masking tape.

259

TEST YOURSELF

1. What is sinking?

   a. When decorative coating seeps down the wall

   b. When decorative coating disappears into the surface

   c. When your ladder is not on an even surface

   d. When decorative coating has an uneven colour

2. What is an oil-based scumble made of?

   a. Water, linseed oil and pigment

   b. Paint and water

   c. Linseed oil, white spirit and pigment

   d. White spirit, water and pigment

3. Why might you use an oil-based ground coat?

   a. Because it is hard-wearing and long-lasting

   b. To avoid yellowing

   c. Because you are using a water-based scumble

   d. Because it's cheaper

4. What can you add to thin out an acrylic scumble?

   a. Drier

   b. Linseed oil

   c. White spirit

   d. Glycerine

5. Which of the following should you use for rag rolling?

   a. Chamois leather

   b. Lint-free cloth

   c. Paper

   d. Any of the above

6. How would you achieve a decorative finish that looks like suede?

   a. Bagging

   b. Stippling

   c. Subtractive rag rolling

   d. Dragging

7. How can you avoid banding or tracking in your work?

   a. Overlap your work by a third

   b. Don't lose your wet edge

   c. Don't press too hard on the surface

   d. Measure and mark your working area first

8. What is a registration mark?

   a. A copyright symbol

   b. A symbol or number that identifies the design

   c. A notch to help you line the stencils up

   d. A stamp to show where you bought the stencil

9. What is creep?

   a. Where paint has rubbed off the stencil

   b. Where paint has bled under the stencil

   c. Where the masking tape has slipped down the wall

   d. Where your stencil has buckled at the corners

10. Why should you use low tack masking tape?

    a. To stop paint coming off the wall when it's removed

    b. To attach your stencil to the wall

    c. To protect edges at the top and bottom of your wall

    d. All of the above

INDEX

A

abbreviations 42
abrading 133
   health risks 139, 140
   using a power tool 157–8
   wet and dry 133–5, 148
abrasive papers 133–4
access equipment and working
   platforms
   carrying out inspections 106–8
   components 103–5
   dismantling 111, 119
   erecting and working from
      108–11, 117–19
   risk assessment 96
   storing 111, 119
access equipment and working
   platforms, preparing for erecting
   94–103, 113–15
   choosing suitable 97–102
   hazards 94–5
   health and safety guidance 97
   hop-ups 101
   ladders 98, 99
   mobile elevated working
      platforms (MEWPs) 101–2
   mobile towers 100
   personal protective equipment
      (PPE) 96
   platform steps 99
   podiums 100
   proprietary staging 100
   protecting work and surrounding
      area 102–3
   risk assessments 95, 96
   step ladders 99
   trestle platforms 100
accident books 2, 9, 17
accident procedures 8–13
accident report forms 10, 96
acetone 128, 144
ACOP (Approved Code of Practice)
   97
additive rag rolling 242
additives
   concrete 70
   in paint systems 174, 175
adhesives for applying papers
   203–6
   defects due to incorrect
      consistency 205
   factors affecting consistency
      204–5

   hazards 205–6
   selecting and preparing 224–5
   types 203–4
aggregates, concrete 70
alternative methods of building,
   sustainability 85–6
Approved Code of Practice (ACOP)
   97
architecture/design
   energy efficiency 91
   sustainability 84, 91
area method 212, 219–20
asbestos 123, 139
   Control of Asbestos at Work
      Regulations 3
assembly drawings 43–4
assembly points 34

B

back filling 146
bagging 242, 243
banding/tracking 243
barrier creams 142, 236
biodegradable materials 86
biodiversity 83
biomass energy 89
birdcage scaffolding 112
bittiness 141, 237, 247
blistering 205, 215, 216
block board 125
block plans 42
bricks and blocks 127
   preparation 133, 151–2
British Standards 6, 41, 180
broken colour effect, producing
   240–4
   application problems 243–4
   bagging 242, 243
   cleaning and storing tools and
      equipment 244
   dragging 242–3, 254–5
   extenders and driers 241
   glazes and scumbles 240–1
   materials, tools and equipment
      240–3
   planning ahead 240–1
   rag rolling 241–2, 251–2
   sponge stippling 242, 253–4
brush keeps 186, 187
brush marks 182, 238
brushes 130, 170
   applying paint 175–7

   cleaning 184–5, 186
   storing 186–7
building design see also
   architecture/design, energy
   efficiency 91

C

carbon, energy sources 88
carbon footprint 84
carded scaffolders 106
caulk, applying 148
cavity walling 74, 75
CCHP see combined cooling heat
   and power units (CCHP)
ceilings
   painting 176
   papering 209
cement, concrete 70
cherry pickers 102
chipboard 125
CHP see combined heat and power
   units (CHP)
cissing 141
cleaning
   brushes 184–5, 186
   contaminated surfaces 143–4
   decorative finish tools and
      equipment 244
   roller sleeves 186, 197
climate 165
coating systems 138–9
colour coded cables, electricity 31
colour systems 178–81
colour wheel 178, 179
combined cooling heat and power
   units (CCHP) 90
combined heat and power units
   (CHP) 90
combustible materials 18, 34–6
common bricks 127
communication 59–63
   appropriate 61–2
   clear/effective 59–60
   diversity 63
   equality 63
   positive/negative 59–60
   responsibilities 61–2
   types 60
   working relationships 62–3
competent 4
concertina folds 213, 227, 228

concrete
  additives 70
  aggregates 70
  cement 70
  foundations 69–71
  reinforcement 70–1
  water 70
concrete floors, formwork 73
Construction (Design and
  Management) Regulations 2007
  42, 95, 97
contaminants 122
contaminated materials, disposing
  of 187
contaminated surfaces, cleaning
  143–4
contamination 18, 19
Control of Asbestos at Work
  Regulations 3
Control of Substances Hazardous to
  Health Regulations (COSHH) 2,
  3, 20, 123, 168, 188
corrosion 126, 132, 136, 149
crawling boards 100
  securing, loading and handling
    110
curtains
  paint defect 141–2
  protecting 167
cutting in 176, 195–6, 259
  irregular 183

D

damp-proof courses (DPC) 76
damp-proof membranes (DPM) 76
dangerous occurrences 9
decanting paint 172, 191
decorative finishes *see* broken
  colour effect, producing; painted
  lines and bands; stencils,
  applying single colour
decorative finishes, preparing
  surfaces for 236–9
  avoiding defects 237
  environmental and health and
    safety regulations 237
  ground coats, choosing 238
  personal protective equipment
    (PPE) 236
  preparation 237–8
  protecting work and surrounding
    area 236
  tools and equipment 238–9
decorator's crutch 209
defects in surfaces and coatings,
  correcting
  common 140–2

health and safety risks 144
materials, tools and equipment
  142–3
primers 149
removing contamination 143–4
repairing *see* repairing and
  making good common
  surfaces
types 132
degreasing 135, 156
delamination 205, 216
dermatitis 20, 21, 32, 122
detail drawings 45
detergents 136, 144, 185, 186
diseases 9
dispersants/emulsifiers 174
diversity, communication 63
documentation 40–9
  drawings and plans 42–5
  manufacturers' technical
    information 48
  organisational 48–9
  policies 47
  procedures 46
  programmes of work 45–6
  schedules 47, 51
  specifications 41–2, 47
  training and development
    records 49
door furniture 167
doors
  applying paper around 209–10
  painting 176–7, 192–4
double pitched roofs 77
DPC (damp-proof courses) 76
DPM (damp-proof membranes) 76
dragging 242–3, 254–5
drawings and plans 42–5
  assembly drawings 43–4
  block plans 42
  detail drawings 45
  isometric projection 45
  location drawings 43, 50–1
  orthographic projection (first
    angle) 45
  scales 50
  sectional drawings 44
driers 174, 175, 241
drop match 207–8, 222
dry coats 249, 259

E

ear defenders 20, 21, 32
efflorescence 140
electricity 28–31
  colour coded cables 31
  dangers 29–30

light fittings 201
Portable Appliance Testing (PAT)
  28–9
precautions 28–9
voltages 30, 31
emergency procedures 8–13, 34–6
end to centre 213, 227, 228
energy conservation 82
energy efficiency 87–91
  architecture/design 91
  biomass energy 89
  building design 91
  combined cooling heat and
    power (CCHP) units 90
  combined heat and power (CHP)
    units 90
  energy ratings 90–1
  heat loss prevention 91
  heat pumps 89–90
  solar photovoltaic systems 90
  solar thermal energy 89
  sustainability 87–91
  wind turbines 90
engineering bricks 127
environment, sustainability 84
equality, communication 63
estimating quantities of materials
  52–7
  formulae 54–6
  measurements 53–4, 57
  paper 212, 218–20
extenders 174, 241
extension poles 172
external walls, construction 74
eye protection 32

F

fillers 136, 147
filling 136, 160
film formers 173, 174
fire extinguishers 35–6
fire procedures 34–6
first aid 12–13
fixtures and fittings 167–8
  replacing 184
flaking or peeling 141
flat roofs 77
floating floors, construction 72
floor construction 71–3
  floating floors 72
  ground floors 71–2
  solid floors 72
  suspended floors 72–3
  upper floors 72–3
flooring, protecting 168
flush 145
flush filling 146

focal walls 207
formulae, estimating quantities of
materials 54–6
formwork, concrete floors 73
foundations 66–71
concrete 69–71
pad foundations 67–9
piled foundations 67–9
purpose 66
raft foundations 67–9
selecting foundations 68–9
shear failure 66
stone 71
strip foundations 67–9
subsoils 66–9
types 67–9
framed walls, construction 74, 75
furniture, protecting 168

G

gable end roofs 77
geothermal heat 89
girthing method 212, 218–19
glazes 240–1, 242
glycerine 241
goggles 32
grinning 182, 183
ground coats 238
ground floors, construction 71–2

H

hand protection 32
handling
access equipment 108–10
Manual Handling Operations
Regulations 4
materials 22–6
hardboard 125
HASAWA see Health and Safety at
Work Act (HASAWA)
hazard identification records 95
hazards 5
Control of Substances Hazardous
to Health Regulations
(COSHH) 2, 3, 20, 123, 168,
188
creating 17–18
of erecting and dismantling
access equipment 94–5
identifying 13–18
method statements 14–15
preparing materials for
application 170
preparing surfaces 122–3
reporting 16–17

risk assessments 14–15
storing paint materials 188
types 15–16
wallpaper adhesives 205–6
head protection 32
Health and Safety at Work Act
(HASAWA) 2, 5
Health and Safety Executive (HSE)
6, 7, 99, 139, 140
health and safety regulations 2–8,
97, 139–40, 168, 187, 237
health risks 21, 122, 139, 140, 144
hearing protection 20, 21, 32
heat loss prevention 91
heat pumps 89–90
heat sinks 89
heights, working at 4, 16, 17
accidents 95
equipment 26–7, 102
medical conditions preventing
108
Work at Height Regulations 2005
4, 97
hipped end roofs 77
hop-ups 101
securing, loading and handling 110
housekeeping 14
HSE see Health and Safety
Executive (HSE)
HVAC (heating, ventilation and air-
conditioning) 82
hygiene 18–21

I

improvement notices 6
information sources
health and safety guidance 97
manufacturers' technical
information 48
selecting information 50–1
infrastructure 81
injuries 7, 9, 10
inspection reports 106
inspections, carrying out 106–8
inspection intervals 107–8
of ladders 116–17
internal walls, construction 74, 75–6
interviews, impressing at 81
isometric projections 45

K

key 122
knife filling 146, 160
knots 132, 135
treating 135, 153

L

ladders 26–7, 117–19
dismantling 111, 119
footing 110
inspection intervals 108
pre-use inspection 116–17
securing, loading and handling
108, 110, 117–19
storage 111
types 98–9
landfill 83
laying off 176, 193
laying on 175, 193
lead paint 137, 139–40
lean-to roofs 77
legislation
health and safety 2–8
personal protective equipment
(PPE) 33
leptospirosis 20, 21
lifting, safe 4, 22–3
light fittings
cutting paper around 211
protecting 167
removal 165, 201
light switches
cutting paper around 211, 232
painting around 176
protecting 167
linear work 177
lining papers 216–17
livering 188
location drawings 43, 50–1

M

major injuries 7, 10
manual handling
access equipment 108–10
Manual Handling Operations
Regulations 4
manufacturers' instructions 97, 115
manufacturers' technical
information 48
marking lines 212–13, 222–5
masking tape 168–9, 170
removal 170, 244
materials
deliveries 51–2
estimating quantities 52–7
handling 22–6
purchasing systems 57–8
quantities 51–8
storing 24–5, 31
measurements, estimating
quantities of materials 53–4, 57

medium density fibreboard (MDF) 125

metal surfaces 126
  ferrous metal preparation 133, 155–6
  non-ferrous metal preparation 133
  primers 149
  rust removal 136

method statements, risk assessments 14–15

methylated spirits 128, 143

millscale 126

mobile elevated working platforms (MEWPs) 101–2

mobile towers 100
  pre-erection inspections 107
  securing, loading and handling 109, 111

mono-pitch roofs 77

mordant solutions 128

mould 142, 151

Munsell colour system 180–1

N

near misses 5, 10, 11

noise 20

O

oil-based paints and coatings 138, 174–5
  brush cleaning 185, 187
  disposal of 185
  environmental considerations 128, 187, 188
  glazes and scumbles 240, 241, 244, 252
  ground coats 240
  roller sleeve cleaning 186
  rollers and brushes 171
  storing 188

opacity 137, 173, 240

opaque 240

opening paint tins 172, 190

orange peel 183

organic materials 86

organisational documentation 48–9

orthographic projection (first angle) 45

outdoors, protecting areas 168

over 7-day injuries 7

P

pad foundations 67–9

paint and coating materials, preparing for application 170–3
  hazards, health and safety and risk assessment 170
  stages of preparation 172–3, 190–1
  tools and equipment 170–2

paint and coatings, applying 173–84
  with a brush 175–7, 192–4
  colour systems 178–81
  defects after 182–3
  paint systems and their components 173–5
  with a roller 177–8, 195–7
  stages of preparation 172–3, 190–1

paint removal 136–7

paint stirrers 171, 172, 191

paint storage 187–8

paint tins, opening 172, 190

painted lines and bands 248–50, 258–9

painted surface, preparing a previously 159–61

papers, adhesives for applying 203–6
  defects due to incorrect consistency 205
  factors affecting consistency 204–5
  hazards 205–6
  selecting and preparing 224–5
  types 203–4

papers, applying
  aligning pasted edges 214
  calculating quantity of materials 212, 218–20
  to ceilings 209
  defects 214–16
  doors, around 209
  external angles 211
  internal angles 211, 230–1
  light switches, around 211, 232
  lining papers 216–17
  marking lines 212–13, 222–4
  paste consistency 214
  'paste the wall' 214
  pasting paper, application sequence for 212–13, 226–8
  patterned wallpaper, working with 207–8, 220–2
  personal protective equipment (PPE) 206
  planning work 206–10, 217–18, 220–2
  power sockets, around 211, 232
  prominent features 207, 211
  ready-pasted 213

shade, measuring and cutting 220–2
  staircases 209, 210
  starting and finishing point 207, 222–4
  to walls 208–9, 228–31
  windows, around 209–10, 233

papers, preparation for applying
  health and environmental hazards 205
  preparing and protecting work area 200–1
  tools and equipment 201–3

papers, removal 137, 154–5

pasting paper, application sequence for 213–14, 226–8

PAT (Portable Appliance Testing) 28–9

personal hygiene 20–1

Personal Protection at Work Regulations 4, 33

personal protective equipment (PPE) 4, 31–3
  applying paint 164
  applying papers 200, 206
  erecting and dismantling access equipment 96
  legislation 4, 33
  preparing surfaces 123
  preparing surfaces for decorative finishes 236

pigment 173, 174

piled foundations 67–9

plaster and plasterboard 126–7
  preparation 133

plastics 127

platform steps 99
  dismantling and storage 111

platforms
  dismantling 111
  pre-erection inspections 107

plywood 125

podiums 101
  pre-erection inspections 107
  securing, loading and handling 110

policies, documentation 47

porous 127

Portable Appliance Testing (PAT) 28–9

power sockets
  papering around 211, 232
  protecting 167

PPE see personal protective equipment (PPE)

primers 135, 136, 137–8
  defective areas 149

priming 135
  spot-priming 136, 137, 148

procedures, documentation 46
programmes of work 45–6
prohibition notices 6
prop 98
proprietary staging 100
   securing, loading and handling
      110
protective clothing 32
protective sheeting 169
proud filling 146
Provision and Use of Work
   Equipment Regulations (PUWER)
   3–4
purchasing systems, materials 57–8
putty, applying 149
PUWER (Provision and Use of Work
   Equipment Regulations) 3–4

Q

quantities, materials 51–8
paper 212, 218–20

R

raft foundations 67–9
rag rolling 241–2, 251–2
ragging off 241–2, 252
raking out 136, 146
registration marks 246
regulations, health and safety 2–8,
   97, 139–40, 168, 187, 237
reinforcement, concrete 70–1
repairing and making good common
      surfaces 144–9
      processes and materials 145–8
      tools and equipment 145
Reporting of Injuries, Diseases
      and Dangerous Occurences
      Regulations (RIDDOR) 2, 8, 9–10
resin 135
resources, sustainability 83, 85
respiratory protection 32, 33
RIDDOR see Reporting of Injuries,
      Diseases and Dangerous
      Occurences Regulations
      (RIDDOR)
risk assessments 14–15
      for access equipment 95, 96
      preparing surfaces 122–3
risks 5
      health 21, 122, 139, 140, 144
rollers 130, 170–1
      applying coatings using 177–8,
         195–7
      cleaning 186, 197
      storing 186–7

roof construction 76–80
      exterior features 78–9
roof coverings 80
      types 77
ropiness 182, 183, 237
rungs 98
runs, paint 141–2, 182
rust removal 136

S

safety notices 36–7
sags, paint 141–2
sandpaper 133–4
scaffolding 26–7, 104–5, 112
      inspections 106, 107
scales, drawings 50
schedules, documentation 47, 51
school studies 58
scissor lifts 102
scoring 136, 154
scraping 145
scumbles 238, 240–1, 242, 244
scuttles 172
sealants, applying 148–9
sectional drawings 44
selecting information 50–1
service providers 81
services 81–2
settling 188
shear failure, foundations 66
shellac/patent 128
signs 36–7
single-pack fillers 128
sinking nail heads 145
site plans 42–3
skinning 188
slip/skid marks 243–4
slung scaffold 105, 112
solar photovoltaic systems 90
solar thermal energy 89
solid floors, construction 72
solid walls, construction 74, 75
solvent-based cleaners 143–4
solvent-based paints and coatings
      138, 174–5
      brush cleaning 185, 187
      disposal of 185
      environmental considerations
         128, 187, 188
      glazes and scumbles 240, 241,
         244, 252
      ground coats 240
      roller sleeve cleaning 186
      rollers and brushes 171
      storing 188
solvent-based primers 137–8

solvents/thinners 128, 174, 187
      'green' 128
specifications, documentation
      41–2, 47
sponge stippling 242, 253–4
spot-priming 136, 137, 148
St Pancras Renaissance Hotel 248
stabilising solution 129
staircases, applying paper 209, 210
starting and finishing points,
      papering 207, 222–4
stencils, applying single colour
      245–7
      application faults 247
      applying paint 247, 257
      marking out 246, 257
      planning considerations 245–6
      positive and negative stencils 245
      securing stencil plates 246, 257
step ladders 99
      inspection intervals 108
      pre-erection inspections 107
      securing, loading and handling
         109
      storing 111
stiles 98
stone, foundations 71
stoppers 127, 136, 146–8
storage
      access equipment 111, 119
      brushes and rollers 186–7
      decorative finish tools and
         equipment 244
      effects of incorrect 188
      hazards 188
      materials 24–5, 31
      paint materials 187–8
      wallpapering tools and
         equipment 203
      wallpapers 217
straight match 207–8
strainers 171–2, 191
stretching 205
strip foundations 67–9
sub-contractors 6
subsoils, foundations 66–9
substrates 124
subtractive rag rolling 241–2, 252
surfaces, preparing a range of
      abrading with a power tool 157–8
      brick 133, 151–2
      coating systems 138–9
      defective areas 132 see also
         defects in surfaces and
         coatings, correcting
      hazards, health and safety and
         risk assessment 122–3

health and safety and
  environmental regulations
  139–40
identifying surfaces 124–7
materials 127–9
metal, ferrous 133, 155–6
metal, non-ferrous 133
paper removal 137, 154–5
personal protective equipment
  (PPE) 123
preparation processes and
  materials 133–7, 151–61
previously painted 159–61
primers 137–8
protecting work and surrounding
  area 131
timber, bare 133, 152–3
timber, painted 133
tools and equipment 129–31
suspended floors, construction
  72–3
sustainability 82–91
  alternative methods of building
    85–6
  architecture/design 84, 91
  carbon, energy sources 88
  carbon footprint 84
  energy conservation 82
  energy efficiency 87–91
  environment 84
  resources 83, 85

T

temperature 165
terebine driers 175
thinners 128, 174, 187
  'green' 128
tie rods 98, 103
timber 124
  preparation of bare 133, 152–3
  preparation of painted 133

preservatives 138
sheet materials 124–5
storage and handling 25
toolbox talks 7, 8, 19
training and development records
  49
translucent 240
trestle platforms 100
  dismantling and storage 111
  securing, loading and handling
    109
tubular scaffolding 104
turpentine 128

U

undercutting 146
upper floors, construction 72–3
utilities 81–2

V

ventilation 166
vinyl papers 204
viscosity 173
adjusting 173
VOCs (volatile organic compounds)
  138, 139, 168, 186, 188

W

wall construction 73–6
  cavity walling 74, 75
wallpapers see papers, applying
water-based paints and coatings
  brushes 130
  cleaning brushes 185
  cleaning rollers 186
  disposal 187
  environmental considerations
    128, 187

glazes and scumbles 240, 241
shelf-life 188
storing 187, 188
systems 138, 173–4
water-based primers 138
weather 131, 165
wet edge, loss of 243
wetting in 136, 146, 154
white spirit 128, 143
window furniture 167
windows
  applying paper around 209–10,
    233
  painting frames 152–3, 177
woodchip paper 208
work area, preparing and protecting
  164–9
  areas and items to be protected
    164
  cleaning and tidying 166
  climate, weather and
    temperature 165
  environmental and health and
    safety regulations 168
  furnishings and fittings 167–8
  light fittings 165, 167
  masking tape 168–9, 171
  other trades on site 166
  protecting from damage 166–8
  protective sheeting 169
  public, protection of 166
  tools and equipment 166–7
  ventilation 166
Work at Height Regulations 2005
  4, 97
working platforms see access
  equipment and working
  platforms; access equipment and
  working platforms, preparing for
  erecting